Entrance to the railway station

Sibelius Monument

Bear statue,
National
Museum

KT-415-412

Esplanade Park (TS) page 242

Enjoying the sunshine, Café Strindberg (NS) page 157

Harbour and Uspenski Cathedral by night (TS)

Lutheran Cathedral (NW) page 233

Ice swimming, Rastila Camping (NW) page 199

Cross-country skiing at Paloheinä (JT) page 198

Nuuksio National Park

(JT) page 263

# Author/Contributors

## AUTHOR

Born in the north of England, Nigel Wallis tumbled out of higher education with a degree in English Language and Literature and immediately pursued a totally unrelated career with a small engineering company, a position which has allowed him to flit around the globe with regularity. Several years later he picked up his pen and started writing again, and has since contributed to various travel guides, including *North Cyprus: the Bradt Travel Guide*, as well as print and online periodicals. When he's not exploring the frozen north for guidebook research, his hobbies include rambling the Yorkshire Dales, prowling the local music scene and fuelling his masochistic streak with a season ticket at Leeds United FC.

## CONTRIBUTORS

Thanks are due to Neil Taylor for writing the section *A day trip to Tallinn* and Pilvi Palonen-Comber for her piece on lakeside cabin holidays.

**First published March 2007**

Bradt Travel Guides Ltd
23 High Street, Chalfont St Peter, Bucks SL9 9QE, England; www.bradtguides.com
Published in the US by The Globe Pequot Press Inc,
246 Goose Lane, PO Box 480, Guilford, Connecticut 06437-0480

Text copyright © 2007 Nigel Wallis
Maps copyright © 2007 Bradt Travel Guides Ltd    Transport map © 2007 Communicarta Ltd
Illustrations © Individual photographers and artists (see below)

**British Library Cataloguing in Publication Data**
A catalogue record for this book is available from the British Library
ISBN-10: 1 84162 184 6    ISBN-13: 978 1 84162 184 5

**Photographs** Neil Setchfield (NS), Tero Sivula/www.kuvakori.com (TS), Jonathan Smith (JS), Juha
Tuomi/www.kuvakori.com (JT), Nigel Wallis (NW)
*Cover* View of city and Lutheran Cathedral (NS)    *Title page* Lutheran Cathedral (JS), Sibelius Monument (JS)
**Maps** Steve Munns based on ITMB source maps, Communicarta Ltd (transport map)
**Illustrations** Carole Vincer

Typeset from the author's disc by Wakewing    Printed and bound in Spain by Grafo SA, Bilbao

# Acknowledgements

The cast behind this guidebook is many and varied. In London, thanks to Riitta Balza at the Finnish Tourist Board for enthusiastically embracing the project and introducing me to Leena Virtala-Pulkkinen at Helsinki City Tourist and Convention Bureau, to whom I am also grateful.

At Helsinki Expert, Enna Paavola and Micaela Roswall-Grägg gave me the latest tourist information and helped ease my course around the city's many museums and galleries. For lightening the load during an extensive research period I owe a similar debt to Johanna Tyynelä at the Palace Kämp Group and Minna Kinnunen of Radisson SAS.

Mikael Jungner and Mika Ojamies welcomed me to their plush offices at YLE, feeding me choice snippets of information that were worth their weight in gold. Similarly, Jouni Mölsä at Helsingin Sanomat greeted me like an old friend – I am especially appreciative of his discerning political and historical eye. Special thanks must go to Antti Virtanen, who got me through the door to many of these places and answered my banal email questions with unfailing gusto and attention to detail.

Thanks also to Sean Nugent, who led me running through Helsinki's Central Park, and Pauliina Siniauer from Radio Helsinki, who thought it was a great idea to interview me at the halfway point. For friendly support and welcoming smiles, *Hei* to Maarit Pitkänen and a big *Moi!* to Nuppu Stenros, who started as a guide and ended as a friend.

I owe a big debt to Tricia Hayne and Hilary Bradt for setting the Helsinki wheels in motion, whilst Anna Moores kept me on the straight and narrow and guided me across the finishing line with good humour and no lack of motivational encouragement. For providing me with reference maps, thanks also to Jack Joyce and Andrew Duggan at ITMB in Vancouver.

This project would never have reached a conclusion without the support of my parents, sister and friends at home, who didn't see me for several months during 2006, and most of all to Sonya, who supported, encouraged, edited and did all the jobs I didn't whilst I was chained to the desk. *Kiitos* one and all.

## FEEDBACK REQUEST

It has been a lot of fun researching this guide to Helsinki. I've paced the streets from dawn until dusk in search of the most up-to-date information, investigating countless museums, cafés, restaurants, bars, hotels, shops, parks, churches and islands. I suffered blistered feet on more than one occasion, froze my brain in an icy pool of water and almost burnt to a crisp under an unrelenting July sun. Hopefully it was worthwhile.

Helsinki is constantly evolving; things change and new opinions are formed. To help improve this guide, please let me know your tips and criticisms by sending an email to e helsinki_guide@yahoo.com. Alternatively, send your scribbles the old-fashioned way to Bradt Travel Guides, 23 High Street, Chalfont St Peter, Bucks SL9 9QE.

# Contents

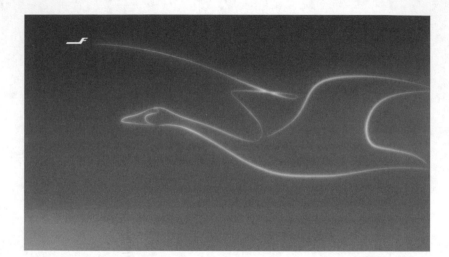

## THE NATURAL WAY TO FINLAND

Fly to Finland the Finnish way – direct, punctually, and on
the blue-and-white wings of Finnair. Finnair flies four times a day
from Heathrow and twice a day from Manchester to Helsinki.
See more at **www.finnair.co.uk**

WHY FLY ANY OTHER WAY

# Introduction

If one word sums up Finland more than any other it's *sisu*, the national characteristic best described as 'guts'. The ability to grin and bear it defines Finnish society, and no surprise. After all, until the 1917 declaration of independence the Finns were prodded, pushed and pulled asunder by their fractious neighbours in Sweden and Russia. They needed *sisu* when Helsinki was burned to the ground in 1654; they needed it again when Tsar Nicholas II launched his Russification of Finland policy in 1899; and they needed it more than ever through the 20th-century war years that shaped Finland as we know it today. No wonder then that *sisu* continues to put fire in the Finnish belly, from the naming of a famous arctic icebreaker to a 70-year-old brand of *salmiakki*, a salted liquorice confection whose consumption requires guts a-plenty.

Blessed with a determination to survive and prosper Finland has emerged as a leading light of the 21st century, with a capital city that radiates charm. Yet Helsinki has not always been on the established tourist trail, blighted by misconceptions of arctic chills and wallet-draining expense, but with airfares falling and the city opening up to the outside world its variety of delights are firmly within reach. Large enough to feel cosmopolitan but easily explored on foot, Helsinki has been handsomely endowed with a unique personality. The Art Nouveau splendour of the Esplanade

Park is the phoenix that rose from the ashes of the Russian invasion, whilst Senate Square depicts strong eastern influences. Another strength is the diversity of culture. Over 80 museums and galleries, from Classical to modern abstract, vie for attention; restaurants cater to all palates and bars rock through the night with the latest sounds. Helsinki is also a city blessed by nature more than most. Lapped by the cool Gulf of Finland, the offshore islands of the archipelago and proximity to expansive wilderness areas give ample opportunities to flit away from the city by boat, cycle or foot.

Summer in Helsinki is a heady mixture of warm days and long nights. Infused with an insatiable *joie de vivre*, the city bursts into life amidst a blaze of outdoor living and constant festivals. Locals laze in the parks, sunbathe by the sea or just indulge in people-watching from the packed café terraces. Winter brings long nights and plummeting temperatures, and the city takes on a wholly different identity. Muffled against the icy chill, this is the time to further your acquaintance with Helsinki's unique blend of Nordic and Russian culture. Marked by oil lamps flickering gently in the still and snowy evenings, cafés, bars and restaurants become snug retreats inclined to induce hibernation. But this is also the time to embrace winter sports, be it cross-country skiing or Nordic walking. In the depths of bleakest midwinter a stroll across the frozen sea is a unique experience, amplified only by a spot of *avanto* (the art of swimming in a hole hacked through the ice). But the highlight of any visit, summer or winter, is the traditional smoke-fired sauna experience, complete with full body scrub. Just leave your inhibitions at home; the unshockable washerwoman has seen it all before.

# How to Use this Book

**MAP REFERENCES** (eg: [2 B3] in Chapters 3 and 5–12) relate to the colour maps at the end of this guide.

**HOTELS** are divided by price range (not area), from luxurious suites to camping by the sea.

**RESTAURANTS** are divided by price, then by style, with further subdivisions for districts or themes. All prices were verified during autumn of 2006, but should serve as a useful comparative guide.

**OPENING HOURS** are included for restaurants, bars, museums, shops and sights.

**CHAPTER 10** (*Walking tours*) includes cross-references to Chapter 6 (*Eating and Drinking*), Chapter 12 (*Natural Helsinki*) and Chapter 11 (*What to See and Do*).

**TIME** is given in local Finnish style, using the 24-hour clock.

## HELSINKI AT A GLANCE

**Location** Southern Finland, on an archipelago jutting into the Gulf of Finland. Three hours by air from London, 2½ hours from Manchester and two hours from Edinburgh. Tallinn, Estonia's capital city, a mere 80km to the south, can be reached in 90 minutes by hydrofoil, or 18 minutes by helicopter.

**Population** 560,000 in the city; 965,000 in the greater metropolitan area

**Language** Predominantly Finnish (92.3%), although Swedish (5.6%) is also an official language

**Religion** Primarily Lutheran, with a small Orthodox community (see pages 27–9)

**Currency** Euro

**Rate of exchange** (Feb 2007) £1 = €1.51, US$1 = €0.77

**International telephone code** Finland: +358 (Helsinki city code: 09)

**Time** GMT/BST +2 hours

**Electricity** 220V AC, 50Hz. Standard northern European round two-pin plug

**Public holidays** The following holidays fall on the same date each year: 1 January, 6 January, 1 May, 6 December, 24–26 December (see pages 33–4 for a full list of all public holidays and festivities, flexible dates included)

**Climate** Warm summers and cold, damp winters. Average maximum temperatures: winter −2°C; spring and autumn 10°C; summer 20°C (see pages 41–3).

# 1 Contexts

## HISTORY

**THE EARLY YEARS** The most significant Finnish archaeological discovery of recent years occurred at Susiluola (Wolf Cave) near the city of Kristiinankaupunki, where several hundred examples of primitive tools have been excavated. Analysis of rock sediment and pollen samples have dated the site at over 120,000 years old, placing it in the Palaeolithic era (200,000–35,000BC) and making it the only site so far uncovered in the Nordic countries that pre-dates the last ice age.

The earliest-known traces of modern man date from the Mesolithic Stone Age period, c8500BC. The oldest find from this period is the Antrea net, a fishing net complete with stone weights found on the Karelian Isthmus in an area now part of Russia. Carbon dating showed the net to be over 10,000 years old. Communities are also known to have existed in Imatra and Joutseno, on the Finnish side of the Russian frontier. Whilst many people believe the earliest post-glacial settlers to be the Sami tribes, little archaeological trace of these ancient northern hunting people has been discovered.

The area around Helsinki was first colonised as far back as 7,000 years ago, although more permanent settlements did not exist until some time later. Centred on Lake Saimaa in southeastern Finland, the so-called Comb Ware Culture (4000–3500BC) was typified by decoratively patterned ceramics. Burial sites and rock paintings from this era have also been discovered; the paintings depict themes often associated with the indigenous animal life and human settlement. A progression of Comb Ware was the Asbestos Ware period (3500BC–AD250), when pottery-firing techniques became more refined and settlers discovered agriculture. Signs of crop cultivation dating from 500BC have been found at Savitaipale, on the shores of Lake Kuolimo, 220km northeast of Helsinki. The Asbestos Ware phase encompassed the era more widely appreciated as the Bronze Age (c1300–500BC), during which settlers from Scandinavia brought new religious ways but made little impact on the austerity of daily life.

With the dawn of the Iron Age (AD250–1320) came increased trade with Scandinavian and Baltic neighbours, which solidified the now well-developed communities of the southern coastal areas. Moving both by water and rudimentary overland tracks, the settlers were building the infrastructure that would help carry Finland into the modern ages.

**THE SWEDISH REIGN** Sandwiched between its powerful neighbours of Sweden and Novograd (Russia), the geographical area comprising Finland had been lacking political direction for the duration of its history. Desirable to both empires, the land was finally divided by a 1323 peace treaty that enshrined the bulk of the territory, the western and southern sections, to the Swedish realm. Novograd was assigned the eastern extremities, and with this partition came the creation of distinct cultural boundaries that would shape the modern Finnish nation. Tied to the Swedish realm, Finland would become inexorably attached to western European philosophies and values.

Despite several visitations of the plague in the early 14th century, life under Swedish rule was generally good. The well-established social principles of the realm granted the same freedoms that were enjoyed by Swedish citizens, and by 1362 the Finns were awarded the right to send representatives to the election of the king in Stockholm. When King Gustav Vasa (1496–1560) introduced the Lutheran Reformation to Finland in the early 16th century, the embedded Catholic faith was swept aside and a groundswell of literary awareness spread across the land as the Church embarked on a widespread programme of education.

**BIRTH OF A NEW CAPITAL** As Finland developed under Swedish rule the southwestern town of Turku emerged as the nation's principal settlement, home to the bishop's seat and crowned with a spectacular cathedral. King Vasa, whilst content that Turku's proximity to Stockholm simplified the administration of Finland, was mindful that the kingdom was suffering due to its lack of an eastern trading post. The king saw the city of Tallinn prospering through Baltic and Russian trade and devised a plan to create his own rival city.

In 1550, a royal decree founded Helsinki (Swedish *Helsingfors*) by the mouth of the River Vantaa in the area now known as Vanhankaupunginlahti (Old Town Bay). Many burghers from Finnish towns such as Porvoo, Rauma and Ulvila were forcibly relocated to the new settlement to fulfil the king's vision of a dominant mercantile port. Unfortunately, nobody had foreseen the severe impediment that was the shallowness of the bay. Blighted by its poor location, the town festered and morale among the traders, who pined for home, ebbed away with each passing tide. Eventually they were allowed to leave and it seemed as if the king's dream had slipped away with them.

During the period of early settlement a whole new generation had been born in depressed Helsinki, a generation who knew no other home. It was these beleaguered few who, through gritted teeth, upped sticks and started again as Helsinki was relocated to its modern-day setting. In 1640, the first settlers came to the harbourside district now known as Kruununhaka, a short way northeast from Senate Square. Beset by yet more problems, not least catastrophic fires that swept through the wooden buildings, by the end of the 17th century Helsinki boasted a population of just 1,600.

**RUSSIA ADVANCES** Helsinki's struggle for recognition was played out against a backdrop of political tension and deteriorating relations between Sweden and Russia. Although the realm had succeeded in pushing its boundary with Russia further to the east, the outbreak of the Great Northern War in 1700 caused grave concern. An allied force of Russian, Norwegian-Danish and Polish-Saxon forces launched a co-ordinated attack against the Swedish Empire, and despite staunch command from Swedish King Karl XII it was clear that their era of dominance was drawing to a close. The signing of the 1721 Treaty of Nystad formally ended hostilities, and with it the empire was lost. Russia, under the command of Tsar Peter I, assumed control of much of the eastern Finnish territory, as well as Estonia, Livonia and Ingria. Northern Europe had a new superpower.

If the western advancement of the Russian Empire was a threat to Helsinki, the founding of St Petersburg was a blow of equal magnitude. The Great Northern War was only three years old when Tsar Peter the Great established his own imperial capital on the shores of the Gulf of Finland. Suddenly, Helsinki found itself further marginalised and ever more vulnerable due to its proximity to the new border. Despite this, development of the city continued and at last some level of prosperity was evident. In 1727, work commenced on the Ulrika Eleonora Church on the site of Senate Square, whilst the imposing sea fortress of Suomenlinna (Swedish Sveaborg) was commissioned in 1748 to nullify the Russian maritime threat.

This latter decision was triggered partly by the so-called War of the Hats of 1741–43, which further took its toll on the political and social fabric of Helsinki but simultaneously infused the city with Russian influence through a renewed military occupation. By now Helsinki was large enough to absorb these moderate shockwaves and by the beginning of the 18th century the population had swollen to 3,000, which made it Sweden's fourth-largest harbour town and a trading post of some magnitude.

As the new century progressed relations deteriorated even further, culminating in the Finnish War of 1808–09. Sweden's refusal to accept the Treaty of Tilsit, an alliance agreement between Russia and Napoleon's France, angered Tsar Alexander I. Although the issues were deep-rooted and complex – Sweden considered Britain its traditional ally – the Tsar was in no mood to negotiate and ordered the invasion of Finland. Facing little resistance, by the winter of 1808 they occupied every Finnish location of strategic note, including a swift capture of Suomenlinna, and were advancing across the frozen Baltic Sea towards Stockholm. King Gustav IV, accused of fundamental mistakes in his handling of the campaign, was dethroned in March 1809 and replaced by his uncle, Charles XIII. The new king quickly struck a truce with Russian leaders. The war was coming to an end, but so too was Sweden's control of Finland.

**FINLAND AS A GRAND DUCHY OF RUSSIA** It was an apprehensive Finland that woke to a new dawn of Russian rule, but outwardly little seemed to have changed. The freshly established Grand Duchy was granted extensive autonomy under Tsar Alexander I, meaning the fabric of society remained under the control of the Finnish people; the highest governing body was the senate, populated by Finns, the Lutheran Church maintained its established role and Swedish continued as the official language. It seemed ironic that after years of living in fear of Russia, Finland was being allowed to develop independently and Helsinki, scene of so much torrid struggle and adversity, was about to hit the big time.

The city's status was cemented in 1812 when the Tsar appointed it capital of the Grand Duchy, succeeding Turku which had itself been ravaged by fire and was considered tainted because of its proximity to Sweden. The Academy ot Åbo, Finland's only university, was also relocated to Helsinki and the city flourished as a programme of reconstruction began to heal the scars of war. Johan Albrecht Ehrenströhm and Carl Ludvig Engel, the team respectively responsible for town planning and architecture, managed the core of the transformation, creating the grand vistas around Senate Square and the Esplanade Park that symbolise the opulent growth of the period. Effectively, the reconstruction of Helsinki amounted to the creation of a new city, including the building of both Lutheran and Orthodox cathedrals, government buildings and the new university. Neither Ehrenströhm nor Engel would live to see the project through to a conclusion, yet the importance of their contributions cannot be underestimated.

**THE FINNISH NATION AWAKES** With the thriving autonomous state came an ever-increasing sense of Finnish nationalism, which began to build an irrepressible head of steam following the publication of the *Kalevala* in 1835–36, Finland's national epic poem compiled by Elias Lönnrot. Tempered somewhat by the Crimean War of 1853–56, the movement gathered pace again in the second half of the century. By 1860 the markka had been established as the official currency, the country operated its own legislation, supported an extensive army and the Language Decree of 1863 marked the beginning of the process by which Finnish would join Swedish as an official language.

The spread of Finnish nationalism did not go unnoticed in Russia and, following disquiet at the way in which the Grand Duchy was apparently separating itself from the empire, a process of Russification was well underway by the onset of the 20th century. Whilst the Russians were distracted by their internal revolution of 1905, the Finns took the opportunity to establish the eduskunta, the most radical parliament in Europe at the time of its inception. Relying on an ethos of universal suffrage the eduskunta empowered Finnish women, and by 1906 they were the first in Europe to be afforded the right to vote, and the second in the world behind New Zealand.

Elections in 1916 returned a small majority for the Social Democrats, and Oskari Tokoi was named as prime minister. Tokoi was keen to co-operate with the Russian government but when no agreement could be reached the shaky relationship was nearing its conclusion. The ensuing mêlée of political infighting, parliamentary turmoil and Russian military action saw bloody murder and bitter recriminations.

**INDEPENDENCE AND THE FINNISH CIVIL WAR** The revolution of October 1917 triggered an official declaration of independence on 6 December 1917. Russia greeted the news with initial good grace, but by January 1918 the military campaign had been re-ignited by the attack on Vyborg that triggered the Finnish Civil War. Separated by political differences, the Finnish people were divided; those who sided with the Russians (the Reds) and those loyal to the government (the Whites), who were led by General Carl Gustaf Emil Mannerheim.

The duration of the war was short, just three months, but violent and catastrophic in its loss of life. For some time it appeared that the socialist dream of the Reds would be realised, as fierce fighting around Helsinki subdued the threat of the Whites. But the tide turned when Imperial Germany sided with the government forces, diverting troops from mainland Europe to finally bring the conflict to an end. It was not to be the end of Finno-Russian hostilities.

In another twist of fate, Germany's defeat in World War I suddenly left the newly independent Finland feeling vulnerable and isolated. With a swift change of policy, the Finns abandoned their plan to emulate the German model and instead chose to establish a republican state. Kaarlo Juho Ståhlberg was appointed president and by 1920 Finland had struck an accord with Russia, the Treaty of Tartu, which once again redrew the borders and hinted at calmer times ahead.

Independence brought swift development during the 1920s, despite sporadic outbursts of violence that threatened the democratic constitution. The Russian border remained a particularly volatile area. Early Finnish foreign policy embraced its closest geographical neighbours – Estonia, Latvia and Lithuania – but with the League of Nations unable to uphold world peace a shift towards Scandinavian orientation was evident by the mid 1930s.

**WORLD WAR II** In November 1939 the ghosts of a troubled past returned. Germany and the Soviet Union had agreed a non-aggression pact, and when Finland refused to allow the Soviets to build military bases on its land the die was cast for fresh military conflict. Revoking a separate non-aggression treaty that had been signed in 1932, the Soviets invaded and initiated what became known as the Winter War.

Finland's resistance in the face of overwhelming force is the benchmark by which the nation judges all other acts of fortitude, and the perfect definition of *sisu* (the traditional Finnish 'guts'). In March 1940 the Treaty of Moscow ended hostilities but Finland was forced to cede significant eastern territory to the Soviets.

Yet still the fragile relationship had not reached equilibrium. With the severity of the Soviets' Finnish campaign diluted by war with Germany, Finland seized the opportunity to launch a military campaign of its own in an attempt to reclaim the lost territory. Crucially the Finns were assisted by Nazi Germany, whose involvement in turn prompted Britain to declare war on Finland. The invasion ultimately proved to be a disaster of colossal proportions. Finland lost yet more ground to the Soviets and was forced to pay war reparations totalling hundreds of millions of dollars. The final act of hostility was played out in the Lapland War of 1944–45, when the Finns opposed German troops who were refusing to leave the distant north.

Despite these setbacks Finland emerged from the war with pride intact; Helsinki was one of only three European capitals not to be occupied during the war, London and Moscow being the others. Commander-in-Chief Mannerheim had struck a skilful balance in his handling of the Nazi relationship and in due course Finland was able to move forward with minimal lasting damage.

**THE MODERN AGE** With the cessation of war came independent Finland's first true period of peace. The Soviet Union was finally placated and the country eventually arrived on the world stage in 1952 as Helsinki played host to the Olympic Games.

Originally scheduled for 1940 but disrupted by conflict, the games served notice that the Finns were now an established nation.

As a whole, the 1950s was proving to be a decade of milestone events. In 1952, war reparations were finally settled, mainly through the divestment of ships that had in turn fostered a solid engineering industry – Finland was the only nation to settle such debts in full. On a more positive note, Finland joined both the UN and Nordic Council in 1955, the latter of which guaranteed a Nordic labour market and freedom of movement for citizens, without passports, between any and all member countries.

The Soviet spectre reared its ugly head again during the Cold War, when Moscow often leant heavily on its western neighbour, but by now Finland was under the leadership of Urho Kekkonen. Elected in 1956, he guided his people through these potentially testing times with grace and wisdom, and would continue to do so for a quarter of a century. Under his presidency Finland blossomed. One of Kekkonen's principal policies became Finnish neutrality on the international stage. By the time ill health forced early retirement in 1981 his place in the nation's heart was already enshrined.

The Finland of the 21st century is a confident and progressive nation that has recovered well from the recession of the early 1990s (see *Economy*, pages 15–17). Powered by a thriving industrial sector, the effect of joining the EU in 1995 cannot be underestimated and the nation is rightly proud of maintaining its border with Russia on behalf of a wider European community. Politically, the Finns continue to move forward through a series of coalition governments (see *Politics*, below) overseen by presidential leadership. It seems fitting that as the new millennium dawned, Finland elected its first female president (Tarja Halonen). In 2006, she was re-elected for a second term in office, exactly 100 years after Finnish women were first afforded suffrage.

## POLITICS

The modern-day political shape of Finland has undoubtedly been influenced by its time spent under Swedish and Russian control, but the seeds of the egalitarian society we know today were sown even before the 1917 declaration of independence.

When the Grand Duchy of Finland was established under the Russian Tsar in 1809, the so-called Diet of Finland (a governing body comprising four provincial estates) was formed to act as the legislative assembly of the autonomous state. The Diet remained in position, albeit meeting irregularly, until the summer of 1906 when, following civil unrest triggered by the Russo-Japanese War, an extraordinary meeting was called to propose radical reforms.

In October 1906 the reforms were enshrined in law and Finland had a democratic parliament that consisted of 200 elected members. The unrestricted right to vote was extended to both men and women over the age of 24, making Finland second only to New Zealand in recognising women's suffrage. Significantly, the reformation also gave the universal right to stand for election, an act by which Finland broke new ground. At the same time, laws were passed guaranteeing freedom of assembly and speech, the latter both in the case of individuals and the press. Turnouts at elections are traditionally high, with over 70% of the electorate voting in the 2003 ballots.

Finland's political party system is rooted in issues of national identity, the bi-lateral language debate, socialism and the representation of rural communities. Throughout its 100-year history, this political make-up has remained stable. There are three major parties – the Centre Party, Social Democrats and National Coalition Party – who have traditionally each received around 20–25% support. The remaining votes have been split between half-a-dozen smaller parties.

The structure relies on a proportional system of voting, which encourages fringe parties to become involved but also means that Finland has never been governed by a single-party majority. Coalition governments are the norm, resulting in peculiar alliances such as the union that was in power from 1995 to 2003, comprising the right-wing National Coalition Party and two extreme left-wing partners.

Matti Vanhanen, a former journalist and newspaper editor, is the current Prime Minister of Finland, leader of the coalition government elected in 2003 that comprises his Centre Party, the Social Democrats and the Swedish People's Party. In opposition, the National Coalition Party are joined by the Green Party who, having risen in popularity in recent years, withdrew from the previous government in protest at the ongoing determination to pursue a policy of nuclear energy. Vanhanen found himself thrust to power when his predecessor, Anneli Jäätteenmäki, resigned after just two months in office following allegations that she used secret leaked documents on the war in Iraq to damage the Social Democratic-led government during the election campaign.

Finland's president has a limited political role, restricted on the domestic front to official state occasions such as the opening and closing of parliament and presiding over regular governmental sessions. Elected for a term of six years, the president also manages Finnish foreign policy and affairs, and is commander-in-chief of the armed forces.

The current president, Tarja Halonen, formerly of the Social Democratic Party, was returned to power for a second term in January 2006. Halonen is Finland's first female head of state, and well loved, being affectionately known as Moominmamma (after the mother-figure from Tove Jansson's children's books). In a display of true Finnish equality she can often be seen queuing in the supermarket with other shoppers. In an age of pumped-up bodyguards and frenzied security alerts, it's a refreshingly temperate attitude.

**FINLAND AND THE EU** There is little doubt that Finland's accession to the EU in 1995 went a long way to eradicating the fiscal problems that had blighted the country since the fall of the Soviet Union. The euro was adopted as the official currency in 2002, replacing the Finnish markka.

On 1 July 2006, Finland began a six-month presidency of the EU. Whilst some view such an accolade with a dubious scepticism, citing the exercise as little more than political backslapping, this term at the forefront of European politics nevertheless represented an important milestone that helped raise the Finns' wider international standing. Over 130 meetings were organised throughout the country, with an emphasis on environmental issues and formal meals prepared with the finest Finnish foods. Needless to say, there was always time for sauna.

## ECONOMY

It is difficult to imagine a country whose economy has been transformed as radically as that of Finland. Endowed with abundant forest resources, the nation excels in the forestry industry although the importance has declined in recent years as the engineering, telecommunications and electronics sectors have grown.

In terms of business competitiveness, economic appeal and transparency of trade, Finland is consistently ranked among the world's leading countries, often ahead of the US and Scandinavian rivals Sweden and Denmark.

Since joining the EU in 1995 Finland has transformed itself from a net importer of wealth to a net exporter. Over 33% of Finland's €160 billion GDP (some €29,500 per capita) is derived from direct exports, principally to Sweden, Germany, Russia and the UK. The harsh climate means agriculture has been traditionally limited to producing the essentials – meat, dairy and grains – and this sector has shrunk steadily since accession to the EU, accounting now for just 2.8% of GDP.

There are currently some 2.5 million Finns in employment, with unemployment running at around 7.5%. Prior to the Soviet collapse of 1991, more than 20% of

Finnish trade was with its eastern neighbour – trade that all but disappeared overnight. Unemployment soared to nearly 17% by 1993, by which time the Finnish markka had twice been devalued in an attempt to remain competitive. Unemployment remains an issue, with official figures distorting the true extent of the problem, but the government is confident of achieving its goal of creating 100,000 new jobs by the time of the next election in March 2007.

Innovation is a national credo in Finland. Education has produced a forward-thinking labour force and, despite the fact that the (free) higher education system is oversubscribed, the economy continues to benefit from the progressive attitude of new graduates. Of Finland's most prominent corporations, Nokia is by far the largest and most famous. What is less well known is that its roots are planted in the manufacture of rubber boots, before it turned to communication cables and finally found its true forte in its current guise at the forefront of wireless communications. Other areas in which Finns shine, or have shone in the past, include paper processing, stylish interior design and modern computer game development.

Approximately 20% of Finland's national income is ploughed into the extensive social welfare network that provides the populace with a high quality of living, including comprehensive pension and healthcare systems.

Since the start of the new millennium, the Finnish economy has been growing steadily at a rate of between 2% and 3.6% per year. The forecast for 2006 is 3.2%, a level which is expected to continue into 2007, although this may be tempered by uncertainty over a possible new government in the run up to the next parliamentary election.

## PEOPLE

The Finnish people are a near living embodiment of their harsh winters; frosty, uninviting, bleak and quiet – so very, very quiet. In mid December you can walk for miles in Finland without hearing a sound, the weather's probably gloomy and you won't ever get properly warm. At best you'll have icy feet, and in all probability you'll be getting cold shoulders as well.

At least, that's winter on the outside. Find a rustic cabin with a crackling log fire, thaw your chilly bones with a magical sauna or snuggle into a café over a steamy mug of coffee and, well, winter's actually pretty great. Stay out in the cold too long and you'll freeze; cosy up inside and you might not want to leave. It's that simple – now all you need is to discover the way to get in.

There's an old joke that runs something like this: 'What's the difference between a Finnish introvert and a Finnish extrovert? A Finnish introvert looks at his feet when he's talking to you. A Finnish extrovert looks at yours!' If you think gags like these are just peddling stereotypes, you're probably right. But most stereotypes develop for a reason and many people would argue that there's more than a grain of truth in this one. Others would say it's patently untrue; why would a Finn be talking to you at all?

Whilst this taciturn nature is often exaggerated in some quarters, it remains one of the defining Finnish characteristics. They are a people of carefully chosen words, on the whole better listeners than speakers, who can maintain a frustrating level of mystery. In Finnish culture it is considered more polite to remain quiet than blabber liberally – trams and buses can be eerily silent places. I could go on, but that would just be rude. Perhaps the finest précis is the (true) tale of the foreign girl who married a Finn. Bemoaning her husband's cool and incommunicative nature, she pined for more affection. 'I have already said that I love you,' said the husband. 'If I change my mind, I shall tell you so.'

Finns have a strong national identity, fuelled by a history of conflict, the struggle against nature and rivalry with neighbouring countries. The principal Finnish trait is *sisu*, the philosophy of triumph against all odds; that what must be done, *will* be done, bound with limitless reserves of endurance, courage and strength of mind. They are intensely proud of the sporting achievements of their small nation. Quite apart from world champion motor racing drivers and some notable footballers, Finland can boast the highest per capita success level in the modern era of the Olympic Games – some 106 medals per million residents.

Which brings me nicely to Sweden. The Swedes are ranked second in the medal table (with a paltry 56.3 per million inhabitants), and my, don't the Finns love that! Having lived under Swedish rule from the 11th century until the dawn of Russian control in 1809, any opportunity to put one over on their old enemy is welcomed with open arms.

The feud isn't particularly political, and like most of the finest modern-day rivalries manifests itself best in the sporting arena. An annual track and field event keeps things bubbling away nicely – in 1992 all six competitors in the 1,500 metres were disqualified for serious foul play – but the real grudge matches come in winter. Finns and Swedes love ice hockey with equal verve, and when the two countries meet this excuse to hit each other with big sticks is an event not to be missed. Sweden has the edge in terms of world titles won, but Finland holds the current bragging rights thanks to victory in the final of the 2006 winter Olympic Games.

Physically, the Finns are a pleasing lot, and you won't have to travel far before you spot your first blonde beauty or handsome hunk who looks like they stepped straight from the pages of a fashion magazine, especially if you hit the town at night. For all you singles out there, Finns are renowned for cutting to the chase. Reserved they may be, but if they see what they want then they won't be afraid to go and get it. Male readers take note; if one comes your way, thank your lucky stars. Beauty *and* silence is a wondrous combination.

## CULTURAL ETIQUETTE

Generally speaking, you would have to work quite hard to offend the average Finn, but here are a few pointers to set you in the right direction.

## FIVE FAMOUS CHILDREN OF HELSINKI

**Tove Jansson** (1914–2001) Gifted novelist, illustrator and painter, most famous for the troll-like adventures of her *Moomin* books.

**Väinö Myllyrinne** (1909–63) Finland's tallest ever man was also the loftiest in Europe, measuring an incredible 2.48m (8' 1½"). Having served in the Finnish army, Myllyrinne is also thought to be the biggest ever soldier.

**Adolf Erik Nordenskiöld** (1832–1901) A member of the high-flying Finnish-Swedish Nordenskiöld family of scientists, Adolf Erik was a renowned geologist, mineralogist and arctic explorer. Uncle of Carl Gustaf Emil Mannerheim, the commander-in-chief of Finland's defence forces who subsequently became president.

**Petri Sakari** (b1958) Classical conductor of opera and ballet who has worked around the world with national orchestras in Stockholm, Gothenburg, Vienna, Singapore, Mexico City, São Paulo, Bucharest, Bilbao, Thessaloniki and Montpellier, amongst others.

**Linus Torvalds** (b1969) World-renowned developer of the Linux computer operating system.

**NUDE OR PRUDE?** Let's get things out in the open straight away – nudity is the norm in the Finnish sauna. Should you be invited to bathe with a Finn, he/she will be unlikely to object if you insist on wearing a swimming costume but will probably have a little chuckle at your embarrassment. Believe me, given the sights I've seen in some Finnish saunas you've probably got nothing to worry about. Equally, being gently 'whipped' with a softened birch branch is a highly pleasurable experience totally devoid of sexual connotation. Enjoy!

**GREETINGS** The customary greeting is a firm handshake accompanied by direct eye contact. Embracing, kissing and other outward signs of affection are reserved for friends. When meeting married couples, the lady should be greeted first.

If you enter a quiet shop or bar, it is customary to exchange a small pleasantry. *Hei* is the most common, which can be used when greeting friends, browsing a boutique or checking into your hotel. More formal greetings are *päivää* (hello), *hyvää päivää* (good day), *(hyvää) huomneta* (good morning) and *(hyvää) iltaa* (good evening). Your host might offer the word *tervetuloa* (welcome), and a useful phrase to remember when making introductions is *hauksa tavata* (pleased to meet you).

*Näkemiin* is the polite way of saying goodbye, although the playful *hei hei* is much more common and is used in most casual situations.

**FORMALITIES** A Finn will introduce him or herself with first name followed by surname. Although titles, qualifications and job descriptions are valued highly, it is

21

considered rude to place emphasis on these at the initial meeting stage. Following introduction (Mr, Mrs, Miss, Sir, Madam, etc are all acceptable) you will soon be on familiar terms with your Finnish friend. After all, if you can strip butt naked together in the sauna, what's in a name?

**WAIT YOUR TURN** I can see British readers across the land (well, hopefully a *few* of you bought this book) nodding in sage understanding of this one – Finns love queuing! Jumping the queue is not the done thing, and at many banks, post offices and supermarket deli counters a strict ticket system will be in operation.

**GREEN MEANS GO** Finns never cross the street unless the little green man tells them to, even if there isn't a single car to be seen. Some rebels (and most foreigners) flout this regulation, a transgression theoretically punishable by a police fine that in reality is seldom imposed.

**SCANDINAVIAN SLIP-UP** Strictly speaking, Finland is considered to be a Nordic country (like Iceland) and does not constitute part of Scandinavia, which comprises Norway, Sweden and Denmark.

**HOME VISITS** Should you be invited to the home of a Finnish friend or business contact, take a gift of wine or good-quality chocolates, or flowers for the hostess. Be careful of flower etiquette – never give bunches comprising an equal number of stems, and avoid white and yellow (the colours used at funerals). Call in advance to ask if you can bring anything for the meal, always arrive on time (Finns love punctuality) and leave your shoes at the door upon entering. Offer to help with preparations (or clearing up), sit in your allocated place, leave your jacket on (gents) unless your host removes his, *don't* talk business, don't eat with your hands (except bread and shrimp), clear your plate *and* accept seconds, when passing condiments place them on the table within the person's reach (not directly to their hand), and when you've finished place the knife and fork (prongs down) with handles facing to the right of the plate. Phew! Did you get all that? There's one more thing; a simple invitation for 'coffee and cake' may well constitute up to seven different sweet delights – you will be expected to sample them all.

**WHOSE ROUND IS IT?** The answer to that is simple; generally, it's nobody's. Being an egalitarian lot, Finns like to buy their drinks individually. Or it could be that buying rounds gets so damn expensive? Whichever, it's not unusual to see a group of friends lined up at the bar, each waiting his or her turn (queuing, remember?).

## LOCAL CHARITIES

**A-Clinic Foundation (A-Klinikkasäätiö)** Paasivuorenkatu 2a; ☎ 622 0290; www.a-klinikka.fi/english. The leading substance abuse service provider in Finland, A-Clinic is a non-profit NGO with 19 outpatient and inpatient facilities specialising in the treatment of alcohol and drug abuse, from detoxification programmes to therapeutic counselling.

23

**Finnish Association for Nature Conservation (Suomen Luonnonsuojeluliitto)** Kotkankatu 9, 00510 Helsinki; ℡ 228 091; www.sll.fi. Finland's foremost nature conservation charity promotes public and political awareness of the need to protect the environment.

**No Fixed Abode (Vailla vakinaista asuntoa ry)** Kinaporinkatu 2; ℡ 701 5338; www.vvary.fi. An organisation for the homeless, by the homeless. No Fixed Abode aims to improve the quality of life for those sleeping rough and in shelters, with the ultimate aim of providing the chance to live independently under their own roof. To raise awareness the group organises the Night of the Homeless on 17 October each year.

**The Finnish Red Cross (Punainen Risti)** Tehtaankatu 1a; ℡ 12 931; www.redcross.fi/en_GB. One of the largest civic organisations in Finland, with 95,000 members and more than 200,000 blood donors.

**The Mannerheim League for Child Welfare (Mannerheimin Lastensuojeluliito)** The Central Office, Toinen linja 17; ℡ 075 324 51; www.mll.fi/in_english. Finland's largest child welfare organisation promotes responsible parenting and the right to childhood for every child. Under the patronage of President Tarja Halonen, the League also co-operates with NGOs in Russia and Estonia, as well as contributing to African aid projects.

## BUSINESS

Being something of an isolated northern outpost, Finland has never really been at the hub of European business but has nevertheless developed into an attractive location for commerce. In a report by the World Economics Forum, Finland was deemed to have the world's best climate for business and also the most competitive economy.

Factors crucial in the award of that accolade included the conditions for sustained growth and the quality of the country's infrastructure. Certainly Finland excels in the latter of these fields, with telecommunications giant Nokia (and a host of other technological pioneers) helping to keep the country at the cutting edge of business technology. Helsinki bulges with excellent business hotels, all kitted out with free WiFi and outstanding conference facilities.

Business etiquette is similar to that in western Europe and the US. The standard attire is a dark coloured, conservative business suit (for the ladies, trouser suit, skirt or smart dress), a firm handshake is used for greeting and business cards are exchanged. There is no particular ritual associated with the exchange of cards, but it is preferable to present it so that it is readable to the recipient. In return treat their card with respect, as this symbolises the way in which you will also treat them.

Punctuality is an important part of the Finnish culture. Always arrange meetings in advance, either by telephone or email, and be sure to arrive on time. If you are likely to be delayed, even by five minutes, telephone and offer your apologies.

Once the introductions have been taken care of, you can expect to get straight down to brass tacks. Finns aren't known for small talk, and neither will they ask many questions during a meeting. Rather, they will expect your presentation to tell them everything they need to know, thus eliminating the need for questions! Direct talking is the norm; be succinct and avoid hyperbole, bragging or any embellished salesman-like spiel.

Finns like to build their business on long-term relationships, but equally they will not be afraid to enter into an agreement if you convince them of your worth. The bonding process quite naturally leads to the sauna, and if invited you should not refuse. Finally, choose your words carefully; in Finnish culture a man's word is taken to be his bond and will be treated as seriously as a written contract.

## USEFUL CONTACTS

**American Chamber of Commerce in Finland** (Managing Director, Natasha Seeley) Vilhonkatu 6a; ☏ 45 136 6303; f 675 387; www.amcham.fi

**Central Chamber of Commerce of Finland** (Managing Director, Mr Kari Jalas, Dr Pol Sc) World Trade Center Helsinki, Aleksanterinkatu 17; ☏ 696 969; f 650 303; e keskuskauppakamari@chamber.fi; www.chamber.fi

**Finlandia Hall** (*www.finlandia.hel.fi*) is the large Alvar Aalto-designed auditorium & convention centre on the shore of Töölönlahti Bay.

**Finnish-British Chamber of Commerce** 5 Arlington St, London SW1A 1RA; ☏ 020 7647 4496; f 020 7408 4426; e assistant@fbcc.co.uk; www.fbcc.co.uk

**Finnish Government** www.government.fi

**Helsinki Stock Exchange** www.hex.com

**Marina Congress Centre** (*www.marinacongresscentre.com*) is on the island of Katajanokka, near the Uspenski Cathedral & South Harbour ferry terminals.

**Ministry of Finance** www.vm.fi

**Ministry of Trade and Industry** www.ktm.fi

# RELIGION

Statistics say that most Finns, 84%, belong to the Evangelical-Lutheran Church, with a minority of 1% belonging to the Russian Orthodox faith. Some 14% have no religious denomination at all, whilst Jews, Muslims and Roman Catholics comprise the majority of the remaining 1%.

In reality, life in Finland is fairly secular and religion plays no great part in everyday life. There are no ostentatious outward signs of religious belief and quite often it is nigh on impossible to separate practising worshippers from their inactive brethren. Despite this, personal religious views are respected and visitors to Finland are unlikely to experience any difficulties. Followers of minority religions may encounter some ignorance, more so in smaller towns, but this is generally the result of a genuine lack of knowledge as opposed to prejudice.

Christianity arrived in Finland around 1,000 years ago, when the Northern Crusades led by Sweden and Denmark aimed to eradicate paganism from countries around the Baltic Sea. Missionaries from western Churches soon followed and by the beginning of the 14th century it was clear that most of Finland was under the Roman Catholic Church. By introducing established European conventions the new administration fostered education and artistic development, and provided an improved quality of life to the sick and needy.

The Protestant Lutheran reformation that swept Finland in the 1520s was notable for one facet above all others. Quite simply, it allowed King Gustav Vasa to nullify the

27

influence of the Church and transfer much of its wealth to the Crown. By 1593 Sweden had accepted Lutheranism as the state religion, a resolute act that severed links with Rome. As Lutheranism took hold Mikael Agricola, Finland's first Lutheran bishop, translated the New Testament to Finnish in 1543 and people became more literate as the Church adopted a cultural role aimed towards nurturing its congregation.

Although Swedish rule ended in 1809, when Finland became a Grand Duchy in the Russian Empire, there was no attempt to impose the Orthodox religion and Lutheranism was allowed to remain the state Church of Finland. In fact, the Ecclesiastical Act of 1869 separated the strict bond between Church and State and allowed the Lutherans enhanced levels of independence.

The 20th century saw the Church become more politicised as Finland found itself embroiled in war. When the nation declared independence in 1917, most clergy sided with the wealthy elite in a move which served to distance religious leaders from the organised working classes. In a sign that the Church was losing its once unilateral powers, the Constitution of 1919 and the 1923 Freedom of Religion Act gave Finns the chance to freely follow their belief of choice for the first time. Prior to the 1889 Act of Nonconformity every Finn was obliged to commit to either the Lutheran or Orthodox faith.

Despite this apparent negation of authority, it was the Lutheran faith that acted as a source of unity during the Winter War with the Soviet Union (1939–40). After peace was agreed, a new edict of social work and youth development carried the Church into the second half of the 20th century. Despite some blips in the 1960s and

1970s, when leaders were derided for their undemocratic and old-fashioned ways, this work has been generally well received and continues to the present day.

Judaism arrived in Finland in the early 19th century, courtesy of merchant traders and men in the employ of the Russian military. During World War II it is a peculiar fact that Finnish Jews were not persecuted, and many even fought alongside German troops. Today, there are about 1,500 Jews in Finland, with synagogues in Helsinki and Turku.

It was the Russian army who also brought the first Muslims to Finland, towards the latter stages of the 19th century, who together with Tatar merchants formed the core of the Finnish Islamic Congregation that was established in 1925. Although small, Helsinki's mosque is active and the population has swollen to around 20,000 in recent years with the influx of refugees seeking asylum.

For details of religious services, see *Chapter 3, Practicalities*, pages 93–4.

## CULTURE

Finland's cultural history bears comparison with any in the world, but with a unique language and reticent personal nature it's a world closed to many who don't speak the lingo.

The single most important literary text is the *Kalevala*, published in two volumes during 1835–36. Compiled by Elias Lönnrot from stirring tales of ancient folklore, the poem is rich with imagery from nature and the spirit world. Faced with the task of intertwining contributions from dozens of poets, Lönnrot chopped and changed stanzas to suit his theme, deleting superfluous passages and writing new sections as required. The text has become known as the *Finnish National Epic*, and such was its impact that it is believed to have acted as a catalyst in the country's awakening that ultimately led to independence from Russia. It would go on to influence every Finnish art form from classical music to interior design, evident most recently in the concept of the KlausKHotel in central Helsinki. Before you rush to the bookshop, tackling the *Kalevala* takes plenty of *sisu*; the poem's 50 chapters comprise an astonishing 22,000 verses!

If Lönnrot became the hero of 19th-century literature, it was the work of Lutheran reformers some 200 years previously that instigated the widespread use of the written Finnish language. Finland's first Lutheran bishop, Mikael Agricola, translated the New Testament to Finnish in 1543 and the Church began an active policy of education. Folklore continued to form the backbone of literature until 1870 when Alexis Kivi's *Seven Brothers* became the first Finnish novel. Kivi was Finland's appointed national writer, playwright and poet, as well as novelist, and the creator of the modern-day literary language. Famous 20th-century literary Finns include Mika Waltari and Frans Eemil Sillanpää, the latter of whom became the first Finnish winner of the Nobel Prize in Literature.

Despite its relative youth, the Finnish language in its written form has blossomed and the people have developed into a population of bookworms. Today there are more than 200 newspapers in production and over 10,000 books are published annually. The literacy rate is 100% and, relative to its population, the provision of library services is amongst the world's best. On average, each Finn withdraws 20 volumes from the library every year.

In music, one name dominates above all others. Jean Sibelius (1865–1957) was the leading composer of his generation, originally influenced by Wagner, whose classical pieces helped shape Finland's strong national identity and have since gained widespread international acclaim. For many years his composition *At The Castle Gate* has formed the theme music for the long-running BBC television programme *The Sky At Night*. Other composers who contributed to the Finnish classical style include Heino Kaski and Leevi Madetoja. Eila Hiltonen's unique monument is a fitting tribute to Sibelius (see pages 240–1).

Finland is also rich in opera and theatre. Kaarlo Bergbom founded the Finnish Opera in 1873, and prior to this the country received occasional visits from touring companies. But despite a lengthy history, true world acclaim did not arrive until the 1970s when new works from Aulis Sallinen promoted the national stage to a new level. Today, the Savonlinna Opera Festival is regarded as a major event in the international calendar and Helsinki boasts a state-of-the-art opera house on the shores of Töölönlahti. Operating an inclusive policy deigned to embrace the nation, tickets cost as little as € 12. Regular theatre productions in Finnish and Swedish happen in various theatres around Helsinki and other major towns.

Two other musical genres that enjoy widespread popularity are jazz and samba. Prominent jazz festivals and buzzing clubs typify this vibrant scene, whilst the love of samba manifests itself in several tuition schools and the annual Helsinki Samba Carnival.

Rock and roll arrived on Finnish shores in the 1950s, leading to the formation of Love Records in the 1960s, Finland's first and most famous record label of the genre. Throughout the 1960s and 1970s bands such as Blues Section, The Hurriganes and Wigwam tore up a storm at home and occasionally in Sweden, but seldom further afield. The late 1970s brought the punk wave that was already sweeping western Europe – all safety pins, spitting and spiky hair.

By the mid 1980s Finland was developing the hard rock circuit that still shapes much of its modern scene. Early runners like Rattus and Dingo were followed by one of the few bands to find international fame, Hanoi Rocks. Their style of power ballads, heavily influenced by the likes of Guns n' Roses, became so popular that at one stage it seemed likely that continental Europe would not be able to keep up with demand for tight trousers, hairspray and dry ice! Leningrad Cowboys operate in a similar vein and remain popular.

The legacy of such rock acts carries over into the modern music scene, which is heavily dominated by death metal groups. Bands of this genre that you probably won't have heard of include Nightwish, Sentenced, Children of Bodom and Sonata Arctica. One band you may be familiar with is HIM, who have achieved modest chart success in the UK and, to a lesser extent, the US. One of the biggest names of the indie music scene is The Rasmus, famous far beyond their own humble borders. Architecture in Helsinki, the quirky indie-pop quartet with the most Finnish-sounding name of all, actually hail from Australia.

Anyone who saw the 2006 Eurovision Song Contest will have seen monster-rockers Lordi triumph for Finland, the nation's first success in the competition. Famed for outlandish costumes, horror-movie latex facemasks and much guttural growling, the band is widely seen as something of a joke but, even so, some 100,000 people packed Helsinki's Market Square to see their glorious homecoming performance. Shortly afterwards, the 'Lordi-gate' scandal caused public outcry when gossip magazine 7 *päivää* (7 days) 'outed' the band, publishing photographs of the singer (Mr Lordi) without his trademark stage garb. Over 200,000 people signed an internet petition, subscriptions were cancelled, advertising campaigns shelved and the flood of protest calls closed the publisher's office for two days.

Amidst all this full-blooded rocking out, it won't surprise you to learn that Finland is the venue for the annual World Air Guitar Championships, a hilarious gathering of middle-aged men in vests, who really ought to know better but are at that dangerous age of just not caring.

If you prefer a little less cliché to your music then there's a vibrant indie, electronic and hip-hop scene pulsing through the bars and clubs of Helsinki, Turku and Tampere. To find the coolest sounds tune in to Radio Helsinki or make a visit to Stupido Records.

## PUBLIC HOLIDAYS

Nearly all businesses close for national holidays, with things pretty much grinding to a halt around midsummer and Christmas, although some shops will be open for part of the day on midsummer's eve and Christmas Eve.

| | |
|---|---|
| **New Year's Day** | 1 January |
| **Epiphany** | 6 January |
| **Good Friday** | 6 April 2007; 21 March 2008 |
| **Easter Day** | 8 April 2007; 23 March 2008 |
| **Easter Monday** | 9 April 2007; 24 March 2008 |
| **May Day** | 1 May |
| **Ascension Day** | 17 May 2007; 5 May 2008 |
| **Whit Sunday** | 27 May 2007; 11 May 2008 |
| **Midsummer's eve** | 22 June 2007; 21 June 2008 |
| **Midsummer's Day** | 23 June 2007; 22 June 2008 |
| **All Saints' Day** | 3 November 2007; 1 November 2008 |
| **Independence Day** | 6 December |
| **Christmas Eve** | 24 December |
| **Christmas Day** | 25 December |
| **Boxing Day** | 26 December |

## FESTIVALS AND EVENTS

Helsinkiites love a cultural gathering and a good excuse for a party, whatever the time of year. Many of these events can be enjoyed free of charge, but where tickets are required the Helsinki City Tourist Bureau will point you in the right direction. The biggest public celebrations are May Day, Helsinki Day, midsummer and Independence

Day. The premier arts bash is the two-week-long Helsinki Festival. The website (*www.festivals.fi*) has a comprehensive countrywide rundown of happening events.

## DOCPOINT *end of January*
Showcasing the most noteworthy documentary films from Sweden, Norway, Russia, Lithuania, Latvia, Estonia and Finland, at cinemas around central Helsinki. See www.docpoint.info/eng.

## RUNEBERG DAY *5 February*
Finland's national poet, Johan Ludvig Runeberg (1804–77), is commemorated with a day of scoffing tasty Runeberg cakes – a delicious cylindrically shaped treat made from wheat and crumbs, spiced with almonds and rum and topped with a ring of icing and a splurge of jam!

## HELSINKI BEER FESTIVAL *around 8–9 April*
Celebrating the best real ales, speciality lagers and Finnish microbreweries. See www.helsinkibeerfestival.com.

## MAY DAY *1 May*
Predominantly a festival practised by students, *Vappu* sees a raucous atmosphere envelop the city as drunken revellers take over the streets. Tree climbing, streaking, copulating and communal sing-alongs are all-important May Day rituals, as is the traditional washing of the Havis Amanda statue in the Esplanade Park.

## WORLD VILLAGE FESTIVAL *around 27–28 May*

Free gathering in Kaisaniemi Park that kicks off the summer festival season. Cultural activities and performances from around the globe are spread across four stages, including music, dance, theatre, literature, sport and food. See www.maailmakylassa.fi.

## NAISTEN KYMPPI *end of May*

Gents, you can sit back and put your feet up for this one. Naisten Kymppi is Finland's biggest sporting event for women, where over 15,000 participants walk, jog and run the rural 10km city course. You can tell there are no men involved – the website declares, 'Naisten Kymppi is not a competition, everyone entering the finish line is a winner!' See www.naistenkymppi.fi.

## HELSINKI DAY *12 June*

To commemorate the founding of Helsinki, people across the city indulge in traditional coffee and rhubarb cake. Special events include free concerts in Kaivopuisto Park, public gatherings in the major squares and free entry to many museums.

## HELSINKI SAMBA CARNIVAL *around 16–17 June*

Samba is surprisingly popular in Finland, and this summer carnival wiggles its way through the city with a variety of outdoor performances and late-night booty shaking. See www.samba.fi.

## HELSINKI PRIDE FESTIVAL *around 25 June–1 July*

A week of partying, parading, exhibitions and workshops (literature, theatre and dancing) for Finland's gay and lesbian community. See www.helsinkipride.fi.

## MIDSUMMER *end of June*

Finland's most important festival, midsummer (*Juhannus*) is celebrated religiously over a weekend at the end of June. Most people leave Helsinki and head for their summer cottages – the majority of businesses and some hotels close – but those who stay can enjoy the big bonfire spectacular on the island of Seurasaari. See www.kolumbus.fi/seurasaarisaatio.

## EUROPEAN CHAMPIONSHIP IN SALMON FISHING AND SALMON MARKET *around 30 June–2 July*

Competitive fishing along the shores of Kaivopuisto Park to determine Europe's top individual, boat and team salmon fishermen. If you're no good with the rod and tackle, simply enjoy the tasty treats on the nearby market.

## KONEISTO FESTIVAL *around 14–15 July*

Hip and happening electronic music festival with top DJs and producers filling several venues around town. See www.koneisto.com.

## HELSINKI CITY MARATHON *around August*

One of the world's most scenic marathon courses, you can follow the Baltic Sea coast past some of Helsinki's greatest landmarks. See www.helsinkicitymarathon.com.

## HELSINKI FESTIVAL *around 18 August–3 September*

Helsinki's big cultural bash, the festival presents theatre, song, dance, cinema, circus and children's events in two-dozen venues across the city, incorporating Art Goes Kapakka, Taiteiden Yö and Viapori Jazz. See www.helsinkifestival.fi.

## ART GOES KAPAKKA *around 18–27 August*

Taking performances of music and theatre into the city's restaurants and clubs. *Kapakka* is the Finnish word for 'tavern'. See www.artgoeskapakka.fi.

## TAITEIDEN YÖ *last Thursday in August*

The annual 'Night of the Arts' festival takes place during the Helsinki Festival, when museums and galleries stay open until late, and various dance, theatre and musical performances take place throughout the night. For some the night brings the curtain down on the summer season, and is marked by exuberant partying and enthusiastic consumption of alcohol – hence the modern nickname 'Little May Day'.

## VIAPORI JAZZ *around 23–26 August*

Finns love a bit of jazz, and this series of concerts presents the best. The festival has a unique location on Suomenlinna, the 18th-century UNESCO World Heritage-listed sea fortress. See www.viaporijazz.fi.

## HELSINKI INTERNATIONAL FILM FESTIVAL *around 14–24 September*
Celebrating the best of cinema, with categories including young European, modern, American independents, contemporary world, gay and lesbian, fantasy, modern documentary and animation. Operating under the title 'Love & Anarchy', it also presents a mix of bizarre, eccentric and controversial films. See www.hiff.fi.

## HELSINKI DESIGN WEEK *around 23 September–1 October*
An international festival presenting new ideas in design and highlighting the brightest current stars, with exhibitions, open studios and events to help the homeless. There's also a two-day design market, where last season's lines are offered at discounted prices before the festival gets underway. See www.helsinkidesignweek.fi.

## BALTIC HERRING MARKET *around 1–7 October*
Practically all Finns love Baltic herrings. The plentiful little *silakka* comprises a staple part of the national diet, and during this week-long festival tens of thousands of visitors come to sample the best recipes and compete in various herring-based competitions.

**FORCES OF LIGHT FESTIVAL** *mid November to early December*
The gloomiest part of the year is illuminated through light installations (neon, diffused colours, candles) that bathe the city in dramatic colours and dancing luminescence.

**INDEPENDENCE DAY** *6 December*
Celebrating the declaration of independence from the Russian Empire, Finland's Independence Day (*Itsenäisyyspäivä*) is a national public holiday involving a service at Helsinki Cathedral, a reception at the Presidential Palace and the lighting of candles across the country.

**VANHA CHRISTMAS MARKET** *around 14–23 December*
In the Vanha Ylioppilastalo (Old Student House), this is the place to get the feel of *Pikkujoulu* (Little Christmas) with over 160 atmospheric gift stalls, parties being organised and much *glögi* (hot punch) being quaffed.

## GEOGRAPHY

Finland is one of Europe's northernmost countries, occupying a territory of 338,000km$^2$, nearly one-and-a-half times larger than the UK and three-times greater than the US state of Ohio. It has approximately 1,100km of coastline, with the Gulf of Finland to the south and the Gulf of Bothnia to the west. The country has borders with Russia (1,340km), Norway (736km) and Sweden (614km). In the far northwest, near the village of Kilpisjärvi, the Finnish, Norwegian and Swedish frontiers, marked with a border stone, meet on an artificial island in Koltajärve Lake.

Finland is a low-lying country; apart from a small highland area in the extreme northwest, the land generally does not rise higher than 180m above sea level. Some 69% of the land is covered in forest. Relative to its size, Finland has more freshwater coverage than any other nation; 10% of the terrain is given over to an astonishing 187,888 lakes. Amidst these lakes and liberally peppering the coastline are myriad islands – 179,584 in total – of which the autonomous Åland Islands off the southwest coast are the most famous.

Helsinki is Finland's capital and situated on the southern coast, located in a strategic position on the Gulf of Finland where trading was easiest and the climate most temperate. The foremost trading route was the King's Road, the 13th-century route that connected the northern capitals of Oslo, Stockholm, Turku and St Petersburg.

## CLIMATE

First-time visitors to Helsinki are often surprised at the city's temperate climate, where the influence of the Gulf Stream contributes to a generally mild environment. Average temperatures are around 17°C in summer, and about –4°C in winter.

Seasonal variations can be extreme. Summer heatwaves can push the mercury above 25°C for days on end, whilst winter cold snaps can see temperatures plunge

41

below −10°C for considerable periods. Northeasterly winds from the Arctic produce the lowest temperatures, when the wind chill may see figures of −20°C or below. Whatever the time of year, the weather can be changeable – warm and sunny one day, cool and raining the next or, in winter, sudden deep frosts and snowfall.

Helsinki's most miserable months are November and December; at these times the gloom is profound. On the winter solstice, 21 December, there is less than six hours of daylight. The sun, should you be fortunate enough to see it, radiates a reddish glow across the horizon. When the snow begins to fall, which is usually in November, the city receives more light. But the first covering usually melts within a couple of days and it is normally approaching Christmas before the snow begins to settle in any depth, shrouding the city in a satisfyingly soft blanket. The contrast between the breezy greens of summer and this icy winter cloak are marked, and present a city whose character is distinctly different in these opposing seasons.

January and February are the coldest months, when frosts are at their most severe and the sea will usually be frozen. The snow cover continues to grow. During this deep midwinter period, there are some spectacularly bright and clear days. At such times, under a deep-blue sky, the best thing is simply to muffle up and walk through the city, across the parks and down to the coast where the air is at its freshest.

By March the days are lengthening rapidly and the snow begins to melt. Spring bursts into life in April, when the thaw produces slushy underfoot conditions. Daytime temperatures begin to nudge above freezing, although nights can still be bitter. Even though days can be warm, the cold sea keeps spring lagging behind the sheltered city, especially around the archipelago.

As summer dawns Helsinki is in full bloom and the days are long. At midsummer, the sun rises before 04.00 and does not set until nearly 23.00. True darkness never arrives, and a walk through the city in the early hours reveals a still bright horizon in the distant north. Long sunny evenings are a delight, with temperatures remaining surprisingly warm until 21.00 and after.

To see if you need long johns or factor 30, check the Finnish Meteorological Society website (*www.fmi.fi*).

**FCO TRAVEL ADVICE**
know before you go
fco.gov.uk/travel

Bradt Travel Guides is a partner to the 'know before you go' campaign, masterminded by the UK Foreign and Commonwealth Office to promote the importance of finding out about a destination before you travel. By combining the up-to-date advice of the FCO with the in-depth knowledge of Bradt authors, you'll ensure that your trip will be as trouble-free as possible.

# www.fco.gov.uk/travel

Bradt

N

**KALLIO**

**KATAJANOKKA**

**CENTRAL HELSINKI**

**TÖÖLÖ**

**EIRA**

Porvoo (50km)

Helsinki-Vantaa Airport (18km)

Hansa Terminal

Helsinki Zoo

Ministry of Foreign Affairs

Tallinn

Tallinn & Stockholm

Gulf of Finland

Tallinn

Stockholm

Suomenlinna

trains to airport, Moscow & St Petersburg

Hotel Finnapartments Fenno

Hakaniemi Market Square

Kuudes Linja

Hilton Helsinki Strand

Korkeasaari

North Harbour

Tervasaari

Accomi Senate

Kanavaranta

Scandic Grand Marina

Katajanokka Terminal

Eurohostel

Valkosaari

Luoto

Särkkä

Hotel Aurora

Kallio Church

Helsinki City Theatre

Botanic Garden

Burgher's House

Military Museum

Presidential Palace

Lutheran Cathedral

Kanava Terminal

Makasiini Terminal

C L Engel

Observatory

Olympia Terminal

United States

France

United Kingdom

South Harbour

Tuomarinkylä Disc Golf Course

Club Liberté

Finnish National Opera

Olympic Stadium (360m)

Eläintarhanlahti

Töölönlahti

Seurasaari (3.5km)

Hakasalmi Museum

Railway station

Kamppi bus station & shopping centre

The Old Church

Ursa Observatory

Liuskasaari

Sirpalesaari

Pihlajasaari

Finnish National Opera

National Museum of Finland

Finlandia Hall

Accomi Parliament

Sibelius Monument

Tram Museum

Scandic Continental

Hietaniemi Cemetery

Sinebrychoff Museum of Foreign Art

Mikael Agricola Church

Confectioner Alenius

Helsinki Car Museum

West Terminal

Copterline helicopter terminal

Tallinn

West Harbour

MANNERHEIMINTIE

HÄMEENTIE

HELSINGINKATU

KAISANIEMENKATU

POHJOISESPLANADI

LÖNNROTINKATU

FREDRIKINKATU

TEHTAANKATU

LAIVASILLANKATU

KANAVAKATU

ALEKSANTERINKATU

ARKADIANKATU

RUNEBERGINKATU

MECHELININKATU

RUOHOLAHDENKATU

0    500m
0    500yds

# 2 Planning

## HELSINKI – A PRACTICAL OVERVIEW

Central Helsinki is compact and for the most part arranged around a series of regular block-like grids. Located on an unusual peninsula protruding from the Finnish mainland, it is surrounded by the sea on three sides.

In the east the well-known tourist areas of Senate Square and Market Square lie at the end of Aleksanterinkatu and the Esplanade Park respectively. Nearby are some of the most expensive shops, cafés and restaurants and the greatest landmarks of the Helsinki skyline, the twin cathedrals serving the Lutheran and Orthodox communities.

Mannerheimintie, the main road in and out of the city, borders Aleksanterinkatu and the Esplanade Park at their western extremity. Heading in a northwesterly direction, the angle of Mannerheimintie dictates that the blocks on its western and southern sides run at 45 degrees to those on the east side. Within these quieter blocks can be found some of Helsinki's most stylish designer boutiques and fashionable nightspots, renowned for their independent spirit and cutting-edge vision.

The grid system becomes somewhat less distinct in other areas of the city. The swathes of Kaivopuisto Park dominate the southeastern corner, a leafy embassy district characterised by ornate wooden villas and private sailing boats. On the southwestern extremity, the commercial ports that handle Helsinki's sea freight form the backdrop to the dignified Jugendstil architecture of the Eira district.

Moving north from the centre, to the west of the railway tracks is Töölönlahti, a beautiful sea lagoon with pleasant parkland with significant landmarks such as Finlandia Hall and the Finnish National Opera. It is possible to meander through the open space as far as the Olympic Stadium and on to the city's large Central Park without hindrance. The neighbouring Töölö district is principally an upmarket residential area.

East of the railway are the working-class quarters of Hakaniemi and Kallio, offering the chance to see everyday Helsinki life, from the best food markets to brawling drunks and some real spit 'n' sawdust bars.

Some 5km north of the city centre is Vanhakaupunki, the 'Old Town'. It is here, by the mouth of the frothy River Vantaa, that Helsinki was founded in 1550.

All around the city are dotted islands of the Helsinki archipelago. There are some 315 in total; the following are ones you are most likely to encounter: Suomenlinna, Seurasaari, Korkeasaari, Harakka, Mustasaari, Pihlajasaari and Uunisaari.

Helsinki-Vantaa Airport is 19km north of the centre. The journey from the city can only be made by road (car, bus or taxi) and takes approximately 30 minutes.

**KATU OR GATAN?** Finland is a bilingual country, and whilst Swedish speakers are very much in the minority (some 6.5% compared with 88.2% native Finnish speakers) democratic Helsinki caters to both.

Most signs give instructions in both tongues, which can be a little confusing at first.

For starters, Helsinki translates into Swedish as Helsingfors, and every district or town (and each individual street) also has a Finnish and Swedish name. Although these are for the most part similar, it's not always the case. For example, we have the districts of Kamppi/Kampen (Finnish/Swedish) and Kaisaniemi/Kajsaniemi, both of which are similar and easily understood. But what about Kallio/Berghall, or Punavuori/Rödbergen? They're nothing like the same!

Streets work the same way. Two words you will soon become familiar with are *katu* and *gatan*, Finnish and Swedish respectively for 'street'. These suffixes are attached to most road names, yielding results such as Aleksanterinkatu/Alexandersgatan, Eerikinkatu/Eriksgatan and Lönnrotinkatu/Lönnrotsgatan. The order breaks when these suffixes are absent, for example Eteläranta/Södra kajen, although these distinctions are the exception and not the rule. Wherever you are in Helsinki the street signs are excellent, with the Finnish name always written above the Swedish.

Throughout this guide, Finnish names are used in conjunction with English translations that may help clarify meanings. The only time you really need to pay close attention is when using a bilingual map, when accurate identification of names can save a lot of wasted time on the ground. To help you on your way, here are a few commonly used words.

| | | | |
|---|---|---|---|
| *katu* | street | *terminaali* | terminal |
| *tori* | square | *lahti* | bay |
| *puisto* | park | *vanha* | old |

| | | | |
|---|---|---|---|
| *silta* | bridge | *uusi* | new |
| *kirkko* | church | *pohjoinen* | north |
| *tuomiokirkko* | cathedral | *etelä(inen)* | south |
| *saari* | island | *itä(inen)* | east |
| *satama* | harbour | *länsi* | west |

## WHEN TO VISIT (AND WHY)

Helsinki is one of those rare capital cities where summer and winter offer two distinct experiences. Between June and August the weather is at its best, with long days, bright nights and temperatures that can make other European countries green with envy. Streets bustle, parks are in full bloom, and the packed summer terraces show a city and people at ease with the world. Accordingly it is also the busiest time, so if you fancy a bit less hustle and bustle then May and September are still good options.

Come winter, it's a radically different picture. October, November and December are often gloomy and damp, with less than six hours of daylight on the shortest day. Come Christmas the snow has usually settled for the winter. From January to March temperatures rarely rise above freezing (and are often well below), but on clear, crisp days Helsinki is a joy to behold. You can cross-country ski through the city forests, try a spot of ice swimming or simply wander off across the frozen sea. The Gulf of Finland freezes during most winters, and to see it for the first time is a thrill. The end of February and beginning of March can also

## A TRIP TO FORGET

All across Helsinki, peppering the city streets with liberal regularity, small metal pegs poke from doorsteps and pavements. Ostensibly designed for the purpose of holding open doors, they serve more to trip unsuspecting tourists on their way to and from shops, cafés and hotels. In summer you can spot them readily enough, but come winter they lurk beneath the surface of fresh snowfall ready to catch the next passer-by unawares. If you are not careful you could find yourself not just with a worm's-eye-view of Helsinki but also a mouthful of *loska*, the dirty city slush that accumulates in the gutter.

be good times to visit – still cold and snowy but with a little extra daylight.

The only downside to a winter visit is that some museums and attractions are closed, but if you muffle yourself against the elements there's more than enough to keep you entertained in the open air. And if that fails, there's always the soothing sauna and the reassuringly cosy cafés.

## HIGHLIGHTS/SUGGESTED ITINERARIES

### JUST HERE FOR THE WEEKEND

- Indulge in the true Finnish passion, sauna, and follow it up with a cool beer (see pages 201–3).

Helsinki glows through the long days of summer, but if you are planning a winter visit here are a few seasonal treats not to be missed:

- Stroll across the frozen sea to Uunisaari.
- Stimulate your circulation with a spot of sauna and *avanto* (ice swimming).
- Explore the city forests on snowshoes or cross-country skis, go skating or catch an ice-hockey match.
- Bump through the icy waters to Suomenlinna, invariably deserted in the depths of winter.
- Visit Santa at the Vanha Christmas Market and get into the spirit of *Pikkujoulu* (Little Christmas) with a few glasses of warm *glögi*.
- Take coffee and cake in a snug café and just watch the snow flutter down.

- Take the ferry from Market Square to the 18th-century sea fortress of Suomenlinna, a UNESCO World Heritage Site (see page 258–61).
- Sip coffee and scoff *korvapuustit* (cinnamon buns) on the summer terrace at one of Helsinki's wonderfully grand cafés (see page 152–7).
- Discover the local markets – Hakaniemi for the best fresh food and Hietaniemi with its secondhand treasures, from clothes to Soviet-era relics (see pages 188–9).

- Explore the city on foot – wander the leafy embassy district of Kaivopuisto (see pages 214–18), follow an architectural tour through Katajanokka (see page 213) or take a gentle stroll around elegant Töölönlahti (see pages 209–12).
- Browse some museums and galleries – satisfy your artistic appetite at the traditional Ateneum Art Museum (see page 229), push the boundaries at the Museum of Contemporary Art Kiasma (see page 230) or visit any number of specialised exhibitions.
- Eat a traditional Finnish dinner of Baltic herrings and mashed potatoes.
- Take to the sea and uncover Helsinki's archipelago. Join a cruise or just nip across to one of the islands – Harakka for its flora and fauna (see page 254), Pihlajasaari for beaches (see page 256), or the open-air museum of Seurasaari for compelling history and friendly squirrels (see page 256).
- Admire the view from the 72m-high Olympic Stadium tower or the 12th-floor Ateljee Bar in Hotel Torni (see page 168).
- Give your flexible friend a workout in the Design District, fit to burst with over 100 different boutiques, galleries and interior design shops (see page 180).
- Stay up late and just enjoy the novelty of long days and bright nights.

## STAYING A FEW DAYS LONGER...

- Embrace nature with an adventure through Central Park (see pages 248–50) or Nuuksio National Park (see pages 263–4).
- Sail across the Baltic for a day trip to medieval Tallinn (see pages 268–73)

51

- Cruise through the archipelago to the old wooden town of Porvoo (see pages 264–7).
- Ride the bus to Vanhakaupunki, where Helsinki was founded in 1550 (see page 253)

## TOUR OPERATORS

Package holidays, city breaks, tailor-made tours and flights are readily available through UK- and US-based tour operators specialising in western Europe and the Nordic countries. In addition to those below, see *Local tours* and *Local travel agents* (see pages 95–7 and 97–9 respectively), some of which can arrange accommodation or travel.

### IN THE UK

**Aeroscope Limited** Scope Hse, Hospital Rd, Moreton in Marsh, Glos GL56 0BQ; ℡ 01608 650103; f 01608 651295; e tours@aeroscope.co.uk; www.aeroscope.co.uk. City breaks, fly/drive itineraries, rail travel, car hire, hotel bookings & cottage reservations.

**Can Be Done** 11 Woodcock Hill, Harrow HA3 0XP; ℡ 020 8907 2400; e holidays@canbedone.co.uk; www.canbedone.co.uk. Specialising in wheelchair-accessible holidays.

**Emagine Travel** 87–89 Church St, Leigh, Greater Manchester WN7 1AZ; ℡ 0870 902 5399; e info@emagine-travel.co.uk; www.emagine-travel.co.uk. One of the most comprehensive portfolios – city breaks, fly-drive tours & brown bear safaris.

**FinnishLakesideCabins** ℡ 01707 256398; e findout@fnnishlakesidecabins.com; www.finnishlakesidecabins.com. Web-based agent with over 250 holiday cabins throughout Finland, some within a short drive of Helsinki.

**Guild Travel** 1A Mornington Court, Lower Ground Floor, Mornington Crescent, London NW1 7RD; ☎ 020 7388 4158; f 020 7529 8750; e mail@guildtravel.com; www.guildtravel.com. City breaks & fly-cruise options — fly to Stockholm, cruise to Helsinki.

**Mantrav International** Meath Hse, 2nd Floor, Crawley, West Sussex RH10 4NU; ☎ 0845 026 6906; f 0845 838 6922; e info@mantrav.eu; www.mantrav.co.uk. Gay & lesbian city breaks.

**Martin Randall Travel Ltd** Voysey Hse, Barley Mow Passage, London W4 4GF; ☎ 020 8742 3355; f 020 8742 7766; e info@martinrandall.co.uk; www.martinrandall.com. Alvar Aalto-themed architectural tours through Helsinki & further afield.

**Travel For The Arts** 12–15 Hanger Green, London W5 3EL; ☎ 020 8799 8350; f 020 8998 7965; e tfa@stlon.com; www.travelforthearts.co.uk. Opera breaks incorporating Helsinki & Tallinn.

## IN THE IRISH REPUBLIC

**Rory McDyer Travel** 49 Clontarf Rd, Dublin 3; ☎ +353 1 833 5100; f +353 1 833 5311; www.rorymcdyertravel.ie. Coach tours & city breaks.

**scandinaviantravel.ie** 1 Wexford St, Dublin 2; ☎ +353 1 4751177; f +353 1 4754683; e info@scandinaviantravel.ie; www.scandinaviantravel.ie. Comprehensive choice of city breaks & special-interest tours.

## IN THE US AND CANADA

**Abercrombie & Kent** 1520 Kensington Rd, Suite 212, Oak Brook, IL 60523-2156; ☎ +1 630 954 2944; f +1 630 954 3324; www.abercrombiekent.com. High-end tailor-made tours for individuals & small groups.

**Brendan Worldwide Vacations** 21625 Prairie St, Chatsworth, Los Angeles, CA 91311-5833; ☎ +1 800 421 8446;

e info@brendanvacations.com; www.brendanvactions.com. Multi-destination tours taking in Helsinki & other Scandinavian capitals, as well as wilderness destinations. Flights, accommodation & car hire.

**Continental Journeys** 5249 Leghorn Av, Sherman Oaks, CA 91401; ✎ +1 800 601 4343; f +1 818 995 8673; e info@continentaljourneys.com; www.continentaljourneys.com. One of the largest selections of independent & guided tours. City breaks, specialist wilderness tours, island getaways, multi-country holidays & self-drive options.

## NATURE AND ACTIVITY SPECIALISTS

**Avian Adventures** 49 Sandy Rd, Stourbridge, West Midlands DY8 3AJ; ✎ 01384 372013; www.avianadventures.co.uk. Worldwide birdwatching tours, including a 2-week trip to arctic Finland & Norway that passes through Helsinki & its surrounding wetland areas.

**Naturetrek** Cheriton Mill, Cheriton, Alresford, Hants SO24 ONG; ✎ 01962 733051; f 01962 736426; e info@naturetrek.co.uk; www.naturetrek.co.uk. Winter weekends in search of owls or bear safaris along the Russian border. Neither trip visits Helsinki.

**Walks Worldwide** 12 The Square, Ingleton, Carnforth LA6 3EG; ✎ 01524 242000; e sales@ walksworldwide.com; www.walksworldwide.com. Trek the forests of the Russian borderland, with cabin, farm & cottage accommodation. Does not visit Helsinki.

## RED TAPE

**ENTRY REQUIREMENTS** European Union (EU) nationals, and citizens of Liechtenstein, Monaco, San Marino, Switzerland and all Schengen Agreement countries can enter Finland with a valid passport for stays of up to 90 days. Citizens of Scandinavian and Nordic countries (Denmark, Iceland, Norway and Sweden) need only an identity card. American visitors are also entitled to a visa-free stay of up to 90 days, although the time period begins at the date of entry to the first Schengen Agreement country. Visitors from South Africa will require a visa.

Anybody planning to visit Russia will require a visa and you are advised to obtain this in their country of residence. Applications may be made in Helsinki, but the process takes eight working days and you must leave your passport at the Russian embassy.

Estonia is now a member of the EU and as such day trips to Tallinn are straightforward, unless you are South African in which case you will once again have to apply for a visa (*www.vm.ee*).

Crossing into Norway and Sweden is possible anywhere along the border, but the Russian border may only be crossed by road at the following points: Vaalimaa, Nuijamaa and Niirala (*open 24 hours*), Imatra (*open 07.00–23.00*) and Vartius, Raja-Jooseppi and Salla (*open 07.00–21.00*). If you travel to and from Russia by train, border formalities will be taken care of as part of the journey.

**CUSTOMS REGULATIONS** There are few problems at Finnish customs. Travellers entering from another EU country may import purchases exempt from tax without restriction on quantity or value.

If you're entering from outside the EU, restrictions are as follows. Visitors aged 17 or over can take 200 cigarettes, 100 cigarillos, 50 cigars or 250g of tobacco (or a combination of the respective amounts), 50g of perfume and 0.25 litres of eau de toilette in and out of Finland. Visitors aged 15 years or over may import 100g of tea (or 40g of tea extract), and 500g of coffee (or 200g of coffee extract or concentrate).

As for alcohol, visitors aged 18 or over can import two litres of aperitif (under 22%) or sparkling wines, two litres of other wine and 16 litres of beer. Adults over 20 years of age can import the same amounts, *or* one litre of spirits or liquor stronger than 22%. Given Finland's relatively high alcohol prices you may well want to take a bottle or two, but home-brew kits of any form are strictly prohibited!

Permits are required for the import and export of products derived from endangered animals (eg: furs from wolves or bears), but this does not apply to the reindeer skins much favoured by many tourists – the reindeer is considered a semi-domestic animal.

Finland has no restriction on the importation of currency.

## Ⓔ FINNISH EMBASSIES OVERSEAS

**Australia** 12 Darwin Av, Yarralumla, Canberra, ACT 2600; ☏ +61 2 6273 3800; f +61 2 6273 3603;
e sanomat.can@formin.fi; www.finland.org.au
**Canada** 55 Metcalfe St, Suite 850, Ottawa, Ontario K1P 6L5; ☏ +1 613 288 2233; f +1 613 288 2244;
e embassy@finland.ca; www.finalnd.ca

**Estonia** Kohtu 4, Tallinn 15180; ☎ +372 6103 200; f +372 6103 281; e sanomat.tal@formin.fi; www.finland.ee

**France** 1 Pl de Finlande, 75007 Paris; ☎ + 33 1 44 18 19 20; f + 33 1 45 55 51 57; e sanomat.par@formin.fi; www.amb-finlande.fr

**Germany** Rauchstrasse 1, 01787 Berlin; ☎ +49 30 50 50 30; f +49 30 50 50 33 33; e info.berlin@formin.fi; www.finnland.de

**Irish Republic** Russell Hse, Stokes Pl, St Stephen's Green, Dublin 2; ☎ + 353 1 478 1344; f + 353 1 478 3727; e sanomat.dub@formin.fi; www.finalnd.ie

**Italy** Via Lisbona 3, 00198 Rome; ☎ +39 06 852 231; f +39 06 854 0362; e sanomat.roo@formin.fi; www.finland.it

**Norway** Thomas Heftyes gate 1, Oslo 0244; ☎ +47 2212 4900; f +47 2212 4949; e sanomat.osl@formin.fi; www.finland.no/fi

**Russia** Kropotkinsky pereulok 15–17, Moscow 119034; ☎ +70 95 787 4174; f + 70 95 247 3380; e sanomat.mos@formin.fi; www.finemb-moscow.fi

**South Africa** 628 Leyds St, Muckleneuk, Pretoria 0002; ☎ +27 12 343 0275; f +27 12 343 3095; e sanomat.pre@formin.fi; www.finland.org.za

**Sweden** Jakobsgatan 6, 6tr, 10391 Stockholm; ☎ +46 8 676 6700; f + 46 8 207 497; e info@finland.se; www.finland.se/fi

**United Kingdom** 38 Chesham Pl, London SW1X 8HW; ☎ +44 020 7838 6200; f +44 020 7235 3680; e sanomat.lon@formin.fi; www.finemb.org.uk

**USA** 3301 Massachusetts Av, NW, Washington, DC 20008; ☎ +1 202 298 5800; f +1 202 298 6030; e sanomat.was@formin.fi; www.finland.org

## GETTING THERE AND AWAY

Finland is vast. The seventh-largest country in Europe extends north to the Arctic Circle over some 338,145km². Sharing borders with Sweden (614km), Norway (736km) and Russia (1,340km), and with coastline winding more than 1,150km around the Gulfs of Bothnia and Finland, entry and exit points are clearly myriad. Nonetheless, unless you plan to roam the wild north à la Baron Adolf Erik Nordenskiöld (Finland's famous 19th-century arctic explorer) it's likely that your first port of call will be Helsinki.

✈ **BY AIR** Traditionally, flying to the Nordic countries has been so expensive that the casual tourist could be forgiven for thinking that they were buying a whole fleet of aeroplanes, never mind a brief encounter with a cramped window seat. For many, this shock to the wallet was harder to digest than the turgid in-flight meal.

So welcome to the 21st century and a change for the better, with increasing choice and decreasing price. Although fares to Finland remain higher than many other tourist routes, the shift in pricing policy that so many airlines have adopted in recent years continues to make the country ever more accessible. With adequate preparation you can easily secure attractive deals, but poor organisation can still leave you seriously out of pocket.

**From the UK** The delineation between the no-frills airlines and major carriers in Finland is less distinct than in many other European countries. Whilst low-cost options have increased in recent years, the prices quoted are still sometimes far from budget. Conversely, and especially if you live close to London, fares with the flagship carriers Finnair and British Airways can almost be as good as those on offer from the likes of Ryanair or Blue1. As always, it's a simple matter of supply, demand and competition.

Currently you can fly direct to Helsinki-Vantaa Airport from London Heathrow, London Stansted, Manchester and Edinburgh (April–September). Additionally, carriers such as SAS Scandinavian Airlines (✆ 0870 607 2727; www.scandinavian.net), KLM (✆ 0870 507 4074; www.klm.com), Lufthansa (✆ 0870 837 7747; www.lufthansa.com) and Air France (✆ 0845 359 1000; www.airfrance.com) will happily whisk you northwards via a network of indirect flights, but bear in mind that this can more than double the duration of the flight, meaning a full day's travelling by the time you hit Helsinki.

**Blue1** www.blue1.com. Part of the Scandinavian SAS group, with twice-daily (*Sun–Fri*) direct flights from London Stansted. *Return fares £105–350.*

**British Airways** ✆ 0870 850 9850; www.ba.com. Numerous daily direct flights from London Heathrow. *Return fares start at a competitive £170.*

**Finnair** ✆ 0870 241 4411; www.finnair.com. Finland's national airline operates daily direct flights from London Heathrow & Manchester, with a twice-weekly direct service from Edinburgh. Paradoxically, ticket prices get gradually more expensive the closer you get to Finland — *the cheapest return fares from these airports are around £175, £210 & £250 respectively.*

**Ryanair** www.ryanair.com. The well-established London Stansted to Tampere route flies daily, although in typical Ryanair style this airport is nowhere near Helsinki (80km northwest). Somewhat atypical is that Ryanair doesn't try to pretend otherwise. Expect to pay from £70 upwards, although in summer 2006 I managed to get a return fare of just £32.50 with only a couple of weeks' notice. The journey from Tampere to Helsinki is straightforward by bus or train. Liverpool to Tampere is also now available.

**Sterling** ✆ 0870 787 8038; www.sterling.dk. In 2006, Scandinavia's largest low-cost airline operated a summer route between Edinburgh & Helsinki. From late June to mid August direct flights departed twice weekly, with fares from under £100. Keep your eyes peeled for a possible expanded service from 2007.

## From the Irish Republic
Finnair flies direct summer flights (*Apr–Sep*) from Dublin to Helsinki. Fares are similar to those from UK airports. Blue1 also offers low-cost direct flights from Dublin.

## From the US
Both Finnair and American Airlines offer direct flights between New York's JFK Airport and Helsinki-Vantaa, taking eight hours. Fares start at around US$600 return. British Airways and SAS Scandinavian Airlines operate indirect flights via London and Copenhagen respectively.

## From the rest of the world
Finnair operates an extensive network of international flights. Direct routes from Helsinki serve most major European cities and many Far East destinations, including Singapore, Bangkok, Beijing, Shanghai, Hong Kong and Tokyo.

Blue1 offers low-cost flights from Helsinki to Amsterdam, Athens, Barcelona, Berlin, Brussels, Budapest, Copenhagen, Gothenburg, Hamburg, Nice, Oslo, Paris, Rome, Stockholm, Warsaw and Zürich.

All of the airlines listed below serve Helsinki-Vantaa Airport.

## Airline/airport contact numbers

**Air France** ↘ +358 9 8568 0500
**American Airlines** ↘ +358 600 140 140
**Blue1** ↘ +358 600 025 831
**British Airways** ↘ +358 9 6937 9538
**Cathay Pacific** ↘ +358 600 140 140
**Finnair** ↘ +358 600 140 140

## Flight information

**KLM** ↘ +358 20 353 355

## Lost luggage

**Lufthansa** ↘ +358 20 358 358
**Qantas** ↘ +358 9 4777 6610
**SAS Scandinavian Airlines** ↘ +358 600 025 831
**Singapore Airlines** ↘ +358 9 680 2770
**Sterling** ↘ +358 9 2313 4853

**Airport transfer from Helsinki-Vantaa Airport into the city centre** Helsinki-Vantaa Airport is Finland's main gateway to the wider world, located 19km north of the city centre. There are two terminals: Terminal I (T1) serves domestic flights, and Terminal 2 (T2) looks after international routes. The two terminals are linked by a walkway. All blond wood and shiny glass, Vantaa is the epitome of sleek, stylish Nordic design. It's also impressively efficient, and all in all a rather pleasant place to be. If you have any spare euros, they'll soon be gone in one of the bars, coffee shops and restaurants, or maybe the painfully tempting mini-galleries of Stockmann, Marimekko and Iittala. There's a 24-hour information office in T2.

Unless you have a car, options for travelling between the airport and the city centre are limited to bus or taxi.

*Public bus* Take service 615 from bus stand 1B outside the terminal building, heading to Railway Square (stand 10). The journey takes 35 minutes and costs €3.40.

*Finnair bus* Finnair's city shuttle bus departs from T1, picking up international arrivals from outside T2 (stand 10) en route to Railway Square (stand 30). On the return journey from the city, T1 is the first stop. Departures every 20 minutes 05.00–01.10. The journey takes 35 minutes and costs €5.20 one-way. The bus picks up/drops off at the Scandic Continental Hotel.

*Taxi* Taxis wait outside the main arrivals hall. Expect to pay around €35 for the 25-minute journey.

**Helicopter to/from Tallinn** Business and tourist travel between Helsinki and Tallinn is on the increase, especially since Estonia's accession to the EU, so if you're strapped for time or just feeling extravagant then you might want to take the chopper. **Copterline** (↘ 020 018 18; *www.copterline.com*) runs this 18-minute shuttle flight up to 14 times daily. Single tickets cost: adult €79–198; child under 12 €44.50–99. Booking online secures the cheapest fares and avoids the €14 per person transaction fee.

Helsinki heliport is at Hernesaari, Hernematalankatu 2 (↘ 0200 19191). Take a taxi from the city or ride tram 1A to the end of Tehtaankatu in the Eira district, from where it's a ten-minute walk.

**BY TRAIN** Only Michael Palin or Paul Theroux would consider taking the train from the UK to Finland, such is the magnitude of this pan-European epic. The buttock-numbing journey traverses France, Belgium, Holland, Germany, Poland, Lithuania, Latvia, Estonia and Russia.

Booking agencies such as Rail Europe (*178 Piccadilly, London W1*; ↘ *0870 830 2000*; e *reservations@maileurope.co.uk*; *www.raileurope.co.uk*) may raise an eyebrow at your barmy request but will happily suggest the best options. They will probably advise a combination of rail and ferry, which could go something like this: train to Newcastle, overnight ferry to Gothenburg (*DFDS Seaways; www.dfds.co.uk*), where you stay the night before taking a high-speed train to Stockholm (*SJ; www.sj.se*) and another overnight ferry to Helsinki (*Silja Line; www.silja.com*). The journey takes three nights and offers no real price advantage over flying. Alternatively, nip through the Channel Tunnel and take a train to Rostock in Germany, and then sail overnight to Helsinki.

A more realistic rail journey is between Helsinki and Russia. At the time of writing, there are three daily international services in each direction. The Finnish-operated *Sibelius* departs Helsinki at 07.42, arriving in St Petersburg at 14.23 (local time). The return journey begins at 16.32, arriving back to Helsinki at 21.18. One-way fares are about €128/86 first/second class. The Russians operate two trains; the *Repin*, also between St Petersburg and Helsinki, and the *Tolstoi* night train from Moscow. One-way fares on these services are around €81/51 first/second class. Contact VR (see below) for exact fares and reservations.

Helsinki's **Central Railway Station** [4 E2] is difficult to miss. Located just off the main Mannerheimintie artery, it not only serves domestic and international train services but also acts as the set-down and pick-up point for the airport shuttle buses. There's also a Metro underground station here, a rattling of trams on terra firma and an omnipresent stagger of drunks in the square.

Trains are operated by **VR** (☏ *0600 41 902; www.vr.fi*) and are almost universally clean, spacious and on time. The network covers the whole country, including the far north, and you can buy tickets at the station, online or over the telephone.

**Rail passes** There are two major providers of discount rail passes for travelling though Europe. **Interrail** (*www.interrail.com*) offers 29 countries and **Eurail**

(*www.eurail.com*) 17 – both cover Finland. However, get into the detail and things seem less attractive. Countries that are not covered by either company include Lithuania, Belarus, Latvia, Estonia and Russia, which effectively separates Finland from the rest of the network. Even the Scandinavian countries seem distant, given that the Gulf of Bothnia does such a good job of keeping Finland and Sweden apart. Bearing this in mind, the average traveller will get little value in Finland from anything other than a single-zone pass (covering Finland, Sweden and Norway), valid for 16 days and costing £206. Discounts are available for youths under 26.

**BY BOAT** Part of Helsinki's charm is the way huge ferries glide directly to the city's core. Even if you don't travel all the way from the UK, there's a possibility that you might want to make a crossing to Tallinn or Stockholm.

There are three distinct harbour areas and six different terminals. The South Harbour (Eteläsatama) is the biggest, home to the Olympia, Makasiini, Kanava and Katajanokka terminals. The North Harbour (Sörnäisten Satama) is home to the Hansa Terminal and the West Harbour (Länsisatama) has the appropriately named West Terminal.

Sailings operate year round on some of the finest cruise ships anywhere in the world. Watch out for weekend crossings, especially to Stockholm, which are something of a rite of passage for teenage youths looking for cheap alcohol (cheaper than the mainland, at least) and nautical naughtiness. But don't tut just yet – the huge revenues from these thirsty party animals help keep the fares down for everyone else.

**To/from Tallinn** Helsinki and Tallinn are only 80km apart. Weather permitting, the quickest crossings are the hydrofoil services. Several companies ply this route, which gives plenty of choice and competitive fares.

**Eckerö Line** Mannerheimintie 10; ℡ 228 8544; f 2288 5222; www.eckeroline.fi. One morning departure every day for this 3½hr crossing. Cabins available. Operates from the West Terminal. *One-way price adult/child/car from €18/12/19. Day cruise price adult/child from €22/15.*
**Linda Line** Makasiiniterminaali, Eteläsatama; ℡ 668 9700; f 6689 7070; www.lindaline.fi. Between 3 & 7 express hydrofoil crossings every day (90mins). Operates from the Makasiini Terminal. *One-way price adult/child from €27/13.50. Day cruise price adult/child from €42/21.*
**Nordic Jet Line** Kanavaterminaali K5; ℡ 681 770; f 6817 7111; www.njl.fi. Up to seven hydrofoil crossings per day (100mins). Operates from the Kanava Terminal. *One-way price adult/child from €27/13.50. Day cruise price adult/child from €56/28. Two adults with car €99 each way.*
**Silja Line** Keilaranta 9; 02150 Espoo; ℡ 180 41; f 180 4402; www.silja.com. Five express crossings every day. Operates from the Makasiini Terminal. *Sliding scale of fares depending on season and also the time of day: one-way adult €20–48, child €10–24.*
**Viking Line** Mastokatu 1; ℡ 123 51; f 123 5292; www.vikingline.fi. Two regular car ferries per day (3hrs). Cabins available. Operates from the Katajanokka Terminal. *One-way price from €33.*

**To/from Stockholm** The ships that cruise to and fro between these two capital cities are floating palaces with bars, restaurants, discos and live entertainment.

**Silja Line** Keilaranta 9; 02150 Espoo; ☎ 180 41; f 180 4402; www.silja.com. There's a daily departure (sailing times are dependent on the season) for this 17hr crossing that calls at the autonomous Åland Islands. Operates from the Olympia Terminal. *Sliding scale of fares depending on season and also the time of day: one-way foot passenger price adult/child from €26/13, one-way cabin fares from €112, cars from €55.*

**Viking Line** Mastokatu 1; ☎ 123 51; f 123 5292; www.vikingline.fi. Similar timetable & exactly the same route as Silja Line. Operates from the Katajanokka Terminal. *One-way foot passenger fare from €33, huge range of one-way cabin fares from €24–403! Car, cabin and 2–4 adults €144–320 each way.*

## To/from Germany

You can take a boat from Hanko, near Helsinki, to Rostock in north Germany.

**Superfast Ferries** Melkonkatu 28 e 18; ☎ 2535 0640; f 2535 0601; www.superfast.com. This 23hr crossing departs daily. Operates from the Matkustaja Terminal at Hanko. *One-way foot passenger price adult/child from €76/46, one-way cabin fares adult/child from €158/79, cars from €118.*

🚌 **BY COACH** The usual suspects in the long-distance coach business don't offer services to Helsinki, suggesting that they think the prospect of such a journey is as ridiculous as everybody else does. Whichever way you try and break it down, it's going to involve a ferry crossing. The most realistic route resembles the journey you could make by train: overnight ferry from Newcastle to Gothenburg (*DFDS Seaways; www.dfds.co.uk*), where you pick up a coach to Stockholm (*Eurolines; www.eurolines.com*) and another overnight ferry to Helsinki (*Silja Line; www.silja.com*).

The journey is likely to take three nights and will offer little (if any) saving over a competitively priced flight.

**BY CAR** As per rail and coach journeys, it is quite inconceivable to drive to Helsinki without taking a ferry crossing. Just in case you're feeling masochistic you could make the journey overland to St Petersburg and then around the Gulf of Finland to Helsinki, but this 3,100km epic would take at least 40 hours. The route would take in Calais, Brugge, Antwerp, Berlin, Poznan and Riga.

**Traffic regulations** Driving in Finland is straightforward. The roads are excellent and many are virtually traffic free, although distances can be long as direct travel is hindered by the proliferation of lakes. In the more remote areas, roads may be surfaced with gravel or dirt. Finns drive on the right and major road signs are consistent with other European countries.

Drink driving is very much frowned upon; the blood alcohol limit is 0.5g/litre (equivalent to a breath alcohol level of 0.22mg/litre), which is lower than the UK. Dipped headlights must be switched on at all times; the use of mobile phones (unless with headset) is prohibited and it is an offence to leave the engine idling on a stationary car for over two minutes (four in winter) unless you are in a traffic jam.

In built-up areas the speed limit is generally 50km/h, although in certain instances this may be 30km/h or 40km/h – in a residential precinct where pedestrians are present you must slow down to walking speed, otherwise 20km/h is the maximum.

Outside of town, the speed limit is 80km/h unless otherwise indicated; on open roads this often increases to 100km/h, and on motorways 120km/h. In winter seasonal tyres (studded or winter-type) must be fitted to all vehicles and speed limits are reduced from 120/100km/h to 100/80km/h respectively.

At all times of year watch out for elk and moose – the threat of collision is very real, and extremely messy (often fatal) for both parties. Finland's Ministry of Transport and Communications publishes the comprehensive booklet *Driving in Finland*. Download it from www.expat-finland.com/driving_in_finland.pdf.

**Car hire** See *Chapter 4*, pages 106–7.

# ✚ HEALTH

Public health services in Finland are excellent and the country has played a pioneering role in the development of primary healthcare. The quality of tap water is amongst the finest in the world and no vaccinations are required, although it is sensible to be up to date with routine vaccinations such as tetanus, diphtheria and polio. There are really only two irritating beasties to concern yourself with: ticks and mosquitoes. Every year there are approximately 30 reported cases of tick-borne encephalitis, mainly in the Åland Islands. If you plan to visit it may be worth seeking immunisation, though it is not readily available in the UK, or at least use a repellent and keep skin covered with long-sleeved clothing, trousers tucked into boots and a hat. Always check yourself – or preferably get someone to do it for you – if you have walked through forested areas or through long grass. If you are travelling with small children remember to check their heads and in particular behind the ears – a body part that is easily forgotten. Around 700 cases of the tick-borne Lyme disease are reported each year in Finland. There is no vaccine to prevent this, but it can be treated with antibiotics.

In a country that comprises almost one-quarter fresh water, a more troublesome problem is Finland's mosquitoes. Known by various names (*hyttynen, itikka, sääski*), these little blighters will drive you mad with incessant buzzing but otherwise are harmless, unless you suffer an allergic reaction. They tend not to be a problem in the city, but the further north you travel during summer then the more noticeable they become. You may wish to take a repellent, pack a head-net or travel with antihistamines.

Finland has marked extremes of weather. Summers can be hot (25°C and upwards), which sounds ideal but with very clean air the sun soon burns unprotected skin. Take sunscreen or pick some up at a supermarket or pharmacy. Icy winter weather can be a major problem – see the *What to take* section on page 75 to make sure you pack properly.

Finnish eating habits have become healthier in recent years. It's still possible to stuff yourself on red meat and stodgy pastries, but with fresh fish and vegetables figuring on most menus there's no reason to eat unhealthily. Middle-aged Finns take more exercise and smoking is decreasing (especially amongst males), but the country continues to battle alcoholic demons. As Europe has become more integrated, Finland has lost some of its strict powers of alcohol control and future health policy is likely to focus on how to address this problem. On a walk around Helsinki you will often see drunks loitering (or sprawled) around town.

## LOCAL MEDICAL TREATMENT

*Jos ei viina, terva ja sauna auta, niin tauti on kuolemaksi* (If tar, liquor and sauna do not cure it, the disease is fatal)

Although it would be churlish to say that this old proverb represents wide-held modern-day beliefs, it does at least shed light on the Finnish inclination for a drink and their wholehearted adoration of sauna. Not only does sauna cleanse the body and soothe the mind, it also treats muscles and limbs weary from a hard day's work.

Many Finns contribute their good health to regular sauna sessions, but if *you* get ill you'll probably want a more conventional form of treatment. European visitors should obtain a European Health Insurance Card (EHIC) before travelling, which entitles the bearer to emergency medical treatment on the same terms as Finnish nationals. Any on-going treatment or non-urgent medical services are covered by the EHIC. Visit www.dh.gov.uk for more details or pick up a T7 form from a post office. The local health system is excellent, English is widely spoken and Helsinki is a frequent evacuation point for emergency cases from the former Soviet states. However, there are still some services that are not free, eg: emergency dental treatment – a standard fee may be charged depending on the procedure. A fixed non-refundable daily charge applies to prescriptions, hospital in-patient or outpatient services. For this reason you should always arrange comprehensive travel insurance that will cover any medical eventualities, and travel with a copy of your policy certificate. In a medical emergency you can either visit a local medical centre (*ensiapuasema*), usually located at hospitals, or dial the general emergency telephone number 112. Private medical company **Mehiläinen** (*Runeberginkatu 47a;* ↘ *010 414 4444/4266; www.mehilainen.fi*) will dispatch a doctor to your hotel around the clock. If private treatment is given, then keep the receipts as some degree of refund may be available.

## SAFETY

**CRIME** Helsinki is very safe and crime levels are low, reflecting Finland's overall status as a secure country to visit. Tourists are rarely the victims of serious crime; pickpockets are the most common nuisance in crowded areas, particularly around major attractions and the railway station, but they are less of a problem than in other European capitals. Exercise the usual precautions against bag snatching and opportunist theft – keep valuables well hidden, don't wave cash around, make sure you can see your belongings, use the hotel safe and never leave anything on show in a hire car.

Alcoholism remains a significant concern for Finnish society. Helsinki has many drunks who, although mostly placid, can be seen fighting one another in broad daylight, throwing punches with gay abandon. You may occasionally be approached in the street or on a tram, but most of these uninvited liaisons are harmless and easily rebuffed. Apart from such disturbances, all forms of public transport are considered safe.

You should keep your wits about you after dark, especially on weekends when groups of young Finnish males are prowling the streets. Loud, brash and sometimes aggressive, they're usually looking for similar groups to rut with and in most instances you'll hear them before they spot you. Take the appropriate detour. Avoid poorly lit areas and you should have nothing to worry about.

**WOMEN TRAVELLERS** Finland's reputation for safety means that female travellers couldn't really choose a better country to visit; women can expect to have a thoroughly enjoyable time travelling either in groups or solo. The worst you can expect is a bit of hassle from over exuberant male drinkers, but Helsinki certainly doesn't have a monopoly on that kind of trouble!

**TERRORISM** Officially, Finland is considered as risky as most other European destinations, but you would be extremely unlucky to travel to Helsinki and become embroiled in a terrorist incident. There is the usual high-profile security visible outside the US embassy.

There were two significant events in 2002. In July a car bomb killed one man outside Hotel Helka, damaging the hotel but without injury to guests. Some three months later Finland suffered its worst act of terror since World War II, when a 19-year-old youth detonated a bomb at the busy Myyrmanni shopping mall near the airport. Seven people died, including the bomber and a young child, and over 80 were injured. Neither of these attacks were deemed to be political or affiliated to terrorist groups, rather they were thought to be suggestive of larger-scale social problems relating to increasing stress levels and mental health problems.

Although these incidents sound shocking, the FCO travel advice for Finland is as low-key as can be expected. Travellers are much more likely to be the target of terrorist activity in their own country than when they arrive in Finland.

**THE POLICE** The Finnish police force generally offers an excellent service. You will notice their presence most heavily around Railway Square and popular hotspots during nights on the town. They are usually helpful, although some speak limited or no English.

Owing to the low crime rate, Finland has one of the smallest numbers of police officers per capita of any European nation. Although this is not noticeable in Helsinki you should be aware that, in more isolated locations, response times to emergency situations can be unpredictable.

Low-level corruption (bribes, etc) between police and tourists is unheard of, and the most common cause of a brush with the law will be for motoring offences (see *Traffic regulations* on pages 68–9).

For **emergency telephone numbers**, see *Chapter 3*, pages 89–90.

## WHAT TO TAKE

Few mainstream tourist destinations offer the possibility of such extremes of temperature as Helsinki. Summers can be long and mild, with near constant daylight, but always pack at least a light jacket or jumper for the cooler days or chilly evenings. Winter is markedly different. Temperatures plummet to well below zero, and when the wind whips in from the frozen sea it feels as if your ears and fingers are about to drop off. A thick coat, scarf, hat and gloves are essential, as well as sturdy boots or shoes for the snow, and maybe even thermals if the mercury really plummets. Pay attention to the advance weather forecasts, but don't worry if you forget something, as everything you could need on a daily basis is available in Helsinki.

You might want to include a swimsuit for the sauna (although a birthday suit takes up less space), a driving licence if you intend to venture further afield or a set of smart togs for a night on the town, although the last is certainly not obligatory. Of course, adequate travel insurance to cover you in the event of accident, illness or loss should be a prerequisite. Carry photocopies of all your important documents.

**ELECTRICITY** The electric current in Finland is 220 Volts/50Hz. Plugs are European two-pin style, but most hotels will be able to provide a three-pin adaptor. If not, head to one of the larger department stores or supermarkets.

75

## NOTES FOR DISABLED TRAVELLERS

*Gordon Rattray www.able-travel.com*

Nordic countries are generally leaders in the integration of disabled people, and Finland is no exception. In Helsinki, standard access for people with limited mobility (wide entrances and ramps instead of steps), along with facilities catering to those with sensory problems, are often in place. This all makes spontaneous decisions easier, and for those who like to plan their travels, information about access is readily available.

**GETTING AROUND** Helsinki-Vantaa **airport** has lifts, accessible toilets and staff trained to cater for passengers needing assistance. Information desks are equipped with induction loops.

Many older and all new **buses** have low floors and ramped access. On timetables, inner-city routes with accessible buses are shown in colour, and adapted inter-city vehicles are shown with the letter 'M'.

**Trams** with lowered floors can be entered where the stop has a platform.

All **Metro** stations are wheelchair accessible and have timetables in Braille for the visually impaired. For information on all these services, ↘ 0100 111 (*Mon–Fri 07.00–19.00, weekends 09.00–17.00; at other times an automated service gives timetable information*).

**Trains** have various accessibility features, and travellers with visual or mobility impairments needing assistance should inform VR (see page 64) about a week before they plan to travel. For information, contact Helsinki station disability service ↘ 0307 21 421 (day), ↘ 0307 20 539 (night).

The following **taxi** companies advertise as being able to accommodate wheelchair passengers: Helsingin Invakuljetus (↘ *350 5200*), Invataxi Iiro's Taxi Service Ltd (↘ *4114 2070, 040 500 6070*), Helsingin Palveluauto (↘ *020 743 2150*) and Iros Taxi (↘ *040 050*).

**ACCOMMODATION AND ACTIVITIES** Many lodgings, hotels and attractions have at least some degree of accessibility, with lifts, ramps and widened doorways commonplace. It is not only mobility problems which are catered for; the Kiasma – Museum of Contemporary Art (Nykytaiteen Museo Kiasma) even has white gloves available for visually handicapped people to feel the objects.

**www.hel.fi** Helsinki's web portal. Information for disabled people with English translation.
**http://esteeton.teho.net** 'Accessible Helsinki'. Gives detailed information about practically everything you'll need.
**www.accessibletravelling.fi** Advice for travellers with disabilities; about Finland as a whole.

# $ MONEY AND BUDGETING

**MONEY** The currency of Finland is the euro, comprising 100 cents. There are seven different banknote denominations, each with a distinctive colour and size (the larger the denomination, the larger the note) to aid identification for the visually impaired.

The denominations, with colour, are: €5 (grey), €10 (red), €20 (blue), €50 (orange), €100 (green), €200 (yellow-brown) and €500 (purple). The most useful notes to carry are 10, 20 and 50 euros, which are used readily in all automated ticket machines.

Coins also increase in size, and therefore weight, with increasing value. The denominations are 1, 2, 5, 10, 20 and 50 cents, 1 and 2 euros.

Surprisingly, some shops and cafés still feel the need to display signs such as 'We do not accept US$', so listen up you American readers – please have the courtesy to use the local currency! Your greenbacks might be enthusiastically welcomed in developing nations but in Helsinki most traders are going to be reluctant to receive dollars, as you would be to receive pounds or euros.

For information on banks, exchanging currency, credit cards, ATMs and travellers' cheques, see *Chapter 3*, pages 81–3.

**BUDGETING** Although Helsinki has a fearsome reputation as a bottomless money drain, there's really no longer any reason why visiting the 'Daughter of the Baltic' should be as expensive as raising a daughter of your own. Yes, it's possible to spend a small fortune, but it's equally possible to find bargains and have a good time without breaking the bank – it might not be a shoestring destination, but I get by every time with a generous boot-string of a stipend. The breakdown below lists daily costs per person, based on two sharing average-priced accommodation during summer. Solo travellers might pay more for a bed, but probably less on swish restaurant and bar bills, which is where real damage can be done. If a breakfast buffet is on offer, and it nearly always is, then eat until you can eat no more!

**Counting the pennies** You can just about live off €30–35 per day if you sleep in a hostel dorm, travel everywhere on foot, look from the outside but don't pay to go in, self-cater at the supermarket, grab a cheap coffee and drink a couple of beers in the park.

**Modest** If you want a private room and a just a little indulgence, you'll get by on €60 per day by taking a private room in a hostel or a cabin at Rastila Camping. You could then visit a museum or gallery, take a good-value buffet lunch, travel all day on public transport and fit in a small café snack and a couple of drinks in a cheap bar at night.

**Comfortable** For around €100 per day you can get a good weekend rate at a tourist hotel or rented apartment. See a few more sights, stop for pastries, drink latte instead of Americano, buy a little souvenir, take a modest meal in a mid-price restaurant and finish up with drinks on a stylish summer terrace.

79

**Indulgent** Now we're getting serious. With an allowance of €200 per day you can really mix it with Helsinki's elite. Book a swish four-star hotel, take a boat tour around the archipelago, stop for cakes, browse the boutiques of the Design District, drink endless coffee, book a table in a top-class restaurant, go to the theatre and drink cocktails in one of the city's most stylish wine bars.

**Ouch!** If money is no object, check into the best room at Hotel Kämp, wine and dine at the Michelin-starred Chez Dominique, get top seats at the opera, flash the cash in the Grand Casino, then buy an original Eero Aarnio ball chair and arrange to have it shipped home. I'm not going to put a budget on this because, like all life's luxuries, if you can afford it you really don't need to know the price.

**TIPPING** Tipping is not a major part of Finnish life. Most restaurant bills will include a service charge as part of the price stated on the menu, but staff at the top places may expect a little something extra. Unless you wish to reward exceptional service, don't worry about it.

# 3 Practicalities

## $ BANKS

Banking services offer the standard range of currency exchange and ATM facilities. Banks are usually open Mon–Fri 10.00–16.30, with longer hours at Helsinki-Vantaa Airport (*open daily 06.00–19.30, until 23.00 in the transit area*) and Katajanokka Ferry Terminal (*open Mon–Fri 09.00–18.00*). The distinctive orange signs of the 'Otto' ATM machines are dotted liberally around the city.

**Aktia** Mannerheimintie 14; ↘ 247 6600 [4 E3] *Open Mon–Fri 10.00–16.30.*
**Nordea** Aleksanterinkatu 30; ↘ 200 3000 [5 G3] *Open Mon–Fri 09.30–16.15.*
**Oko** Aleksanterinkatu 19; ↘ 255 9021 [3 F3] *Open Mon–Fri 10.00–16.30.*
**Sampo** Kaivokatu 6; ↘ 513 5928 [4 E2] *Open Mon–Fri 10.00–16.30.*

**EXCHANGING CURRENCY** The currency of Finland is the euro. There are many bureaux de change booths in the central area of the city, at major travel hubs and some department stores. Most hotels will offer an exchange facility, or simply utilise one of the plentiful ATM machines.

American visitors who try to use US dollars are likely to receive short shrift, especially in the small cafés and gift shops around the major tourist sights.

**Forex at main railway station** Rautatientori; ☎ 669 001 [4 E2] *Open Mon–Fri 08.00–21.00, Sat–Sun 09.00–19.00.*
**Forex** Mannerheimintie 10; ☎ 647 008 [4 E3] *Open Mon–Fri 10.00–18.00.*
**Forex** Pohjoisesplanadi 27; ☎ 636 256 [5 G3] *Open Mon–Fri 09.00–19.00, Sat 09.00–15.00.*
**Tavex** Fabianinkatu 12; ☎ 68 149 149 [5 G3] *Open Mon–Fri 09.00–18.00, Sat 10.00–16.00.*

## TRAVELLERS' CHEQUES

If you still prefer paper over plastic, you can cash cheques at banks and bureaux de change throughout the city. Generally speaking, Forex offer a faster and cheaper service than the banks. Buying cheques in denominations of euro, before you leave home, makes most sense.

## VISA TRAVELMONEY

Visa TravelMoney is the 21st-century alternative to travellers' cheques, essentially a pre-paid electronic debit card. Accessed by PIN, you simply use the card to withdraw cash from ATM machines or pay bills, as with any other Visa card, until the balance expires. Then, simply toss the card away and start again. You can load up to a maximum of around £6,000 per card. Contact your local bank to find out the options.

## CREDIT CARDS

Finns survive on credit cards, and use them liberally in establishments from youth hostels to late-night bars. Major cards are American

Express, Diners Club, Visa and MasterCard. Debit cards, such as Visa Electron, Cirrus, Plus and Maestro, can be used to withdraw cash from ATMs and banks. Withdrawals for foreign cardholders incur a transaction fee, so the fewer uses the better.

Smaller museums, cafés and shops may be not be equipped to accept plastic, so keep a few euros to hand. If you plan to drive, be especially wary of petrol stations. Many pumps are automated and only accept Finnish credit cards, rendering them useless to travellers. To be stranded in the Finnish wilderness with a bunch of rejected cards is a pickle not to be relished.

## MEDIA

**PRINT** Finns love to read. In a country of little more than five million people there are some 53 newspapers that are published daily or every other day, and a further 153 that appear weekly. The biggest-selling daily, and the only one to be distributed nationally, is *Helsingin Sanomat*, with an average circulation of almost half a million. The most popular tabloid-style publication is *Ilta-Sanomat*, with the usual mix of major news and celebrity gossip. *Hufvudstadsbladet* is the main Swedish-language newspaper.

Finland's political parties are well represented by their own newspapers. The Centre Party publication is *Suomenmaa*, the Social Democrats have *Uutispäivä Demari* and the National Coalition Party publishes *Nykypäivä*.

## DONALD, WHERE'S YOUR 'HOUSUT'?

For years one of Finland's most popular comic-book heroes had been *Aku Ankka* (Donald Duck), and not just amongst children. First published in 1951, so widespread has been the phenomenon that it is not uncommon for married men to subscribe to the adventures of the grumpy quacker, and the comics have won high praise for their clever use of Finnish. Indeed, for students new to the language they are considered an invaluable learning tool, but it wasn't always the case.

Scandal engulfed the Disney favourite in the late 1970s when, faced with mounting financial difficulties, Helsinki councillors suggested cutting back on the number of subsidised comics being distributed to youth centres. As so often in politics and the murky world of tabloid journalism, rumour subjugated fact and before long it was being reported that little *Aku* had been banned in Finland for his insistence of parading *sans* pants – 'Donald, Where Are Your Trousers?' screamed US newspaper headlines.

Of course, like all the best rumours it was completely unfounded, but the story persists in some quarters to this day. Surely somebody ought to have thought that, in a land of rampant nudity in the sauna, *Aku's* proud stance could be a lesson to us all.

**English-language press** The **Academic Bookstore** (see page 191) holds the most comprehensive range of international newspapers, whilst the numerous **R-kioski** convenience stands stock a more limited selection.

Online news in English is available courtesy of Helsingin Sanomat (*www.hs.fi/english*) and the Finnish Broadcasting Company **YLE** (*www.yle.fi/news*).

Useful free newspapers with a mix of cultural, entertainment and tourist content are *SixDegrees* (*www.6d.fi*), *City in English* and *Helsinki This Week* (*www.helsinkiexpert.fi/helsinkithisweek_eng*). Pick them up from hotels, bars, restaurants or the main tourist office.

**TELEVISION** Finland's state-operated television company is **YLE** (*www.yle.fi*), which has been broadcasting since 1926. Commanding 53% of the viewing audience, YLE is comparable to Britain's BBC in structure and is similarly funded by licence payments. Major channels available to all are **TV1** and **TV2**, with a mixed bag of general news and entertainment programming such as sport, drama, satire, film, real-life and children's programmes. Additional channels, currently digital only, include **YLE Teema** (documentaries), **YLE24** (news) and **YLE FST** (Swedish-language programming).

The largest commercial rival to YLE is **MTV Media** (*www.mtv3.fi*), who offer the hugely popular **MTV3** and **Subtv** channels. The content is much the same as other commercial European stations, being high in glitz but often low on substance. *Big Brother* or special celebrations such as *Miss Baltic Sea & Scandinavia* are typical broadcasts.

**Nelonen** is another commercial rival to YLE, whilst special-interest stations include sports-based **Urheilukanava** (*www.urheilukanava.tv*), music channel **The**

**Voice** and **TV Finland** (*www.yle.fi/tvfinland*), the last being a joint venture digital service between YLE and MTV3 that offers programming for Finnish expats in Europe.

Finns watch an average of almost three hours' TV per day, and favourite current programmes that will be familiar to many readers are *Lost*, *Rome* and, bizarrely, *Emmerdale* – goodness only knows what they made of Seth Armstrong.

The most popular regular broadcasts are the news programmes, which attract almost a million viewers, an impressive 20% of the population. But one event outstrips all the others by a country mile – the annual **Independence Day reception** hosted at the Presidential Palace, which is broadcast on nearly every channel. Finns love to watch people eating and dancing with Tarja Halonen; the talk of who has and has not been invited is hot gossip.

Across the networks, foreign programmes are shown with subtitles so you can always find something in English. All business hotels have at least a basic selection of international channels from the likes of the **BBC** and **CNN**. For news in English, **YLE1** and **YLE24** broadcast at 09.09 daily, and **Euronews**, shown on YLE24, has news in four languages (English, German, Russian and French) at 10.00, 12.00, 14.00 and 23.00 (*Mon–Fri*), and 12.00, 14.00 and 23.00 on weekends.

Always ready to embrace new technology, Finland will pass two memorable televisual milestones in 2007. Firstly, in February owners of the latest generation DVB-H mobile phones will be able to receive all channels from YLE, and up to 35 other stations, as free real-time broadcasts. Then, in September, Finland will become a completely digital TV nation as analogue antennae across the land are switched off simultaneously.

**RADIO** For a nation of little more than five million people, Finland has more than its fair share of radio stations. Once again the national broadcaster, **YLE**, leads the way and boasts 50% of the market with myriad channels.

Culture, art and factual talk shows are broadcast on **YLE Radio 1**. Popular culture, including new pop and rock, can be heard on **YLEX**. The so-called 'national' station is **YLE Radio Suomi**, which has middle-of-the-road music and chat content. Swedish programmes can be found on **YLE Radio Extrem** and **YLE Radio Vega**, and in the far north **Sámi Radio** is a joint venture channel with Swedish and Norwegian networks that serves the minority Sámi community.

Other popular channels include **SuomiPOP** (general pop and rock), **Sävelradio** (Finnish *Iskelmä* music – a kind of light, jolly folk style), **Radio Nova** (middle-of-the-road general listening broadcaster) and, catering to the small population of Russian speakers, **Radio Sputnik**. The best station for modern independent music of all genres, with no defined playlists or commercial slant, is **Radio Helsinki**; listen online at www.radiohelsinki.fi.

For English-language broadcasts, YLE's foreign-language radio channel is **YLE Mondo**, available through digital TV services or on 97.5FM in Helsinki. A five-minute English news bulletin is presented daily at 07.30 and 08.55 (*08.55 only on weekends*), and the network also carries information in Special Finnish, a simplified form of the language designed for immigrants and students. A shorter bulletin is also broadcast daily on **YLE Radio 1** (87.9FM) at 15.55.

Classical scholars might be interested to hear **Nuntti Latini** (News in Latin). Commissioned in 1989, the broadcast is a joint project between YLE and Helsinki University and the weekly five-minute bulletin (major news headlines, arts stories, sport, etc) is the only international broadcast of its type anywhere in the world. In Finland, tune in to YLE Radio 1 or find it on the internet at www.yleradio1.fi/nuntii.

# ℓ COMMUNICATIONS

**TELEPHONE AND FAX** The telephone area code for Helsinki is 09; drop the zero if calling from outside Finland. Local Helsinki numbers have between five and eight digits (after the 09). Mobile phone numbers are generally seven digits long, with a prefix of between three and five digits. All prefixes begin 04, with the exception of the three-digit prefix 050.

As one of the most mobile phone-friendly nations in the world, public telephones are gradually disappearing from the streets of Helsinki. In keeping with the modern way, coin-operated booths are very thin on the ground – most accept plastic phonecards or credit cards. You can buy phonecards (local and international) from post offices and R-kioski convenience stands.

For foreign calls, dial the international access code 00 followed by the relevant country code and number. Occasionally, alternative international access codes such as 999, 994 or 990 are still used in a hangover from the old exchange system. These differing codes attract slightly dissimilar rates, so check prior to dialling. Calls are cheapest off-peak, usually between 22.00 and 08.00.

Some country codes are as follows:

| | | | | | |
|---|---|---|---|---|---|
| Australia | 61 | Germany | 49 | Norway | 47 |
| Canada | 1 | Greece | 30 | Russia | 7 |
| Estonia | 372 | Ireland | 353 | UK | 44 |
| France | 33 | Italy | 39 | USA | 1 |

## Useful/emergency telephone numbers

**Airport information line (arrivals and departures)** ↘ 2001 4636 (premium-rate line)

**Ambulance/fire brigade/police** ↘ 112

**Domestic operator and directory enquiries** ↘ 118

**Hotel bookings** ↘ 2288 1400

**International operator and directory enquiries** ↘ 02 02 02

**Long-distance bus information (Matkahuolto)** ↘ 0200 4000 (premium-rate line)

**Lost property office** ↘ 189 3180

**Medical emergencies (Helsinki University Central Hospital)** ↘ 4711

**Medical non-emergency information** ↘ 10023

**Police non-emergency** ↘ 10022

**Public transport information** ↘ 0100 111 (premium-rate line)

Taxi – automated booking line ☎ 0100 7007
Taxi – central reservation office ☎ 0100 7000
Tourist information ☎ 169 3757
Train information (VR – Valtion Rautatiet) ☎ 0600 41 902 (premium-rate line)

**Cellphones/mobiles** Show me a Finn without a mobile phone and I'll show you a character on the verge of collapse. Finland is home to telecommunications giant Nokia, and consequently the country has one of the world's highest densities of mobile usage.

There are several service providers (including Sonera and Telering), and so long as your handset is compatible with the European 900/1800 GSM network you can use any of them.

If you plan to use your own phone for extended periods, it pays to invest in a local SIM card. Not only do you get cheaper calls, but you can also benefit from a range of other services available to subscribers to the local networks. The dextrously fingered amongst you can buy public transport tickets, get airline flight information or book a taxi in a mere matter of seconds.

✉ **POST OFFICES** Helsinki's main *posti* (post office) is located between the main railway station and Kiasma Museum of Contemporary Art, housed in the large yellow Postitalo building at Elielinaukio 2f [4 E2]. The hours of opening are Mon–Fri 07.00–21.00, Sat–Sun 10.00–18.00. This is also where to find the poste restante service.

Smaller branch offices are scattered around the city. You can also buy stamps at R-kioski convenience booths, as well as the train and bus stations.

**e INTERNET** No country in the world is more internet friendly than Finland. This tech-savvy nation has embraced the web with verve and you'll have no problem gaining a connection, often for free.

WiFi is standard almost everywhere you go, from hotels to cafés and even outdoor public spaces, including a complimentary network in the Esplanade Park. It must be said, however, that each time I tried to access the service whilst researching this guide, I couldn't get a connection.

If you don't have your own laptop, fixed terminals are available at Helsinki City Tourist Bureau at Pohjoisesplanadi 19 [5 G3] and Kirjakaapeli Library at Mannerheimintie 22–24 [4 D2]. Again, both of these offer free access.

Here's a quick tip – if you're looking for the @ symbol on a Finnish keyboard, just hit AltGr+2.

**Internet cafés** With free web access so readily available, Helsinki doesn't have a wealth of internet cafés. The following are the best options if you want a beer, coffee or sticky bun whilst you surf.

**mbar** Mannerheimintie 22–24; ☎ 6124 5420; e info@mbar.fi; www.mbar.fi [4 D2] Strictly speaking this is a cool alternative bar & club, but it melds seamlessly into a groovy daytime café. With 13 fixed PCs, WiFi &

printing service. WiFi free, fixed PCs €5 per hr (minimum €2), printing €0.20 per A4 sheet. *Open Mon–Tue 09.00–midnight, Wed–Thu 09.00–02.00, Fri–Sat 09.00–03.00, Sun 12.00–midnight.*

If you think that's too trendy, try any of the following branches of Robert's Coffee:

Aleksanterinkatu 21; ✆ 6228 1960 [4 E3] *Open Mon–Fri 07.00–20.00, Sat 09.00–18.00.*
Forum Shopping Centre, Mannerheimintie 20b [4 E3] *Open Mon–Fri 07.00–20.00, Sat 10.00–18.00.*
Stockmann, Aleksanterinkatu 52b; ✆ 121 3759 [4 E3] *Open Mon–Fri 09.00–21.00, Sat 09.00–18.00.*
Olympia Ferry Terminal, Olympiaranta 1; ✆ 662 958 [5 J7] *Open daily 09.00–20.00.*

## E EMBASSIES AND CONSULATES IN HELSINKI

**Canada** Pohjoisesplanadi 25b; ✆ 228 530; f 601 060; e hsnki@international.gc.ca [5 G3] *Open Mon–Fri 08.30–12.00, 13.00–16.30. Summer opening hours (Jun–Aug) Mon–Thu 08.00–12.00, 13.00–16.30, Fri 08.00–13.30.*
**Estonia** Itäinen Puistotie 10; ✆ 622 0260; f 622 02 610; e embassy.helsinki@mfa.ee [7 J8] *Consular section open Mon–Fri 10.00–13.00; entrance from Kallionlinnantie. Closed public holidays and Estonian national holidays.*
**European Commission Representation** Pohjoisesplanadi 31; ✆ 622 6544 [5 F3] *Open Mon–Fri 10.00–16.30.*
**France** Itäinen Puistotie 13; ✆ 618 780; f 618 783 42; e ambassade.france@kolumbus.fi [1 C4] *Open Mon–Fri 09.00–13.00, 14.00–16.00.*
**Germany** Krogiuksentie 4b; ✆ 458 580; f 458 58 258; e info@deutschland.fi. *Open Mon–Fri 09.00–12.00. Telephone enquiries may also be made in the afternoon.*

**Ireland** Erottajankatu 7a; ☎ 646 006; f 646 022; e helsinki@dfa.ie [7 F5]

**Norway** Rehbinderintie 17; ☎ 686 0180; f 657 807; e emb.helsinki@mfa.no [6 E8] *Open Mon–Fri 10.00–14.00.*

**Russian Federation** Tehtaankatu 1b; ☎ 661 876, 661 877, 607 050; f 661 006; e rusembassy@co.inet.fi [7 H7] *Open Mon–Fri 09.00–12.00 for visitors; Mon–Thu 08.30–12.30, 14.00–18.00, Fri 08.30–12.30, 14.00–16.45.*

**South Africa** Rahapajankatu 1a; ☎ 6860 3100; f 6860 3130; e saembfin@welho.com [5 K3] *Open Mon–Fri 09.00–14.00.*

**UK** Itäinen Puistotie 17; ☎ 2286 5100; f 2286 5262; e info.helsinki@fco.gov.uk [1 C4] *Open Mon–Fri 09.00–17.00. Summer opening hours (Jun–Aug) Mon–Fri 08.30–15.30.* Consular and visa section open Mon–Fri 09.00–12.00. For emergencies outside normal opening hours, ☎ 0500 817 242.

**US** Itäinen Puistotie 14a; ☎ 6162 5730; f 6162 5800 [1 C4] Appointments only. Consular telephone enquiries answered Mon–Fri 14.00–16.00 (for non-immigrant visa information e helsinkiniv@state.gov; for immigration information e helsinkiiv@state.gov). The embassy operates an American Citizens Service Unit (ACS) to help nationals with issues such as passport applications and renewals, as well as emergency services citizens in distress – ☎ 6162 5701; e helsinkiacs@state.gov. ACS telephone enquiries answered Mon–Fri 08.30–17.00.

## RELIGIOUS SERVICES

Helsinki's **Lutheran Cathedral** (Tuomiokirkko [5 H2]) holds daily services and daytime prayer. Expect a regular Sunday service every week at 10.00 or 11.00, but call ☎ 709 2455 for detailed information.

Anyone wishing to experience a service at the atmospheric **Uspenski Cathedral** [5 K3] can attend vigil at 18.00 every Saturday (and the day before festivals) or liturgy at 10.00 every Sunday (and on festival days). Proceedings are conducted in Finnish (✆ *634 267*).

The unique **Temppeliaukio Church** (Temppeliaukion Kirkko) at Lutherinkatu 3 [4 B1] is home to services of the International Evangelical Church, every Sunday at 14.00 (✆ *586 8770*; *www.church.fi*). Consecrated in 1826, the beautiful wooden **Old Church** (Vanhakirkko) is, as the name suggests, the oldest church in Helsinki. Services in Finnish are held at 10.00 on Sundays and holidays, whilst the Swedish congregation meets shortly afterwards at 12.00. The church is at Annankatu 14c (✆ *709 2255*) [4 E4].

The **Helsinki Mosque** is at Fredrikinkatu 33a (✆ *643 579*) [6 E6] and holds prayer meetings daily at 12.30.

Services in Hebrew are conducted every Saturday at 09.00 at **Helsinki Synagogue** at Malminkatu 26 (✆ *5860 3121*) [4 B3].

# *i* TOURIST INFORMATION

**Helsinki City Tourist Bureau** Pohjoisesplanadi 19; ✆ 169 3757; f 169 3839; e tourist.info@hel.fi; www.hel2.fi/tourism [5 G3] The main tourist office is a well-stocked Aladdin's Cave of maps, leaflets & accommodation information, staffed by an excellent multi-lingual team. Buy transport tickets, the discount-offering Helsinki Card or book guided tours & excursions. Two free internet terminals. *Open May–Sep Mon–Fri 09.00–20.00, Sat–Sun 09.00–18.00; Oct–Apr Mon–Fri 09.00–18.00, Sat–Sun 10.00–16.00.*

**Finnish Tourist Board** Eteläesplanadi 4; ☏ 4176 9300; **f** 4176 9301; **e** mek@mek.fi; www.mek.fi [5 G4] General information covering the whole of Finland, including tour-booking service. *Open May–Sep Mon–Fri 09.00–17.00, Sat–Sun 11.00–15.00; Oct–Apr Mon–Fri 09.00–17.00.*

**Hotel Booking at main railway station** Rautatientori; ☏ 2288 1400; **f** 2288 1499; **e** hotel@helsinkiexpert.fi [4 E2] Arrived in town without a room? These folks, located in the central hall of the station, can help you find a bed. *Open Jun–Aug Mon–Fri 09.00–19.00, Sat 09.00–18.00, Sun 10.00–18.00; Sep–May Mon–Fri 09.00–18.00, Sat 09.00–17.00.*

**HELSINKI HELPERS** From mid June to late August watch for the distinctive green uniforms of these roving ambassadors who trawl the streets ready to assist with any tourism-related queries. They also patrol the ferry terminals to meet visitors arriving by sea.

## LOCAL TOURS

Take to the water, pound the streets, ride the rails, run through the forests or even quaff beer on a variety of guided tours around the city.

**BizarreOne** Mannerheimintie 33a; ☏ 438 8091; **e** info@bizarreone.fi; www.bizarreone.fi [1 A1] Bizarre by name, bizarre by nature – this is tourism with a twist. Go on a date with a drag queen, free your artistic side as a human paintbrush, compete to build the best ice sculpture or do your Christmas shopping with the 'fun' Santa. Ideal for stag or hen parties.

**Citysherpa** www2.hs.fi/extrat/citysherpa. The best choice for getting under the skin of the city. Organised by the *Helsingin Sanomat* newspaper & Radio Helsinki, a group of specially selected volunteers show you *their* Helsinki. In 2006, you could go running in Central Park, tour the best record shops, have dinner with the city's former boss of EU affairs, learn ancient folk-tales, tour fantastic flea markets or just hit the coolest bars. All tours need to be arranged in advance & are subject to the volunteers being available on your chosen dates, but you get an unbiased view of local life.

**Easy Living** Käpylänkuja 1; ☎ 8683 5630; f 8683 5631; e easyliving@easyliving.fi; www.easyliving.fi. Guided cycle tours, Nordic walking & snow-shoe walking in & around Helsinki.

**Helsinki Expert** Helsinki City Tourist Bureau, Pohjoisesplanadi 19; ☎ 2288 1500; f 2288 1599; e tourshop@helsinkiexpert.fi; www.helsinkiexpert.fi [5 G3] The city's undisputed tourism specialists cover all bases with guided audio coach trips & themed walks featuring prominently. Audio tour adult/child €23/11; tour takes 1½ hours, in English, German, French, Spanish, Swedish, Italian, Russian & Japanese.

**Sightseeing Tram 3T/3B** This regular public-service tram runs a figure-of-eight route & covers most of the areas of interest in the city, hence its 'sightseeing' tag. From the central areas around the Market Square & Senate Square, the tram loops around the outlying districts of Kallio, Töölö, Eira & Kaivopuisto — the tourist board even publishes a leaflet detailing all the sights *en route*. It's the cheapest tour you can take without walking, costing adult/child €2.20/1.10; full tour takes 1hr.

**SpåraKOFF** This distinctive bright-red, 1950s' pub-tram has become a Helsinki landmark over the last 10 years, plying a route around the city that passes major sights like Railway Square, Senate Square, Parliament House & Finlandia Hall. Of course, your eyes will be on the beer, but nevertheless this is a novel way to get your bearings — or lose them altogether. *Adult/child €7/3.50; full tour takes 50mins. Operates mid May to mid Aug, Tue–Sat 14.00–20.00, departing from Mikonkatu near the Railway Square.*

Three companies offer boat trips around the archipelago with unique views of the city, operating between May and September from the Market Square. Trips generally run from 10.00–18.00, usually with lunch and dinner options, and occasionally evening cruises.

**IhaLines** ✆ 6874 5050; www.ihalines.fi [5 H4] Tours take 1½ or 2½hrs. *Tickets adult/child from €14/7, family ticket from €28.*
**Royal Line** ✆ 612 2950; www.royalline.fi [5 H4] Tours take 1¼, 1½, 2 or 2½hrs. *Tickets adult/child from €16/8, family ticket from €34.*
**Sun Line** ✆ 727 7010; www.sunlines.fi [5 H4] Tours take 1½hrs. *Tickets adult/child from €16/8, family ticket from €34.*

## LOCAL TRAVEL AGENTS

If you want to explore further afield, any number of local agencies will take you out of town on a variety of contrasting excursions.

**Arch-Tours** Linnankoskenkatu 1a2; ✆ 454 3044; e archtours@archtours.fi; www.archtours.fi. Exploring the full gamut of Finnish architecture, these tours combine obvious highlights such as the work of Alvar Aalto & the Suomenlinna Sea Fortress with the less-explored delights of wooden churches, Finland's industrial heartlands & cutting-edge 21st-century modernism. Also trips to Tallinn & St Petersburg. These multi-day tours generally operate from May to September, but some run all year round.

**Finnish Country Holidays** Eteläesplanadi 22c; ✆ 5766 3350; f 5766 3366; e sales@lomarengas.fi; www.countryholidays.fi [5 F4] Large selection of Finnish log cottages, fishing retreats & even private islands for rent, ranging from the southern archipelago to the northern Lappish wilderness.

**Fishing Lords** ✆ 041 530 7727, 041 530 7726; f 777 3126; e mika.viitanen@fishinglords.fi, tuomas.ollikainen@fishinglords.fi; www.fishinglords.fi. Sea, river & lake fishing in Helsinki & around southern Finland. Standard excursions including all equipment & accommodation, or tailored packages upon request.

**Fun Action** Meripellontie 11c; ✆ 343 6800; f 344 3501; e funaction@funaction.fi; www.funaction.fi. A wide range of adventure- & action-based activities, such as jet skiing, snowshoeing & off-roading.

**Haruspurjekuunari Zangra** Lönnrotinkatu 35 d 47; ✆ 626 210; e info@kuunarizangra.com; www.kuunarizangra.com [6 C5] Sail around the archipelago on day cruises or overnight trips aboard this 57ft Finnish-built schooner. Suitable for groups of 8–15.

**Helsinki Expert** Helsinki City Tourist Bureau, Pohjoisesplanadi 19; ✆ 2288 1500; f 2288 1599; e tourshop@helsinkiexpert.fi; www.helsinkiexpert.fi [5 G3] As well as guided city tours, Helsinki's number-one operator will take you to the charming wooden-town at Porvoo, through the tranquil lakes & forests of Nuuksio National Park, by rail to imperial St Petersburg & medieval Tallinn, on a cultural tour to Tampere & Turku or on a visit to see Santa up in Lapland. Also sea fishing, winter sports & accommodation booking. In short, a finger in every pie.

**Inara** Siamintie 2b; ✆ 8684 3660; f 8684 3661; e ohjelmapalvelut@inara.fi; www.inara.fi. Coastal rafting, country sauna & nature programmes close to Helsinki.

**TTE – The Travel Experience** Rahapajankatu 1 f 37; ✆ 622 9810; f 6229 8120; e info@travel-experience.net; www.travel-experience.net [5 K3] This Helsinki agent offers cycle touring around southern

Finland, golf breaks, self-drive holidays & winter packages to the arctic north. They can also arrange accommodation & transport.

## DISCOUNT CARD

The tourist board maintains a relentless campaign of promotion for the **Helsinki Card**. The considerable list of benefits includes free entry to all major sights and over 50 museums, unlimited travel on public transport within the city, free travel and all entries to Suomenlinna Sea Fortress, and a free audio city tour. In addition, discounts are offered on the Finnair airport shuttle (30%), entertainment such as concerts and opera (up to 50%), selected restaurants (up to 20%), day trips to Tallinn and activities such as swimming and sauna.

Think carefully about whether you'll get value for money, because the card is quite pricey, and there are only so many museums you can visit, trams you can ride and meals you can eat in a day. Available for periods of 24, 48 and 72 hours, it costs adult/child €29/11, €42/14 and €53/17 respectively. If you plan to go hell for leather, it's worth it. If you just want to wander at your own pace, you'll be better saving those euros for extra cinnamon buns and frothy coffees.

Buy the Helsinki Card from the tourist bureau, airport, ferry terminals, hotels, Stockmann department store or, for a discount of €3, via their website at www.helsinkiexpert.fi/helsinkicard.

# PUBLIC TOILETS

Helsinki's official public toilets can be expensive (around €1–2), and not always open when you need them. If you get caught short, your best bet is to dash for one of the following places: the department stores of Stockmann (Aleksanterinkatu 52b [4 E3]) and Sokos (Mannerheimintie 9 [4 E2]); the large shopping centres at Kamppi (Level 1 [4 C3]), Forum (Mannerheimintie 20a [4 E3]) or Kluuvi (Aleksanterinkatu 9 [5 G3]); or any of the large business hotels around the centre, where you can usually slip in and out unnoticed.

The public toilet on Sofiankatu [5 H3] is open Mon–Fri 09.30–16.00 (€0.50). For extreme emergencies, incongruous alfresco cubicles can be found dotted around town (€0.40).

# 4 Local Transport

## PUBLIC TRANSPORT

A combination of trams, buses, boats and an underground Metro system cover practically all corners of Helsinki with regular efficiency and a uniform pricing structure. You can transfer with ease between different modes of transport, and electronic display boards keep travellers updated with the latest information. For disabled passengers, low-access doorways are usually found at the front of buses and trams, and seats near the doors are reserved for those with restricted movement. The Metro system and Suomenlinna ferries are also wheelchair accessible (see pages 76–7).

There are several ticket choices. Basic single tickets are valid for one hour (long enough to get anywhere in central Helsinki), tourist tickets are prepaid cards allowing unlimited transport and regional tickets allow longer journeys into the neighbouring municipalities of Espoo, Kauniainen, Vantaa and Kerava. Buying tickets from automated machines is cheaper than paying the driver.

Ticket prices are as follows:

| | | |
|---|---|---|
| Single ticket from machine | adult/child | €2/1 |
| Single ticket from driver | adult/child | €2.20/1.10 |

| Tram ticket from driver | adult | €2 |
|---|---|---|
| Tourist ticket 1 day | adult/child | €6/3 |
| Tourist ticket 3 days | adult/child | €12/6 |
| Tourist ticket 5 days | adult/child | €18/9 |
| Suomenlinna ferry ticket (valid for 12 hours) | adult/child | €3.80/1.90 |
| Mobile phone e-ticket | adult | €2 |

Children are classified as between seven and 16 years of age; children under seven travel for free. Automated ticket machines are usually found at tram stops, at all Metro stations and at the Suomenlinna ferry terminal. Prepaid tourist tickets can be purchased from R-kioski, the Helsinki City Transport service booth in the main railway station and the Helsinki City Tourist Bureau. One-day tourist tickets may be purchased from the driver on trams and buses. Ticket machines accept coins and banknotes; the Helsinki City Transport service kiosk accepts credit cards; drivers deal with cash only, but are not obliged to accept notes of greater denomination than €20. You can also use the Helsinki Card (see *Chapter 3*, page 99) for free transport around the city. Ticket inspections are random; the penalty for being caught without a valid ticket is €66.

Travellers with mobile phones operating on the Sonera, Elisa, DNA, Saunalahti and Tele Finland networks can purchase tickets electronically. Simply send the SMS text message A 641 (AS 641 for message in Swedish) to the number 16353 and you will receive the e-ticket by return.

Although the Helsinki transport system has two zones, the overwhelming majority of tourist journeys will be taken in Zone 1. You can plot your route around Helsinki with the journey planner at www.hel.fi/HKL.

**TRAMS** Helsinki's excellent tram network is the main mode of transport within the city. One of the oldest electrified systems in the world, there are currently 11 lines:

| | |
|---|---|
| 1 | Kauppatori–Käpylä |
| 1A | Eira–Käpylä |
| 3B | Eira–Kauppatori–Kallio–Töölö–Eira |
| 3T | Eira–Töölö–Kallio–Kauppatori–Eira |
| 4 | Katajanokka–Munkkiniemi |
| 4T | Katajanokka Ferry Terminal–Munkkiniemi |
| 6 | Hietalahti–Arabia |
| 7A | Senaatintori–Sörnäinen–Vallila |
| 7B | Senaatintori–Pasila–Töölö–Senaatintori |
| 8 | Salmisaari–Sörnäinen–Vallila |
| 10 | Kirurgi–Pikku–Huopalahti |

Of these numbers 3B and 3T offer an excellent overview of Helsinki, performing a figure-of-eight loop that takes in many of the major sights (see page 96). Lines 2 and 5 have been retired, whilst a new line (number 9) is in the pipeline.

**BUSES** More than 100 bus routes connect the various districts of Helsinki, linking well with tram and Metro services. Most regional buses (including services from the airport) terminate at Railway Square, whilst long-distance services and shuttles to Espoo use the new Kamppi terminal. One of the most useful tourist buses is the number 24 to Seurasaari, which operates from the Swedish Theatre on Mannerheimintie.

**METRO** Helsinki has one underground Metro line. It runs from Ruoholahti in the west, through Kamppi, the main railway station and Hakaniemi, and forks at the Itäkeskus shopping centre. The only time you are likely to go further than this is to visit the campsite at Rastila, in which case take a train heading towards Vuosaari. Metro stations are signified by a white 'M' on an orange background.

**BOATS** The Helsinki City Transport service operates shuttle boats to the sea fortress of Suomenlinna. Tickets are valid for 12 hours and come either in card or paper form. Cards are valid from the time of the first journey, whilst paper tickets are valid from the time of purchase.

**AIRPORT TRANSFER** See *Chapter 2, Getting there and away*, page 62.

**TAXIS** Although taxis have illuminated yellow lights to signify their vacancy, most will be heading for a designated rank and hence trying to hail one on the streets can be

## PUBLIC TRANSPORT INFORMATION

Helsinki's public transport network is supported by an extensive array of telephone and web resources. The following will help you plan your journey with effortless efficiency:

**Travel Information** ☎ 0100 111. *Open Mon–Fri 07.00–19.00, Sat–Sun 09.00–17.00.*
**Travel Card Advice** ☎ 472 4000. *Open Mon–Thu 07.30–19.00, Sat–Sun 09.00–17.00.*
http://www.hkl.fi Timetables, routes & ticket news.
http://www.reittiopas.fi Route planning service.

If you're already pacing the streets, you can visit the **Customer Service Point** in the Metro station underneath the Central Railway Station (*open Mon–Thu 07.30–19.00, Fri 07.30–17.00, Sat 10.00–15.00*).

For lost property contact **Suomen Löytötavarapalvelu** (*Mäkelänkatu 56;* ☎ *0600 41006; http://www.loytotavara.net; open Mon–Fri 09.00–18.00*), and for general feedback or complaints call ☎ 0800 111 811 (e *palaute.hkl@hel.fi*).

a challenge. Late at night and during winter snowstorms are also difficult times to find a cab. Journeys are in general more expensive than other western European countries, but the cars are of good quality, the meter is always used and drivers (by and large) don't try any tricks. A journey from the city centre to the airport will cost in the region of €35. Tipping is not necessary. For taxi contact details see *Chapter 3, Useful/emergency telephone numbers*, pages 89–90.

**CAR HIRE** With such an efficient public transport system there's really no need to use a car in the city, especially given the high rental prices. Even in summer, for the most basic of models you should expect to pay around €100 per day with the international agencies, dropping to around €80 per day for extended rentals. Cheaper deals are available with local companies.

The only reason to pick up a car would be to visit some of the outlying nature reserves or to take off to a wilderness cabin for a few days. If you *do* take the plunge, pay attention to tram tracks and bus lanes, and expect a bumpy ride over the cobbled streets.

**AK-Rent Centre Ltd** Porthaninkatu 7; ✆ 726 2884. Irregular privately operated place near Hakaniemi Metro station. Rates here are cheap (from around €70 per day), & pick-up & return time flexible, but you need to call in advance to make the necessary arrangements.
**AVIS** Hietaniemenkatu 6; ✆ 441 155; e budget@budget.fi; www.budget.fi. *Open Mon–Fri 09.00–17.00.*
**Europcar** Helsinki City Holiday Inn, Messaukio 1; ✆ 403 062 803; e info@europcar.fi; www.europcar.fi. *Open daily 08.00–midnight.*
**Hertz** Mannerheimintie 44; ✆ 0200 112 233; e hertz@hertz.fi; www.hertz.fi. *Open Mon–Fri 07.00–17.30, Sat 08.00–14.00.*

**Transvell Ltd** Työpajankatu 2; ☎ 350 5590; rent@transvell.fi; www.transvell.fi. Rates from €40 per day including 100km, or €69 with unlimited kilometres (weekly from €233). Good-value weekend packages (*16.00 Fri to 09.00 Mon, with 500km*) start from €95. Transvall come in to their own at nights – call ☎ 08000 7000 at any time for express delivery service. Located between the Sörnäinen & Hermanni districts, northeast of the city centre. *Open Mon–Fri 08.00–17.00, Sat 09.00–13.00.*

**PARKING IN HELSINKI** Many of the streets where it's possible to leave a car are reserved for permit holders. If you must drive in the city, try one of the underground car parks.

**Autohotelli** Olympia Terminal M2; ☎ 177 107; www.autohotelli.com. 120 spaces. Fee €4 per hr, €25 for 12hrs, €30 for 12–24hrs. Intended for boat passengers. *Open daily 07.00–21.45.*
**EuroPark P-Kamppi** Olavinkatu; ☎ 6969 3000; www.europark.fi. 255 spaces, maximum height 2.7m. Fee €1 per hr, €27 for 24hrs. *Open daily 06.00–midnight. Exit possible 24hrs.*
**EuroPark P-Presidentti** Eteläinen Rautatienkatu 4–6; ☎ 6969 3000; www.europark.fi. 100 spaces, maximum height 1.8m. Fee €1 per hr, €27 for 24hrs. *Open daily 06.00–midnight. Exit possible 24hrs.*

# 5 Accommodation

Since Helsinki emerged from the northern gloom and began to develop both as a tourist and business destination, the number of excellent hotels in the city has increased dramatically. For a city that ranks among Europe's smaller capitals, the choice is comprehensive.

Having said that, many of the options seem to be carbon copies of one another. We all know that sleek Nordic style has swept through the world of interior design, but there are only so many white-wall and blond-wood hotel rooms you can visit before they start to meld into one. International business-class hotels rule the roost here, along with a decent crop of tourist places in wannabe imitation style, meaning that it's actually quite tricky to pick a bad hotel. Whichever one you choose, you can usually be assured of a clean and comfortable stay. Prices are reasonable and on a par with other major cities in northern Europe.

Helsinki has only two hotels awarded five-star status by the tourist board, the decadently opulent Hotel Kämp and the Hilton Strand. Some of the four-star hotels are superb. Indeed, two are so good that I've elevated them to the illustrious ranks of the 'Luxury' section on the grounds of historical elegance and modernist style respectively. There are others that compete on service but, on the grounds of either showing their age or adopting a soulless identikit design, they didn't quite make it to the big league.

If you've already studied your maps in the back of this guide, you will have seen that Helsinki is built on a promontory that pokes southwards into the Gulf of Finland. What this means is that a room with a sea view is not overly difficult to find. Granted, your view may be of the docks or ferry terminal but the point is that a watery vista doesn't necessarily command a huge premium, so don't snap up the first one that comes along.

If you like the hustle and bustle of the city centre, you will be well catered for. Many hotels are in or around the middle area of town, with the prime shopping and entertainment complexes right on your doorstep. Most other places are within a 10–15-minute walk of the action, usually in more peaceful areas. Two or three options lie a little further out, yet still within the city and with striking locations, and for these you will probably want to take a bus or tram to the centre.

Helsinki is a compact city so accommodation is not arranged by area. Instead, listings have been subdivided by price range, beginning with the no-expense-spared luxury options and then working down through business- and tourist-class establishments. Self-catering apartments have a separate section, even though some are as swish as the higher-end hotels. Finally, bringing up the rear is a clutch of hostels and the city's solitary campsite. Don't read anything into the order of listings; this is purely alphabetical and does not suggest any preference.

The prices listed are for standard high-season rack rates. High season in Finland is slightly different from other countries, as rates tend to fall in midsummer (mid

June to early August) when Finns take their annual holidays and business across the country slows down. At these times some of the top-end hotels will have tempting deals. The low season tends to run from December to February (with the exception of Christmas and New Year). Rates tend to be highest at all other times of year. Be particularly aware of big celebrations such as *Vappu* (May Day), Helsinki Day (12 June) and *Itsenäisyyspäivä* (Independence Day, 12 December). Not only will rates be high, but also availability will be low. On most weekends of the year business-class hotels will be offering advantageous rates as they aim to fill thousands of otherwise empty rooms. Check directly with the hotels for any special offers. Internet-only offers can be good value, as can reservations for long weekends that span Friday and Saturday nights, even if the stay spills over into the working week.

Like most Nordic nations Finland's relationship with the credit card is a passionate affair, and practically every establishment (including hostels) will accept payments by plastic. Rates are usually quoted inclusive of VAT (8%). If travelling independently, it can pay handsome dividends to scan websites such as www.tripadvisor.com and www.ebookers.com.

Standards are good across the board. Most tourist- and business-class hotels offer extensive buffet breakfasts that keep you firing all day, whilst nearly every establishment offers free sauna and internet (often WiFi).

Two common features take a bit of getting used to. Firstly, wetroom-style bathrooms that mean the whole floor turns into one big puddle after you've been in the shower; invariably you will forget and walk in there in just a pair of socks. Secondly, doors which open out into the corridor. If that seems inconsequential, just wait until someone opens one straight into your face as you're casually strolling to breakfast.

## 🏠 HOTELS

**LUXURY** When I was compiling this section on accommodation, I thought it was a little unfair on all the competition to list Hotel Kämp as the sole luxury hotel in Helsinki. Yes, it's the most sumptuous, best known and, undeniably, the most expensive, but one man's luxury heaven is another man's pretentious hell so to offer a bit more choice I'm throwing in a contemporary design hotel, a classy boutique number (both centrally located), and Helsinki's plushest international chain. Expect top-notch comfort and excellent service wherever you choose.

🏠 **Hilton Helsinki Strand** (192 rooms) John Stenberginranta 4; ↘ 393 51; e helsinkistrand@hilton.com; www.hilton.com [1 C2]

Discretion is always a good indication of class, & whilst some lesser hotels thrust themselves upon you with all the subtlety of a late-night Finnish hot-dog stand, others are happy to watch from afar & wait to be discovered. So it is with the Strand, Helsinki's number-one chain hotel, which sits confidently by the waterside near Hakaniemi, a 10min stroll north of the city centre. Bland from without, the soaring marble-clad lobby makes a striking first impression, & the airy Bridges Restaurant is one of the more lavish hotel dining rooms in the city, with rich hues of autumnal browns & golds, & huge expanses of gleaming glass. What can I say about the facilities? Swimming pool, fitness centre, beauty salon & even a barbershop leave you wanting for nothing. Bedrooms are large (30m²), suitably comfortable &, whilst not the most stylish in town, have everything you would expect of a Hilton. The emphasis is one of comfort over cool, which is sometimes the more reliable option. All have decent views, but if you're pushing the boat out to stay here you really need to go for the ones facing towards the harbour, which is especially beguiling when illuminated at night. *Dbl from €242. Special-internet weekend rates from dbl €125.*

⌂ **Hotel Kämp** (179 rooms) Pohjoisesplanadi 29; ☎ 576 111; e hotelkamp@luxurycollection.com; www.hotelkamp.com [5 G3]
From the outside it's easy to miss the Kämp, not because it's bland but rather because its surroundings are equally impressive. Located on the Esplanade Park, the leafy tree-lined boulevard at Helsinki's heart, this elegant neoclassical street houses some of the city's swishest boutiques & grand old cafés. Negotiating your way past the top hat 'n' tails doormen, the opulent vaulted foyer with its circular balcony is an eloquent introduction to the hotel's class. The sumptuous rooms feature every conceivable luxury, from fluffy bathrobes to an optional butler service. Suites are so decadent they should carry a health warning, whilst the facilities of the spa (with pool) & gym are second to none. Originally opened by restaurateur Karl Kämp in 1887, & rekindled in 1999 after a long hiatus, the Kämp's success epitomises Helsinki's emergence as a desirable destination. A member of the Starwood Hotels group, in 2005 the hotel was named 'Luxury Collection Hotel of the Year' & received the finest customer feedback ratings of any of their 850 worldwide establishments. Quite simply, if you want to celebrate a lottery win, propose marriage or just scare the pants off your bank manager, this is the place to do it. *Dbl from €285, jnr suite from €580, Kämp suite from €750; closed for Christmas (usually 22–26 Dec).*

⌂ **Hotel Rivoli Jardin** (55 rooms) Kasarmikatu 40; ☎ 681 500; e rivoli.jardin@rivoli.fi; www.rivoli.fi [5 G4]
The most understated of the luxury options, the Rivoli Jardin is a family-run boutique hotel just a block from
the Esplanade Park. From the outside, the green plastic canopy & dreary 'Hotelli' sign are unassuming — some
would say tacky — but press on through the little courtyard because what lies within is worth discovering. The
subtle décor has distinct French & Oriental influences, but the styles never clash & the result is one of
Helsinki's most tasteful & relaxing interiors — pitched halfway between the stark Finnish minimalism of many
business hotels & the unabashed grandeur of Hotel Kämp. The rooms have individual themes so what you get is
potluck in a way, but there's no danger of drawing a dud. You get satellite & pay-TV, minibar & internet access;
there's no gym but this is Finland so sauna is very much on the menu. The service is perhaps the most
attentive of the 3 luxury hotels (this being the smallest) & you shouldn't miss b/fast, taken at marble-topped
tables amidst the beautiful leafy conservatory. *Dbl from €237 (internet specials from €169).*

⌂ **KlausKHotel** (138 rooms) Bulevardi 2–4; ☎ 770 4700; e rooms@klauskhotel.com; www.klauskhotel.com
[5 F4]
Opened in the winter of 2005, KlausK brought some much-needed contemporary flair to Helsinki's hotel scene,
on one of the most upmarket streets. Based loosely on themes drawn from Finland's national epic text, the
*Kalevala*, this is an ambitious project comprising equal measures of style & substance. From the über-chic
lobby area with sleek white surfaces, subtle lighting & receptionists plucked straight off the catwalk, it's clear
that you're on fashionable ground. I actually felt as if my unsophisticated presence was disrupting the whole
*chi* of the place, but I soon forgot this by collapsing on a pile of deep-red cushions that were laid seductively
across my custom-made bed. Nice & comfy, I investigated delights such as LCD TV, DVD player, MP3 stereo
system & WiFi internet before freshening up in the trendy shower room, complete with KlausKHotel-embroidered

towels & bathrobe. The rooms have been given stirring, emotional monikers; Passion & Mystical, Desire, Envy, Envy Plus & Envy Suite. All you need to know is that they're all plush & these names are classier than calling them small, medium, big, bigger & biggest. Each type has a different colour theme, from racy reds to cooling creams. If you've got a preference, just let them know. Equally, if space is an issue then the Passion & Mystical rooms (up to 20m²) could be a touch tight. There's a sauna & small gym, & also direct access to the Helsinki Day Spa, one of the city's finest (although treatments cost extra). B/fast is a reassuringly swanky buffet affair served in one of the 3 excellent restaurants. *Dbl from €207. Special spa packages from dbl €150 (Fri–Mon).*

**BUSINESS** Helsinki's forte is catering to the business market, with a host of centrally located chains vying for your euros. They also do a good job of catering to tourists; from long-term Japanese tour groups to casual weekend escapees, it's not unusual to see a mixed crowd jostling around the breakfast buffet. As standard, you can expect en-suite rooms with bath and/or shower, TV with satellite and pay channels, safe, minibar, internet access, air conditioning, bar and restaurant. Some may have fitness facilities, and unless stated all will have at least one sauna. Breakfast will usually be a hearty buffet, including fruits, cereals, meats, pastries, hot dishes, porridge and the obligatory several gallons of coffee. The amount some people can pack away is a sight to behold.

⌂ **Hilton Helsinki Kalastajatorppa** (235 rooms) Kalastajatorpantie 1; ✆ 458 11; e helsinkikalastajatorppa@ hilton.com; www.hilton.co.uk/kalastajatorppa

Located away from the city, 5km from the centre, this Hilton monster offers understated luxury by the Gulf of Helsinki. Impressive facilities include swimming pool, tennis courts, gym & a private beach that makes the most of the seaside setting. Rooms are standard business type, with floor-to-ceiling picture windows & the muted grey/white/black colour tones that define Nordic style, set against warm wooden floors. Bathrooms feature smoked-glass doors & those freestanding basins on dark wooden plinths that are currently all the rage. It's all very comfortable & well thought out, & there are some lovely sea views. Restaurant Meritorppa offers stylish waterside dining, especially under the sunset of a midsummer eve, whilst the contemporary Vista Bar is just waiting to tempt you into parting with a few more euros. Service is slick & although out of town, you are actually closer to some attractions (Seurasaari, Gallen-Kallela Museum, Sibelius Park) than many central hotels. *Dbl from €242. Special internet weekend rates from dbl €110.*

🔺 **Hotel Seurahuone** (118 rooms) Kaivokatu 12; ➘ 691 41; e helsinki.seurahuone@restel.fi; www.hotelliseurahuone.fi [4 E2]

Directly opposite the railway station, Seurahuone is one of Helsinki's few remaining grande dames where period elegance still rules over modern minimalism. With a distinct personality, it's also infinitely more memorable than many of the international chains. A *seurahuone* is a traditional meeting house for the Finnish aristocracy, where ladies & gentlemen could glide across the parquet floor of the graceful Art Deco ballroom & dine on gourmet dinners beneath glittering chandeliers, & a place for visiting dignitaries to lay their heads amidst convivial surroundings. So high ceilings, ruffled curtains & elaborate gold flourishes are the order of the day – the design of the public spaces & galleries is particularly striking – whilst rooms feature dark-wood furniture & romantically rich fabrics. There's no shortage of mod cons either, with LCD TVs & WiFi throughout, together with that most British of requirements, the hospitality tray in every room. The clientele may have changed these days, but the spirit remains & the service is as attentive as it ever was. Ask for a quiet room, although with Station Square to the front & a nearby nightclub at the rear you might be hard pressed to find one. *Dbl €197–247. Weekend rates dbl €127–179.*

🏠 **Palace Hotel** (39 rooms) Eteläranta 10; 🔧 1345 6656; e palacehotel@palacekamp.fi; www.palacekamp.fi [7 H5]
From the outside, the Palace looks like a design born out of the architect's waste paper basket — to call it an ugly block would be polite. The huge sprawl that occupies a significant section of prime waterfront also houses offices & the Japanese embassy, & the hotel itself is a relatively small portion of the structure. But let's not judge the book by its cover; come on, we're going inside. And what a difference! Opened for the 1952 Olympic Games, whilst some hotels of this period now appear dated the Palace is an example of 1950s modernist style par excellence. The lobby area resembles the inside of a sleek design shop, with simply arranged furniture in pleasing creams & browns & a symmetrical reception desk that is a work of art in itself. These themes continue into the bedrooms themselves, albeit with a splash more colour on the quilts & easy chairs. Bathrooms are spacious & include luxurious (& large) walk-in shower enclosures. If you can stretch to a sea-view room, the hotel's superb location by the harbour & Market Square affords a panoramic outlook with especially fine views of the Uspenski Cathedral. If you can't stretch, why not enjoy your complimentary afternoon tea in the Sea Lounge? The vistas here are equally special. *Dbl from €235–350. Special internet rates dbl €210–260. Weekend rates dbl €130–260.*

🏠 **Radisson SAS Plaza** (291 rooms) Mikonkatu 23; 🔧 775 90; e info.plaza.helsinki@radissonsas.com; www.radisson.com/helsinkifi_plaza [5 F1]

This has one of the best locations of any central hotel, tucked away at the end of a little street running away from Railway Square. It's the kind of place you only find if you're going to look for it, but yet it's still just a couple of minutes from the railway station & National Theatre, whilst the green space of Kaisaniemi Park & the University Botanical Gardens are right on the doorstep. Wonderfully Art Deco in style, there are 3 basic room types that vary in décor from sleek Nordic to the more colourful Italian style. Even the smallest are large enough (23m$^2$) & all have AC & free broadband. Some business rooms have their own private sauna, whilst all benefit from marbled bathrooms with powerful walk-in showers, essential for banishing those deep February chills. Keep-fit fanatics can pound the treadmill in the gym or simply jog through the park, where in winter you can also build snowmen to your heart's content. Interestingly, the hotel has been used as a set for the Finnish soap opera *Secret Lives* – keep it a secret for yourself. *Dbl €125–195. Special internet rates dbl €100–156.*

🏠 **Radisson SAS Royal Hotel** (262 rooms) Runeberginkatu 2; 📞 695 80; e info.royal.helsinki@ radissonsas.com; www.radisson.com/helsinkifi [4 C3]

I have to admit a soft spot for Radisson hotels. They may be an international chain, but they have a great knack for converting old buildings into interesting, individual hotels that remain faithful to their original architecture & design. This one, however, was built from scratch in 1991 & is easily recognised with its circular glass atrium & sleek lines. Admittedly, since the neighbouring Kamppi shopping centre opened it has been somewhat overshadowed, but that breezy interior remains as welcoming as ever. The beds here are one of the best features & receive regular praise from visitors. Those with a shower aversion should note that each bathroom has a full-size tub to soak away the stress of work or alleviate a dose of tourist's foot. Superior rooms boast the extra touches of tea & coffee facilities & free movies, whilst WiFi internet streams throughout the hotel & this is yet another place with huge buffet b/fasts that defy belief. For luxurious pampering with a city view, book the 8th-floor VIP sauna with roof terrace. *Dbl €115–185.*

🏠 **Radisson SAS Seaside Hotel** (364 rooms) Ruoholahdenranta 3; ☎ 693 60; e info.seaside.helsinki@ radissonsas.com; www.radisson.com/helsinkifi_seaside [6 A6]
When I first discovered that this hotel was actually opposite the docks & Helsinki's western ferry terminal, I thought that Radisson were stretching the boundaries of reasonability by using the name 'Seaside'. True, the sea *is* across the road, but it's full of commercial vessels bobbing against a backdrop of cranes & multicoloured containers. But it must be said that this converted cheese factory is a winner; modern & stylish, it's quiet & only a brisk 10min walk to the heart of the city. Rooms come in a variety of sizes, from somewhat pokey to more than generous — some with lounge area & microwave. The b/fast buffet will sate the fiercest of appetites & this is also one of the closest hotels to the appealing Hietalahti flea market. Book yourself into the top-floor sauna & enjoy the panoramic views. My only quibble would be the slightly pokey & low-key bathrooms, but that hasn't stopped me staying here on more than one occasion. *Dbl €110–165. Special internet rates dbl €88–132.*

🏠 **Scandic Continental** (512 rooms) Mannerheimintie 46; ☎ 473 71; e continentalhelsinki@scandic-hotels.com; www.scandic-hotels.com/continentalhelsinki [1 A1]
Showing its age somewhat, the 1970s Continental could do with a facelift but merits inclusion as one of the few hotels in the Töölö area of town, overlooking the beautiful Töölönlahti sea inlet & convenient for attractions such as the Opera House & Olympic Stadium. Some rooms seem a little cramped & the lack of opening windows can feel restrictive in warmer weather & really this leaves me a little apathetic; I've certainly stayed in (many) much

worse places but I'd be disappointed if I chose this for a special occasion. It's popular with business visitors & is a convenient stop for the Finnair airport bus, & if you like the outdoors life you can skip straight across into the leafy park by the water's edge, where on summer evenings martial arts are practised, bongos bashed & beer supped alfresco. *Dbl from €182. Special internet rates from dbl €99.*

🏠 **Scandic Grand Marina** (462 rooms) Katajanokanlaituri 6; ☎ 166 61; e grandmarina@scandic-hotels.com; www.scandic-hotels.com/grandmarina [I D3]
Not only is this converted early 20th-century monolith convenient for the Katajanokka & Kanava ferry terminals, it also serves as a great base for exploring Katajanokka Island, blessed with some of Helsinki's best Jugendstil architecture, quiet streets & a couple of recommended restaurants. The Grand Marina itself is the former Harbour Magazine building, a brick-clad beast of more than 140m in length that served as warehouse space during Helsinki's boom trading years. Remodelled as a hotel between 1989 & 1992, today its primary role is to cater to boat passengers & visitors to the adjacent convention centre, whose bulky presence blocks views of the harbour. Inside, the rooms are fine but lack either the plush luxury or sleek modern panache of some rivals, being rather utilitarian in style; the stark bathrooms (some solely with shower) are a case in point. The architecture of the warehouse lends some curiosities. Owing to its vast length, the corridors can feel like never-ending tunnels; improved lighting would be of benefit. Of more pertinence are the variations in window size. Some are perfectly fine, others way too small & likely to cause claustrophobia. On the upside, the service is excellent, b/fast unnecessarily immense & there's a gym to work it all off. *Dbl from €166. Special internet rates from dbl €99.*

🏠 **Scandic Simonkenttä** (359 rooms) Simonkatu 9; ☎ 683 80; e simonkentta@scandic-hotels.com; www.scandic-hotels.com/simonkentta [4 D3]

Locations don't come much more central than this. Situated slap-bang next to the glittering Kamppi centre, Helsinki's brand-new shopping, dining & entertainment mega-mall, & a 5min walk to the railway station or Esplanade Park, this is a great choice for being amidst the action. Befitting its stylish location, the Simonkenttä is all sleek glass & brushed metal, with a huge reception area where the dark tiled floor contrasts moodily with curvy brown leather sofas & deep vivid red rugs. The lobby bar overlooks the Kamppi square, & is a great place to nurse a soothing drink as you watch the world go by. This is especially true in winter as people scuttle to & fro through the snow as you sit snug as a bug on the inside. Rooms are modern & airy affairs, with laminate floors & neutral colour schemes punctuated by splashes of blues or reds. There's a small but well-equipped gym. *Dbl from €175. Special internet rates from dbl €152.*

⌂ **Sokos Hotel Torni** (154 rooms) Yrjönkatu 26; ☏ 020 1234 604; e torni.helsinki@sokoshotels.fi; www.sokoshotels.fi [4 E3]
One of Helsinki's most iconic hotels, this stately 12-storey tower was the city's first skyscraper when it opened in 1931. Even today, the fact that it still offers spectacular views from the rooftop Ateljee Bar speaks volumes about the city's low-rise development, & its prominent spike can be seen from far & wide. A favourite with more mature travellers & those in search of nostalgia, the Art Deco style runs deep, from the rich wood-&-marble-adorned lobby to the warm atmosphere of soft-gold & rich brown colours in the guest rooms. The white-walled modern rooms have simple blinds with colourful bed covers to add definition, mirrored walls to create the illusion of space & curious bathrooms with glass walls & doors. Meanwhile, *Kyllikki* rooms are decorated in Jugend style, which means antique-style touches, period wallpaper & gilt-edged mirrors. Offering a comprehensive rundown is tricky, however, as all the rooms have individual charms just waiting to be

discovered. It can be worth shelling out a few extra euros to secure a larger superior room, with tea & coffee facilities & (occasionally) a freestanding bathtub. Even if you don't want to stay here, take a trip up to the roof bar for the views. Girls, your bathrooms up there have the best view of all. *Dbl from €243. Special internet rates from €158. Weekend rates from dbl €117.*

**TOURIST** Helsinkiites have never really embraced the concept of guesthouses or B&Bs, so whilst many travellers in Europe are snuggling up in a cosy family home, visitors to the Finnish capital can feel left out in the cold. Whilst the service at the large business-class hotels is usually faultless, you can still feel like a number as opposed to a guest and so, for those seeking a little more character and friendliness, the tourist hotels can be a good bet. They still cater to business guests, and mostly have en-suite bathrooms, internet access, TV and sauna. Some will also have restaurants, bars and fitness facilities. You'll notice that rates can be startlingly high, so it really does pay to shop around.

⌂ **Hotel Anna** (64 rooms) Annankatu 1; ☎ 616 621; e info@hotelanna.com; www.hotelanna.com [7 F6] Peacefully located in a quiet central suburb, & a 10min walk to the beautiful south shore. This is one of the most pleasant areas of town, quiet & laid-back but close to a number of decent bars & restaurants. Some may be put off by the tackiness of nearby Iso-Roobertinkatu, but it really doesn't affect the hotel, where rooms could best be described as homely & a little dated. Don't bother looking for any booze in the minibars — Anna is run by the Finnish Free Church & the strongest brew on offer is the b/fast coffee. High rates mean this is probably best suited to families sharing one of the larger corner rooms. *Dbl €160–175.*

🏠 **Hotel Arthur** (144 rooms) Vuorikatu 19; ✆ 173 441; e reception@hotelarthur.fi; www.hotelarthur.fi [5 G1]

Friendly Arthur wasn't blessed with the best location, situated on a main road running from the station towards Kaisaniemi Park. In mitigation, the staff are friendly & accommodation reliable, if unspectacular. Standard rooms are a touch small, looking uncannily like oversized ferryboat cabins, but all are more than comfortable & tastefully decorated. Superior rooms offer considerably more space. Try to secure one of the 17 new rooms that were opened in mid 2006. They have similar footprints to the regular rooms, but with modern décor & touches including minibar, LCD TV & sleek shower rooms. Family rooms (for up to 5 guests) are superb value for groups. *Dbl €114–134. Weekend rates dbl €92–108. Family rooms €174 (€152 weekends).*

🏠 **Hotel Aurora** (70 rooms) Helsinginkatu 50; ✆ 770 150; e reservations@hotelaurorahelsinki.com; www.hotelaurorahelsinki.com [1 B1]

Located in the north of the city, close to Töölönlahti, the Olympic Stadium & Linnanmäki (Finland's oldest & most popular amusement park), Aurora is a dull building on a busy 4-lane road that hides an altruistic secret. Operated by a charitable child welfare trust, your room rates help fund the nearby children's hospital. In addition to the feel-good factor, you can treat your body to a workout in the pool, gym or on the squash court, & treat your wallet to very decent summer rates (*dbl €69*). With parquet flooring throughout, the hotel has a certain distinguished air, & features satellite TV, AC & en suite bathrooms. Some larger rooms have self-catering kitchenettes & WiFi internet is also available. Although slightly dated, there are some winning views across Töölönlahti & for the price it's an attractive option. *Specials from €69, weekends from €98, standard rates €138.*

🏠 **Hotelli Helka** (150 rooms) Pohjoinen Rautatiekatu 23A; ✆ 613 580; e reservations@helka.fi; www.helka.fi [4 B2]

Totally renovated in 2006, Helka has embraced the Finnish panache for sleek design & melded it with an appreciation of the great outdoors. What we get are subtle tones of greys, blacks, earthy browns & soft greens, whilst walls throughout the lobby areas & restaurant carry photographic wallpaper of nature scenes. Be careful, the first time I tried to find the lift on the top floor, I couldn't – it was well camouflaged in a thick forest. This theme continues in the bedrooms, where huge canvases hanging from the ceilings show similar calming images, & also in the dining room where birch trunks run floor to ceiling. The beds are super-comfy & en-suite shower rooms modern & efficient. Add in minibar, free internet & a decent b/fast spread & you have everything you need. Rooms around the courtyard are quietest. *Dbl €159. Weekend rates dbl €102. Special internet rates dbl €96–139.*

🏠 **Martta Hotelli** (44 rooms) Uudenmaankatu 24; ✆ 618 7400; e info@marttahotelli.fi; www.marttahotelli.fi [6 E5]

On trendy Uudenmaankatu, Martta has gained something of a reputation for the friendliness of its welcome & homely quality of the bedrooms, despite a slightly lived-in appearance. It reminds me of visiting old friends who are always glad to see you; they don't much care what you look like &, in return, you don't mind if they're a touch on the shabby side themselves. Try to grab one of the newer rooms, where such concerns aren't really an issue. The attractive restaurant serves up a splurge of a b/fast, & the roof terrace is a good place to hang out above the pavement. Set back from the street, through an unusual sloping-glass entrance, this is a quiet & pleasing retreat. *Dbl €155.*

🏠 **Palace Hotel Linna** (48 rooms) Lönnrotinkatu 29; 📞 10 3444 100; e linna@palacekamp.fi; www.palacekamp.fi [6 C5]

Located near the Hietalahti flea market, the façade of Linna must surely be one of Helsinki's most romantic. The name translates to 'castle' in English, a perfect description of the stout Jugendstil architecture with chunky arched doorways & prominent turret. Hewn from impressive chunks of granite, the craftsmanship is detailed & typical of the national romantic style. In winter, with snow on the ground & oil lamps flickering by the entrance, the scene is especially charming. Inside, apart from the impressive period reception area, sophisticated guest lounge & medieval-style basement restaurant, the hotel is surprisingly contemporary. The rooms, housed in a modern annexe, are reached through a twinkling glass corridor & epitomise Finnish cool. Flat-screen TVs, curvaceous furniture & comfortable beds complement the well-equipped bathrooms, whilst modernist art adorns the walls. The hotel is the former students' union building of Helsinki Polytechnic; not surprisingly, it was deemed too good for scholarly recreation. *Dbl €210. Weekend rates dbl €116.*

## SELF-CATERING APARTMENTS

Helsinki has short- and long-term apartment lets available, from plush modern designs with all creature comforts to more basic places akin to university accommodation.

Dotted around the city, if you want to look after yourself these can be an attractive option. Furthermore, as many have no minimal rental, they can be excellent value for a weekend break, when rates tend to be lowest. The tourist office keeps up-to-date lists of the best options.

⌂ **Accome Parliament** Museokatu 18; ✆ 2511 050; e helsinki@accome.com; www.accome.com [1 A2]
Readers with a long memory might remember these apartments as Accome Tölö, in the beautiful Jugendstil
residential district near Temppeliaukio Church. Well, the name may have changed (an upmarket rebranding
exercise), but the style & service on offer in the 43 4-star apts remains the same. Ranging from 26–75m², these
are probably Helsinki's most comfortable self-catering choices, very well equipped without being overbearing in
style. Short of nothing, you can take a sauna, do the washing or surf the net all day long whilst relaxing on
your soft sofa. Kitchens have fridge, stove & microwave, but if you don't fancy cooking there are several good
eateries in the neighbourhood. *Daily rates: studio apt €90–128, studio superior apt €95–136, studio twin apt
€101–144, 1-bedroom apt €112–160, superior 1-bedroom apt €123–176, 2-bedroom apt €129–184.*

⌂ **Accome Senate** Kauppiaankatu 5; ✆ 2511 050; e helsinki@accome.com; www.accome.com [1 D3]
The second Accome option is across town on the stately island of Katajanokka, close by the Uspenski Cathedral
& ferry terminals for crossings to Tallinn & Stockholm. Like its cousin, Senate has also been rebranded & the 52
apts (ranging from 28–70m²) share the same spawned-in-IKEA appearance. Suffice to say, you have identical
features & benefits as well, although Senate probably has the inferior location. Yes, it's close to the Market
Square, Esplanade Park, the city cathedrals & Suomenlinna ferries, but then Parliament is better placed for the
railway station, shopping centres, museums, galleries & a wider, more budget-friendly choice of restaurants. *Daily
rates: studio apt €84–120, studio queen apt €90–128, 1-bed apt €101–144, superior 1-bed apt €106–152,
executive 1-bedroom apt €112–160, superior 1-bedroom twin apt €123–176, executive penthouse €168–240.*

⌂ **Apartment Hotel Niko** Eerikinkatu 48; ✆ 2709 1690; e info@apartmenthotelniko.com;
www.apartmenthotelniko.com

Stay in real Finnish homes on a short- or long-term basis. Hotel Niko act as agents for a group of two-dozen apts around the city, from a compact 21m$^2$ to a spacious 115m$^2$. Some have balconies, others car-parking spaces & several their own sauna. Styles vary considerably across the board, from basic to plush, so it's worth checking the website before committing. With less of a hotel-style atmosphere these are probably better suited to long-term lets, but if you fancy a more authentic experience at a decent cost then these could suit you down to the ground. *Daily rates: 1-room apt €45–92, 2-room apt €60–110, 3-room apt €90–173, 4-room apt €110–173.*

🏠 **Apartments Rivoli Jardin** Korkeavuorenkatu 39; 🔌 681 500; 📧 rivoli.jardin@rivoli.fi; www.rivoli.fi [7 F5] These are some of Helsinki's swishest DIY digs but you wouldn't guess from the outside. Only the number '39' light cube above the doorway marks the location, so keep your eyes peeled or you'll easily miss it. Apts range from studio (31m$^2$) to 2-bedroom (68m$^2$) & act as a lesson in perfect Finnish design. Once again, clean lines dominate a palette of white, black, soft greys & focused bursts of colour. Furniture is of classic Nordic style. Everything you need is here: TV, DVD, telephone, hairdryer, iron, broadband internet (on request), laundry, sauna & well-equipped kitchen. The largest apts, which sleep up to 6, even have dishwasher & freezer. I want to move in! With a minimum 6-night rental the Rivoli caters mostly to the business market, but could be perfect value for a longer city break. *Daily rates: studio apt €75–108, small 1-bedroom apt €85–115, large 1-bedroom apt €89–130, 2-bedroom apt €175–225.*

🏠 **Hotel Finnapartments Fenno** Kaarlenkatu 7; 🔌 774 980; 📧 reception@hotelfenno.fi; www.hotelfenno.fi [1 C1] The low-cost choice, Fenno is an uncompromising Soviet-style block of a place near Kallio Church, 2km north of the railway station. It has the austere feel of an academic institution, but tempered by helpful staff this draws a mixed crowd of budget travellers who brighten the atmosphere. Rooms are small & basic, with tiny bathrooms together with simple cooking facilities (microwave, stove, fridge), but you get a decent buffet b/fast & morning sauna included in the price. Economy rooms have shared bathrooms & cooking facilities. Laundry, café, restaurant, internet access in the lobby. Summer deals (€32.50–55 pp) are particularly attractive. *Daily rates: sgl economy €50–56, sgl €65–72, dbl €77–88.*

## HOSTELS

What do you expect from a youth hostel? If it's shabby dorms with dog-eared carpets, raucous late-night partying and a bohemian decadence, then generally you won't find it here. On the whole Finland's hostels are clean, crisp affairs that offer great low-cost accommodation, in some instances even for families, but tend to lack the atmosphere that backpackers love. There are a couple of places where you can meet like-minded souls, swap travellers' tales and have a few beers, but these are the exception rather than the norm.

Many of these establishments have private rooms with bathroom, whilst internet access, spotless self-catering kitchens and decent cafés are not unusual either. With those kinds of facilities, they complement the more expensive tourist hotels nicely. If you're planning to travel in summer it's worth knowing that despite near 24-hour daylight decent curtains are a rarity. If you want a good night's sleep, take eye patches.

🏠 **Eurohostel** Linnankatu 9; ☎ 622 0470; e eurohostel@eurohostel.fi; www.eurohostel.fi [1 D3]

Ideally situated for the ferry terminals on Katajanokka, this bustling place is more budget hotel than true youth hostel, which makes it a great place to secure a low-cost room (families as well as couples) but not the best for solos or those seeking a good time. It's also popular with visitors from the Baltics & Russia, which can leave English-language speakers feeling isolated, especially as there's no common area to meet fellow travellers. On the plus side, it's clinically spotless, friendly & choc-full of useful information. Facilities include internet, laundry & a great café serving good-value set lunches for around €8. The Eurohostel rooms command an extra premium for features like TV & improved soundproofing. All have shared facilities. *Backpacker rooms: sgl €39.20, twin/trpl €23.50, family room €57.90, extra bed €13.90. Eurohostel rooms: sgl €45.20, twin/trpl €26.60, family room €65.30, extra bed €15.10. B/fast €6.30.*

🏠 **Hostel Erottajanpuisto** Uudenmaankatu 9; ☎ 642 169; e info@erottajanpuisto.com; www.erottajanpuisto.com [6 E5]

Finland's 'Hostel of the Year' in 2005 is *the* place to go if you want the true hostel experience: no curfew, muddled furnishings & the laid-back, sociable atmosphere that give it the feel of a student house. It's also got a superb location on trendy Uudenmaankatu, just a few minutes from all the worthwhile action. Popular with younger backpackers, Erottajanpuisto has rooms from sgl to 8-bed dorms. Some might find the bathrooms a squeeze but overall the cleanliness & friendly welcome make this place a winner. *Dorm bed €22.50, sgl €47, twin €30, trpl €26, quad €21. B/fast €5.*

🏠 **Hostel Stadion** Pohjoinen Stadiontie 3; ☎ 477 8480; e stadion@hostel.inet.fi; www.stadionhostel.com

Most of us can only dream of going to the Olympics. In Helsinki, you can go there *and* dream at the same time. Located in the striking Olympic Stadium in the north of the city, Hostel Stadion benefits from a wonderful location by the Central Park & a whole host of outdoor activity opportunities. Unfortunately, the modernist design that so suits the exterior of the stadium appears cold & dated on the inside. The dorms themselves are OK, sleeping from 1–5, but the shared showers are a real throwback to the worst white-tiled communal affairs from schooldays. Café, laundry, TV room, internet station & WiFi, as well as ample free parking. *Dorm bed €16, sgl €32, twin/trpl €22, quad €20. Sheets €4 (or use your sleeping bag), towel €1, b/fast €5.60. Closed daily 10.00–16.00, late Jul to mid Aug and Christmas (24–27 Dec).*

🏠 **Hostel Suomenlinna** Suomenlinna Island C9; 📞 684 7471; e leirikoulu@pp.inet.fi; www.leirikoulut.com [1 D5] If hostels were rated solely on location, then Suomenlinna would win hands down every time. Situated on the historic 250-year-old sea fortress, you need to catch a boat from the Market Square to get here, & don't expect bright lights & booming nightlife. This is all about history, tranquillity & the novelty of staying on one of the archipelago islands. In rooms sleeping 2–10, the facilities here are basic with shared bathrooms & a slightly draughty feel. There's a café, common room, laundry & internet access & the island has a small shop, but for a great Suomenlinna experience just grab some friends, pick up a *pussikalja* (traditional Finnish carrier bag stuffed with beer bottles) & head off to catch the midnight sun from your own secluded, rocky promontory. *Dorm bed €20, sgl €40, dbl/trpl €25. B/fast €4.50.*

## CAMPING AND CABINS

Helsinki has but one campsite, but it's well worth a visit. On weekends you can pitch a tent free of charge on the island of Pihlajasaari (see page 256). For cabin accommodation within striking distance of the city, see the boxed text on pages 266–7.

**⚊ Rastila Camping** Karavaanikatu 4; 📞 321 6551; e rastilacamping@hel.fi; www.hel.fi/rastila

This very well kept site offers everything you could want from city camping. With a waterside location & forests of fir trees in the vicinity Rastila has an archetypal Finnish setting, yet the Metro stop is only a 5min walk away & the ride to the centre of town takes just 15mins. If you want to roll up with a tent, go ahead, but the best options are the cabins. The 4-person bunk-style camping cabins are single-roomed affairs with no private facilities, but for a few extra euros you can move upmarket to a log cottage with TV, lounge area, kitchenette, bathroom & terrace. Sleeping 6, they're still pretty basic but unbeatable for the price, & romantic amidst the winter snows. Top of the pile are the holiday cottages, complete with private sauna. In addition, a summer hostel operates from mid June to early August. You can rent canoes or bicycles, use the sauna, loaf on the beach, go for a swim or dine in the on-site restaurant. In winter, Rastila is one of the only places visitors can try the invigorating ice-swimming experience. Reception is open round the clock in summer (08.00–22.00 at all other times). *Camping: adult €5, child (<15 years) €1. Summer hostel dorm bed €19, summer hostel sgl/db/trpl/quad €30/55/75/90, 2-/4-bed camping cabin €45/64, log cottage €120, holiday cottage €180.*

# 6   Eating and Drinking

*Elämä on epävarmaa, syö jälkiruoka ensin* (Life is uncertain, so eat your dessert first)

## FOOD AND DRINK

At the July 2005 G8 summit in Edinburgh French President Jacques Chirac was overheard telling Gerhard Schroeder and Vladimir Putin that Finnish food was the worst in Europe and only marginally worse than that in Britain, of which Chirac allegedly said, 'one cannot trust people whose cuisine is so bad'.

Whilst Finland's gastronomical star has never ascended to the self-proclaimed heights of French excellence, it does rather beg the question of just what Chirac ate that was so bad? Yes, there are some shockers – take for example *maksalaatikko* (minced liver casserole) or *mustamakkara* (a type of local blood sausage) – but every nation has its epicurean pariahs and for each Finnish dish that makes you blow your cheeks out in revulsion there are many more that leave you craving seconds.

To be fair to Chirac the Finns are a pretty easy lot to please when it comes to food. One of the most popular delicacies is *lenkkimakkara* (ring sausage), the traditional fast food that is scoffed heartily across the land. After a sauna, on the summer barbecue or at the end of a night out, any time is a good time for *lenkkimakkara*. If you add beer to the equation, all the better.

With over 180,000 lakes and a considerable coastline, fresh fish also features heavily on the menu. Spawned in beautifully clean and cool waters, Finnish fish are some of the finest in the world, and most Finns eat at least one variety on a daily basis. The most famous is the *silakka* (Baltic herring), which is celebrated at the annual Baltic Herring Market (see page 39) and can be prepared in dozens of ways. Favourites include *silakkarullat* (marinated and rolled into tight coils), *silakkalaatikko* (casserole with potato, onion, egg and milk) and *suutarinlohi* (literally 'shoemaker's salmon' – salted and pickled in brine or vinegar). Fried herrings with mashed potato is a delicious and hearty meal served in local restaurants up and down the land. Other fish commonly available include salmon, pike, burbot, perch and trout. August to September is crayfish season and the *rapujuhlat* (crayfish party) is the only way to celebrate such a delicacy. All you need is an ample supply of crayfish, a bunch of friends and gallons of schnapps. It's really just another in the long list of Finnish excuses for a party.

If you like meat and game, Finland won't disappoint. *Sianliha* (pork) is a perennial favourite due to its high fat content, ideal for Nordic climes, and *naudanliha* (beef), although sometimes allowed to mature a little too long for some palates, has never once seen a sniff of BSE. For something more traditional you could try *poronliha* (reindeer) or *hirvanliha* (elk). Reindeer sautéed in lard and served with mashed potato, lingonberries and pickled cucumbers is a delicious treat, if somewhat heavy on the stomach. Russian restaurants in Helsinki commonly offer bear steaks. Smoked meats are common and reindeer and *kinkku* (ham) are among the tastiest.

If you're wondering about vegetables, the Finns maintain the most northerly self-sufficient agricultural society in the world. The long cold winters restrict growing seasons to a few short summer months, but the long days and warm climate result in booming crops come July time. The deep frosts also eradicate pests without the need for pesticides, keeping Finland's fields truly organic. Market stalls groan under fresh produce, the best of which are fresh chanterelle mushrooms and piles of juicy strawberries, blueberries and raspberries, as well as lingonberries and cloudberries. The cloudberry is so synonymously associated with Finland that it is displayed on the Finnish-minted €2 coin.

When it comes to choosing a meal in Helsinki, you can be as Finnish as you wish. The style of eating and the timing of meals are similar to other western European cities. All international styles are represented across the dynamic restaurant scene, from Michelin-starred excellence to greasy-spoon takeaway. With so much choice, even Monsieur Chirac should be happy.

## ALCOHOLIC DRINKS

*Ei Tippa tapa ja ämpäriin ei huku* (A drop does not kill, and a barrel won't drown you)

Finland has a long-standing love affair with boozing. Although their intake is less than some other European countries, Finns tend to treat drinking as a sprint as opposed to a marathon. Binge drinking, whilst less of a problem than in former years, is commonplace and socially tolerated. Until 2004 the average alcohol tax in Finland stood at over 50%, but following cuts in line with European legislation the current average is around 28% – still high, but a reduction which saw sales of wines and spirits soar. Alcoholic drinks of greater than 4.7% strength are sold in state-owned alcohol shops, somewhat unfortunately called *Alko*, whilst supermarkets promote cut-price beer in order to entice customers through the door. Whilst the cost of a beer in a Helsinki bar might be €5, you could pick up 12x33cl bottles for around €11 in the supermarket.

Finland's cold northern climate is about as grape-unfriendly as it could be, and it is no surprise that Finnish wine is non-existent. Perhaps in an attempt to compensate for this misfortune of nature the Finns have embraced what resources they *do* have to develop a booming industry in berry spirits, liqueurs and fortified wines. Three liqueurs are particularly worth trying: *lakka* (from cloudberries), *mesimarja* (from the arctic bramble) and *polar* (from cranberries). Koskenkorva is the most readily available grain alcohol, distilled from barley but different in style from vodka, which Finland also produces in the form of the famous Finlandia brand. Somewhat less palatable is *salmiakkikossu*, a vodka-based spirit containing *salmiakki*, that rather dubious salt-liquorice confection that contains ammonium chloride.

Finnish beer (*olut*/*kalja*) is good and should not be overlooked for more familiar international options. Popular brands include Koff and Lapin Kulta (Lapland's Gold). Other names to watch out for are Karhu, Olvi, Karjala and Kukko. Foreign brews such as Becks, Amstel, Heineken, Corona and, inevitably, Guinness are widely available but tend to command a premium price.

Drinking has always been an important element of Finnish culture; the key to every major social occasion and the grease that smoothes the turning of society's wheel. Years of practice in this fine art have also spawned one of the wisest of all Finnish proverbs: *kännissä ja kihloissa on kiva olla, krapulassa ja naimisissa yhtä helvettiä* (it is pleasant to be drunk and engaged, but a hell to be hung-over and married).

*Kippis!*

**NON-ALCOHOLIC DRINKS** There are no surprises in the market for Finnish soft drinks (*virvoitusjuoma*); all the regular mainstream brands are available. For something local try Jaffa, a fizzy orange drink similar to Fanta that has weaned generations of young Finns and is considered a cure for many ailments. Other popular brands are Smurffi (carbonated pear drink), Muumi (strawberry lemonade) and Pirkka Cola. Finnish tap water is among the world's purest, but for a bottle of the fizzy stuff ask for *soodavesi* (soda water).

# ✖ RESTAURANTS

For a small city Helsinki is loaded with restaurants, cafés and bars. There are well over 800 options, catering to all tastes and budgets. Cheapest are the myriad fast-food joints and late-night *grilli*, dishing up a variety of sausage, kebab, burger and pizza options – a good bet after a beer or two. There's a strong Finnish element across the board, which frequently melds international styles with local produce and seasonal ingredients. Restaurants serving purely Finnish fare – heavy portions of reindeer, bear meat, lake fish and hearty plates of mashed potato – tend to cater to the tourist market, although several old stalwarts are perpetual features on the local scene. Elsewhere, a wide selection of international cuisine is represented – Russian, Italian, Japanese, Thai, Spanish, Chinese, Tibetan, Indian – the list goes on.

The major concentration of restaurants and cafés is in the central area of the city, in a strip that runs south from the train station along Mannerheimintie, spreading to the Market Square in the east and around the Kamppi area in the west. Further south, towards the districts of Eira and Kaivopuisto, options become more limited yet pockets of activity still burst forth and several places are worth travelling to. In summer the cafés in the south of the city are particular favourites, as are the island restaurants in the city's archipelago (see pages 140–1). If you're staying in the Töölö area, refer to the boxed text on pages 154–5 for some recommendations.

The amount of overlap between different categories of venue is considerable, and a headache for the guidebook writer. Many cafés are also great restaurants; some restaurants have fantastic cocktail bars; certain bars will happily serve you breakfast, whilst others will offer you a sauna whilst you sip a beer. Meanwhile, places that operate as bistros by night will dish up light snacks during the day; in one place you can even do your laundry whilst munching fresh pastries! The best of these diverse options have been collated in the boxed texts on pages 146–7 and 170–1.

Eating out in Helsinki can still be a major expense, but it needn't always be the case. An average main course in a mid-range restaurant will cost you around €12–18, starters and desserts around €5–10. Of course, you can splurge a considerable amount more than this, but it's alcohol that does the real damage. A bottle of wine will cost €25–30, and a half-litre beer can easily gobble up another €5 or so. If you know where to look you can find some decent cheaper eateries, with mains for less than €10, but booze is universally expensive in the city centre and can often cost as much as, or more, than the meal itself.

Two useful websites can help you sort the wheat from the chaff: www.eat.fi is a real-time restaurant database showing which establishments are open at any time of day or night, and includes maps and customer reviews; www.helsinkimenu.info is the website of the HelsinkiMenu programme, whereby participating restaurants offer promotional menus with a focus on innovative Finnish cuisine.

As the centre of Helsinki is compact, listings have not been divided by area. Instead, with an eye on the purse strings, entries are arranged by budget and then subdivided by style.

## FINE DINING

✘ **Chez Dominique** Rikhardinkatu 4; ☎ 612 7393; www.chezdominique.fi [5 F4]

You need to book well in advance for a trip to Helsinki's only 2-starred Michelin restaurant, which specialises in French-Finnish dishes — don't expect to arrive on the weekend & just get a table. If *haute cuisine* is your style, this is the best place to go, although time will tell whether standards will transcend the late-2006 relocation to larger premises. *Mains €39–48, set menu €85–129. Open Tue–Sat 18.00–midnight.*

✗ **G W Sundmans** Eteläranta 16; ✆ 622 6410; www.royalravintolat.com/sundmans [5 H4]
Wonderfully romantic, Michelin-starred harbourside restaurant next to Market Square. With frilly tablecloths, high ceilings, period cornice work & ornate chandeliers, it's not as smooth as its rivals, but for classical dining opulence it can't be beaten. *Mains €31.50–38.50, set menus €47/65/81. Open Mon–Fri 11.00–14.30, 17.00–midnight, Sat 18.00–midnight.*

✗ **George** Kalevankatu 17; ✆ 647 662; www.george.fi [4 D4]
The third & final Michelin-starred establishment, George is a more traditionally formal restaurant. The square dining room has neutral colours, soft candlelight & sufficiently elegant table settings, but the food is anything but conventional. The menu changes frequently — expect delights such as fillet of reindeer with Jerusalem artichoke purée & caramelised apple or white chocolate buckthorn berry tart with fudge sauce & mandarin sorbet! Respectably priced wine list. *Mains €29–32; set menus €49/78/112. Open Mon–Fri 11.00–midnight, Sat 18.00–midnight.*

✗ **Savoy** Eteläesplanadi 14; ✆ 684 4020; www.royalravintolat.com [5 G4]
Designed by Alvar & Aino Altar, food at the stylish Savoy tastes as good as the venue suggests it should. Serving world-class food since opening in 1937, this was a favourite haunt of Field Marshal Mannerheim & to this day uses the best seasonal ingredients in its dishes. Food aside, the roof terrace overlooking Esplanade Park & the city skyline offers the best dining view anywhere in Helsinki. *Mains €36–40, set menu €89. Open Mon–Fri 11.30–14.30, 18.00–midnight.*

## MIDDLE OF THE ROAD
### Finnish

✕ **Ilmatar** Bulevardi 2–4; ✆ 020 770 4714; www.ravintolailmatar.fi [5 F4]

In the KlausKHotel at the foot of upmarket Bulevardi, Ilmatar serves modern Finnish food in a classy open-plan area that forms a tantalising backdrop to the hotel reception. Rich greens & browns suggest strong natural influences, & the stylish tableware & decorations come courtesy of Iittala & Alvar Aalto. *Mains €12–31, set menu €49/58/65. Open b/fast Mon–Fri 06.30–10.00, Sat–Sun 07.00–11.00; lunch Mon–Fri 11.30–14.00; dinner Mon–Thu 18.00–23.00, Fri 18.00–midnight.*

✕ **Kolme Kruunua** Liisankatu 5; ✆ 135 4172; www.kolmekruunua.fi [1 C2]

Traditional Finnish cuisine in the Kruununhaka district, at the eastern end of Liisankatu near Tervasaari. Enjoy tasty meatballs & mounds of mash in the stately 1950s environment. *Mains €11.50–16.80. Open Mon–Sat 16.00–03.00, Sun 14.00–03.00.*

✕ **Kosmos** Kalevankatu 3; ✆ 647 255; www.ravintolakosmos.fi [4 E3]

The same family has operated the classiest of Helsinki's traditional restaurants since opening in 1924. Steeped in history, Kosmos is a melting pot of Helsinki life, rich & poor alike. Join them for delicious fried herrings. *Mains €12–26. Open Mon–Fri 11.30–01.00, Sat 16.00–01.00.*

✕ **Lappi** Annankatu 22; ✆ 645 550; www.lappires.fi [4 D4]

One of the clutch of 'traditional' restaurants aimed squarely at the tourist, this faux log-cabin place with Lappish nature scenes is expensive but for a one-off you could do a lot worse. Top of the bill is snow goose with creamy chanterelle mushroom risotto. *Mains €16–37. Open Mon–Fri 12.00–22.30, Sat–Sun 13.00–22.30.*

**✕ Saaga** Bulevardi 34; ☎ 7425 5544; www.ravintolaopas.net/saaga [6 D6]
Another tourist place, Saaga sits towards the western end of Bulevardi, away from the city centre. Venturing through thick door curtains, you discover huge pictures of Lappish wilderness scenes, reindeer furs & an annoying lady in traditional costume banging a big drum. It's fun for kids & American businessmen, & the reindeer & mash portions are huge, but it's far from authentic. *Mains €17–42. Open Mon–Sat 17.00–midnight.*

**✕ Salve** Hietalahdenranta 11; ☎ 603 455 [6 B6]
One of the better options in the Punavuori district, Salve sits next to Hietalahti flea market & does great fried

## ISLAND RESTAURANTS

If you fancy dinner with a different view of Helsinki, there are several islands close to the city with unique restaurants that operate through the summer season. Between May and September you can take a short boat ride to the inner archipelago and dine in style.

The menus offer an inventive range of fish and meat dishes, and whilst not as refined as some of the restaurants in the city these relaxed venues are nonetheless a cut above average. Unsurprisingly, so are the prices. You should expect to pay €20–25 for a main course, or from €50 for a four-course set menu, and that doesn't include the boat ticket! That will cost you another €3.50–5, but this is about the experience as a whole and unfortunately that means the wallet suffers accordingly.

herrings & other honest staples. Nothing flash, but *not* touristy & recommended for a good square meal. *Mains €10.30–25.50. Open Mon–Sat 09.00–midnight, Sun 09.00–23.00.*

✕ **Sea Horse** Kapteeninkatu 11; ☎ 628 169; www.seahorse.fi [7 F8]
This is probably the best of the old-style Finnish restaurants, serving Helsinki since 1934. In typically Finnish style, the clientele who jabber away in the lively dining room transcends society – you could be sat next to an old sailor boy or an MP taking a lunch break. Best fried herrings in town. *Mains €12–29. Open Mon–Thu 10.30–midnight, Fri–Sat 10.30–01.00, Sun 10.30–midnight.*

Three of the restaurants – **Boathouse** (*Liuskasaari;* ☎ 6227 1070 [1 C5]), **Klippan** (*Luoto;* ☎ 633 408 [1 D4]) and **Särkänlinna** (*Särkänsaari;* ☎ 1345 6756 [1 D5]) – are operated by the Palace Kämp group (*www.palacekamp.fi*). **NJK** (*Valkosaari;* ☎ 639 261 [1 D4]) is owned by Royal Ravintolat (*www.royalravintolat.com*), and **Saari** (*Sirpalesaari;* ☎ 7425 5566 [1 B5]) by AS Restaurants (*www.asrestaurants.com*).

The summer restaurants are extremely popular and bookings are recommended throughout the season, especially on weekends when the islands are popular venues for wedding celebrations. You can view menus and make table reservations online. (*Opening hours are generally Mon–Sat 17.00–midnight. Boathouse also opens Sun 15.00–22.00, and Saari Jun–Aug daily 11.30–midnight.*)

✕ **Zetor** Kaivopiha, Mannerheimintie 3–5; ☎ 666 966; www.ravintolazetor.fi [4 E3]
Low down & loud, this is Helsinki's answer to Hard Rock or TGI Friday, but with added earthiness & the kind of grit that can only be formed through excessive boozing. A lot is made of the tractors that adorn the interior, & the hearty menu has a heavy slant on hefty meat portions — steak, meatballs, reindeer stew & pork fillet, for example. *Mains €10–27. Open Sun–Mon 15.00–01.00, Tue 15.00–03.00, Wed–Fri 15.00–04.00, Sat 11.00–04.00.*

## Russian

✕ **Restaurant Bellevue** Rahapajankatu 3; ☎ 179 560; www.restaurantbellevue.com [5 K3]
Opened in 1917, Helsinki's original Russian eatery is believed to be the oldest outside Russia, & fittingly lies in the shadow of the majestic Uspenski Cathedral. The dark, moody candlelit interior is the setting for fine first-rate blinis, kievs & meat dishes (including pot roast bear steak), set to the accompaniment of soft Russian music. Highly recommended. *Mains €17.50–64.80. Open Mon–Fri 11.00–midnight, Sat 17.00–midnight.*

✕ **Romanov** Yrjönkatu 15; ☎ 642 394; www.romanov.fi [4 E4]
Helsinki's Russian restaurants are held in higher esteem than most that can be found across the border, a result of culinary stagnation in the Soviet era. Romanov is one of the newer establishments in the city, offering traditional dishes but also more contemporary platters such as baked duck breast with orange sauce & buckwheat kasha. *Mains €15–42. Open Mon–Fri 11.00–midnight, Sat 16.00–midnight.*

✕ **Saslik** Neitsytpolku 12; ☎ 7425 5500; www.asrestaurants.com/saslik [7 G8]
Across from the Russian embassy, Saslik uses stained glass, authentic music, a deep rouge décor & Tsarist-era

paintings to create the ambience of the 1950s Soviet east. The food is good — try Ivan's Sword (skewer of beef, lamb & bacon) — but despite being frequented by locals this restaurant is pushed heavily to the tourist market. *Mains €19–76. Open Mon–Sat 12.00–midnight, Sun 13.00–21.00.*

## Asian and Indian

✕ **Gorkha** Vuorimiehenkatu 12; ☎ 676 106; www.gorkha.fi [7 F8]
Consistently praised for its quality, friendly service & value for money, this Nepalese beauty near the junction of Vuorimiehenkatu & Korkeavuorenkatu in Ullanlinna is a little off the beaten track, but well worth discovering. *Mains €11–18. Open Mon–Fri 11.00–23.00, Sat–Sun 12.00–23.00.*

✕ **MaiThai** Annankatu 31–33; ☎ 685 6850 [4 D3]
Incongruously overlooked by the huge Kamppi centre, cosy MaiThai is often stuffed full with hungry diners, which is no surprise as it's the finest Thai restaurant in the city. Small, steamy & dimly lit with flickering candles, you'll be knocking elbows with your fellow diners but that won't matter a jot — the powerful, aromatic green curry will keep you focused. If it doesn't, just turn to the side & pinch something from the adjoining table. *Mains €12.50–18. Open Mon–Fri 11.00–23.00, Sat 12.00–23.00, Sun 14.00–23.00.*

✕ **Namaskaar** Bulevardi 6; ☎ 6220 1155; www.namaskaar.fi [4 E4]
British curry aficionados won't be disappointed here. The prices might be higher than you're used to at home, but this is a stylish restaurant (not a curry house) & the quality doesn't disappoint, although you won't get a chicken bhuna. What you could have is kofta made with Finnish lake fish, a fine balance of light fish & fragrant spices. *Mains €10.50–20. Open lunch Mon–Fri 11.00–15.00; dinner Mon–Thu 15.00–22.00, Fri 15.00–23.00, Sat 12.00–23.00, Sun 14.00–20.00.*

**✕ Villa Thai** Bulevardi 28; ✆ 680 2778; www.villathai.com [6 D5]
This rather unassuming place, on the ground floor of a somewhat bland apartment block, is probably Helsinki's swishest Thai restaurant. Prices are a touch higher than the competition & the atmosphere can occasionally be flat, but the quality can't be faulted. *Mains €11–16. Expansive 7-course set menu for 2 €70. Open Mon–Fri 11.30–14.00, 18.00–23.00, Sat 18.00–23.00.*

**✕ Zen Sushi** Kämp Galleria, Kluuvikatu 4; ✆ 671 367; www.zensushi.fi [5 F3]
Great sushi just next door to Hotel Kämp, but easily overlooked due to its reclusive location on the top floor of the swish Kämp Galleria. Service can be a touch tardy but the prices, especially at lunchtime, are great for the city centre. There's also a smaller sushi bar at Snellmaninkatu 16 *(open Mon–Fri 11.00–19.00). Prices from €10 (8 pieces) to €34 (24 pieces). Lunch specials from €7.70 (8 pieces). Open Mon–Fri 11.00–20.00, Sat 11.00–19.00.*

## European
**✕ Coma** Korkeavuorenkatu 2a; ✆ 677 655; www.coma.fi [7 F7]
Not a great name for a restaurant, admittedly, but Coma uses organic ingredients to make delicious pasta & risotto dishes. Typical Mediterranean feel – terracotta floor tiles, rustic presentation & a friendly, relaxed ambience. *Mains €10.90–21.50. Open Mon–Thu 11.00–23.00, Fri 11.00–midnight, Sat 15.00–midnight.*

**✕ Demo** Uudenmaankatu 11; ✆ 2289 0840; www.restaurantdemo.fi [6 E5]
Stylish fusion restaurant, flavour of the month with the young professional crowd & with an interior to match. Wonderfully creative dishes but priced on the high side. *Mains €22–27. Open Tue–Sat 16.00–23.00.*

✖ **Filmitähti** Erottajankatu 4; ✆ 020 770 4712; www.filmitahti.fi [5 F4]
Excellent salads, burgers, sandwiches & soups served in an atmospheric diner setting. Part of the KlausKHotel, Filmitähti's *raison d'être* is to show classic Finnish cinema on various screens whilst you dine. *Open Mon–Thu 11.00–23.00, Fri 11.00–02.00, Sat 12.00–02.00.*

✖ **FishMarket** Pohjoisesplanadi 17; ✆ 1345 6220; www.palacekamp.fi [5 H3]
Just a stone's throw from the South Harbour, this new place has been making waves with its superb contemporary fish dishes. Try eel mousse on iced salad or sashimi of swordfish with lime & ginger. The monkfish with Provençale risotto comes recommended; as do the daily oyster & seafood catches. Beautiful interior with a calming mix of soft cream décor & smartly set chunky wooden tables. *Mains €19.60–25.90; set menu €28/34/41. Open Mon–Sat 17.00–midnight.*

✖ **Restaurant Henri'x** Tehtaankatu 21; ✆ 4114 5370; www.henrix.fi [7 F8]
Stylish Scandinavian cuisine in the south of the city (Ullanlinna district). Sleek, dark wood, exposed brick walls & enticing dishes like fried turbot with crayfish tails & horseradish froth. *Mains €20.50–28. Open Mon–Fri 11.30–14.30, 18.00–midnight, Sat 18.00–midnight.*

✖ **Rivoletto** Albertinkatu 38; ✆ 607 455; www.rivolirestaurants.fi [6 C5]
Modest place on the ground floor of a residential block, a 10min walk west from the Swedish Theatre & Esplanade Park. This Italian place is renowned for some of the best pizzas in the city amidst a welcoming & very relaxed atmosphere. *Mains €8.40–25.50. Open Mon–Thu 11.00–midnight, Fri 11.00–01.00, Sat 13.00–01.00, Sun 13.00–23.00.*

## DINING FOR THE INDECISIVE

We've all been there. It's getting late, you're in a strange city and you just can't agree on where to eat. All of a sudden even McDonald's starts to look tempting, but don't go scuttling off to the golden arches just yet.

Helsinki has a number of eating and entertainment complexes that blend a whole host of styles and offer casual café-bar bites, lunchtime specials or upmarket bistro dining all under one roof. To round off the night, some even offer late-night bars and clubbing as well.

✗ **Baker's** Mannerheimintie 12; ☏ 612 6330; www.ravintolabakers.com [4 E3]
Predominantly a meat lover's paradise, you can chomp steak, towering burgers or tasty reindeer with blackcurrant sauce & mashed potato. Also salads, fish &, during the day, café snacks. *Mains €13–28.50. Restaurant open Mon–Tue 11.00–22.00, Wed–Fri 11.00–23.00, Sat 13.00–23.00; café bar open Mon–Fri 07.00–04.00, Sat 10.00–04.00, Sun 13.00–04.00; bar open Tue–Thu 16.30–23.30, Fri–Sat 16.30–04.00; nightbar open Fri–Sat 22.00–04.00; pub open Mon–Thu 17.00–02.00, Fri 16.00–04.00, Sat 18.00–04.00.*

✗ **Bank** Unioninkatu 20; restaurant ☏ 1345 6260; bistro ☏ 1345 6271; www.palacekamp.fi [5 G4]
Forget the contemporary evening bistro at Bank, just go for the incredible lunch offers; nowhere will you get

✗ **Rivoli** Albertinkatu 38; ☏ 643 455; www.rivolirestaurants.fi [6 C5]
The upmarket sibling of Rivoletto – the two are next door to one another & share a kitchen. The style here leans heavily towards French cuisine (bouillabaisse, garlic snails, country meat pâté, etc), but you could equally

such style for so few euros. Typical dishes include green Thai curry with turkey, cabbage bake with lingonberry purée & herb chicken with sun-dried tomato & potato wedges. The price includes bread & dessert/coffee. *Bistro mains €14–24, lunch club €8.20. Restaurant open Mon–Fri 08.00–17.00 (lunch club 11.00–14.00); bistro open Mon–Thu 11.30–23.00, Fri 11.30–midnight, Sat 16.00–midnight.*

✗ **Mecca** Korkeavuorenkatu 34; ☎ 1345 6200; www.mecca.fi [5 F4]
Popular with the suit set, Mecca oozes cool & is well revered but style & quality come at a price. Excellent wine list & trend-setting DJs in Mecca Lounge. If you can stretch to a set menu (the 10-course €75 per head extravaganza is the pinnacle) you'll see the kitchen at its most creative, otherwise regular mains cost €14.90–24.90. Styles include Oriental & meat such as veal entrecôte with corn pasta, liquorice-spiced onions & soy butter. *Open Mon–Tue 16.00–midnight, Wed–Thu 16.00–02.00, Fri–Sat 16.00–04.00.*

✗ **Teatteri** Pohjoisesplanadi 2; ☎ 681 1130; www.ravintolaopas.net/teatteri [5 F4]
Excellent mixture of salads, meat & fish dishes in one of the city's most stylish locations. Recommended summer terrace & a cool upstairs club for warm summer nights. *Mains €13.90–25.30. Open Mon–Tue 09.00–01.00, Wed–Fri 09.00–04.00, Sat 11.00–04.00.*

choose Alaska king crab with dill butter, a local plate of fried herrings or Russian dishes such as blini with vendace roe. Excellent but quite pricey. *Mains €8.70–40. Open Mon 11.00–22.00, Tue–Fri & Sat 17.00–midnight.*

✵ **Sasso** Pohjoisesplanadi 17; ☏ 1345 6240; www.palacekamp.fi [5 H3]
Italian restaurant that sits above FishMarket near Market Square. Highly modern & contemporary styling complements the creative food. Portions are a touch small, & prices high due to the location, but dishes such as ocean perch & cuttlefish ragout with sardel & potato purée are well received by diners. *Mains €17.80–24.90. Open Mon–Fri 11.30–midnight, Sat 13.00–midnight.*

✵ **Tony's Deli** Bulevardi 7; ☏ 020 7424 268; www.tonysdeli.fi [6 E5]
Down a flight of steps off Bulevardi, Tony's has a small deli & wine bar that open out into a large, glass-ceilinged dining room — the roof casts a diffused light throughout the basement when the winter snow settles. They do good pizzas & much more adventurous, contemporary Italian fare such as roast duck breast with duck salsiccia & rosemary sauce. The style is decidedly swish, favoured by business types, but the food needn't break the bank. Lunch offers the best value. *Mains €8–24. Open Mon–Wed 11.00–23.00, Thu–Fri 11.00–midnight, Sat 12.00–midnight.*

## International
✵ **Elite** Eteläinen Hesperiankatu 22; ☏ 434 2200; www.royalravintolat.com/elite/ [1 A2]
Culinary Helsinkiites seem to hold an endearing affection for Elite, a venerable elder statesman of the gastronomic scene. Serving writers, musicians & actors since 1932, a dignified air means dining here is as much about the ambience as it is the food, which comprises thoughtfully prepared meat & fish dishes such as roast arctic char served with lemon potato terrine & forest mushroom sauce. *Mains €15.50–26.80. Open Mon–Thu 11.00–01.00, Fri 11.00–02.00, Sat 14.00–02.00, Sun 13.00–23.00.*

✘ **Henri'x BBQ House** Urho Kekkosenkatu; ✆ 010 270 1700; www.henrix.fi [4 C3]
One of the bustling new venues in the swish Kamppi centre, the name gives this away – Henri'x BBQ is all about meat, & plenty of it. If you want a 30oz porterhouse steak, this is the place to come. *Mains €15–65. Mon–Sat 11.00–01.00, Sun 12.00–19.00.*

✘ **Kappeli** Eteläesplanadi 1; ✆ 681 2440; www.ravintolakappeli.com [5 G4]
This beautiful glass palace at the foot of Esplanade Park is one of Helsinki's landmarks, & dining here won't disappoint. Anything from salads to sandwiches, seafood to vegetarian risotto or even reindeer with elk sausage. Great style & unparalleled location, but expensive. Popular in summer for its outdoor terrace & lively bandstand. *Mains €13–28. Open Mon–Sat 09.00–02.00, Sun 09.00–midnight.*

✘ **Via** Ludviginkatu 8–10; ✆ 681 1370; www.viaravintola.com [7 F5]
A real mix of styles here – salads, bruschettas, Asian stir-frys, Indian & Thai curries, noodles, pasta, grilled fish & meat dishes. The period dining room has been spruced up with straight-edge modern tables & benches in dark wood, & although the mix of style doesn't always hit the right note (Italian dishes are more reliable than the Asian offerings) the service is generally reliable. The summer grill, with tasty meats, is the best option. *Mains €11.90–17. Open daily 11.00–midnight.*

## JUST MAKE IT CHEAP!
✘ **Bar No 9** Uudenmaankatu 9; ✆ 621 4059; www.bar9.net [6 E5]
Bright & spacious, the menu at Bar 9 reads better than it eats, although the salads, toasted sandwiches & stir-frys are still good value nonetheless. *Mains €4.90–14.90. Open Mon–Fri 11.00–02.00, Sat–Sun 12.00–02.00.*

**✕ Beefy Queen Jambo** Pieni Roobertinkatu 13; ↘ 611 071 [7 F5]
The signs are all there – big bottles of Heinz Tomato Sauce, a smattering of ruddy-faced labourers & the smell of honest, no-nonsense food. This is Finnish greasy spoon par excellence & a great advert for good old substance over style. Just don't expect the menu to be in English. *Prices €5–10. Open Mon–Fri 10.30–18.00, Sat 11.00–18.00.*

**✕ Four Seasons Salads & Delicatesses** Kapteeninkatu 24; ↘ 611 220 [7 F8]
Bringing a touch of French elegance to the Eira district, this is a place for a wonderful salad, lasagne or risotto. Made using fresh ingredients, portions are more than generous & great value at around €8–9 – also decent latte at €2.50. It's only a small place so try to grab a table in the window to avoid the lunchtime squeeze. *Open Mon–Sat 11.00–19.00.*

**✕ Iguana**
Pulling a mainly young crowd, 4 branches of Iguana play a varied mix of rock tunes whilst you tuck into munificent plates of pasta, burritos, fajitas or salads; tasty, recommended & never far away when you need it. *Mains €7.20–13.80.*
Aleksanterinkatu 48; ↘ 652 147 [5 F3] *Open Sun–Thu 11.00–01.00, Fri–Sat 11.00–03.00.*
Kalevankatu 23; ↘ 680 1865 [4 D4] *Open Sun–Thu 11.00–midnight, Fri–Sat 11.00–02.00.*
Keskuskatu 4; ↘ 663 662 [4 E3] *Open Mon–Thu 11.00–01.00, Fri–Sat 11.00–02.00, Sun 12.00–23.00.*
Mannerheimintie 12; ↘ 680 1855 [4 E3] *Open Sun–Thu 11.00–01.00, Fri–Sat 11.00–03.00.*

**✕ Namaskaar Express Aleksi** Aleksanterinkatu 36b; ↘ 278 136; www.namaskaar.fi [5 G3]
Close to Senate Square, this is the smaller brother to the renowned à la carte restaurants & ideal for

grabbing a whopping lunch plate between sightseeing. Daily specials come with rice, naan & poppadom — it's cheap but they don't scrimp on flavour. How the staff in the adjoining opticians concentrate is anybody's guess. *Mains €6–8. Open Mon–Fri 11.00–19.00, Sat 12.00–19.00.*

### ✕ NoriSushi Bar Wanha Kauppahalli; ☏ 260 0027; www.ravintolaopas.net/norisushibar [5 H4]
Situated by the South Harbour at the foot of Esplanade Park, the Old Market Hall (Wanha Kauppahalli) is a favourite on the tourist trail for its range of fresh delicacies, & this cute cabin-like affair is the most interesting of its smattering of eateries. The fish is fresh & there's good miso soup. Aside from using cheap plastic chopsticks & serving green tea from a bag, it's a winner. *Prices from €3.50 (2 pieces) to €19 (13 pieces). Open Mon–Fri 08.00–18.00, Sat 08.00–16.00.*

### ✕ Quick and Tasty Kamppi Centre [4 C3]
On the lower floor of the swish shopping mall & bus terminal, this smart food court serves up a range of tasty fast-food-style dishes for around €10 or less, such as noodles, chilli con carne, sandwiches, pizza & sushi. *Opening hours vary – generally Mon–Fri 10.00–21.00, Sat 10.00–19.00, Sun 11.00–19.00.*

### ✕ Tori Punavuorenkatu 2; ☏ 6874 3790 [6 E6]
Tori means 'square' & that's exactly where this is set, in Fredrikintori on the corner of Punavuorenkatu & Fredrikinkatu. Although not the great secret it used to be, this laid-back café-bar still has good-value staples like meatballs, toasted sandwiches & pasta dishes. Somewhat smoky, it attracts a mainly youngish art crowd. *Mains €5–10. Open Mon–Fri 10.00–23.00, Sat 12.00–23.00, Sun 14.00–23.00.*

## ✕ UniCafe

Primarily aimed at students, there are 11 of these refectory-style buffets around the city. Offering a range of warm dishes & cold snacks, salads, b/fasts & vegetarian/lactose-free options. The surroundings are austere, but this is all about value for money. Following an old Finnish tradition, Thursday is pea soup day! *Mains €5.20–6.90.*

**Metsätalo** Fabianinkatu 39; ☎ 1912 1603 [5 G1] *Open Mon–Thu 09.00–16.00, Fri 09.00–15.00.*

**Topelias** Unioninkatu 38; ☎ 1912 4309 [5 G2] *Open Mon–Thu 09.30–15.00, Fri 09.30–14.00.*

**Ylioppilasaukio** Mannerheimintie 3; ☎ 260 9491 [4 E3] *Open Mon–Fri 11.00–19.00, Sat 11.00–18.00.*

## COFFEE AND CAKE

**PÂTISSERIES AND CAFÉS** The Finns are irrevocably hooked on coffee, on average consuming around six mugs per day; that's 12kg per year for every man, woman and child – more than any other nation. They are also equally fond of buns, cakes and pastries of all descriptions, which usually come in stomach-straining proportions. Café culture is engrained in society, with elegant old establishments choc-full of tempting treats and heady with freshly ground beans. Busy day and night, many also act as graceful restaurants and refined wine bars. Although not always cheap – a latte could easily be €4, cakes and pastries around €5 – the following are some of the best and you should try at least one as part of the authentic Helsinki experience.

☕ **Café Ursula** Ehrenströmintie 3; ☎ 652 817; www.ursula.fi [1 C4]

My favourite, the original Ursula has a gorgeous seaside setting at the edge of the leafy Kaivopuisto embassy

## CAKES AND PASTRIES

If you stop for a lazy latte or cream cappuccino, you might be tempted by one of Helsinki's broad range of traditional Finnish cakes and pastries. Slacken the belt and tuck into these beauties…

**Korvapuusti** A giant cinnamon bun, literally meaning 'a smack on the ear'
**Munkki** Similar to a sugared jam doughnut
**Mustikkapiiraka** Wonderful blueberry pie made with *pulla* dough pastry
**Omenapiirakka** A type of apple pie commonly served with a creamy vanilla sauce
**Piimäkakku** Soft buttermilk cake made with cloves, ginger and cinnamon
**Pulla** Sweet dough coffee cake, spiced with cardamom
**Puolukkapiirakka** Similar to a *mustikkapiiraka*, but with seasonal lingonberries
**Wienerleipä** Finland's answer to a Danish pastry

district. The sun terrace is open year round, covered with a large sail-like white canopy, & can be deceptively warm on sunny winter days — just take a coat, grab a blanket & ponder a post-latte walk on the ice. Occasional live jazz. *Open daily summer 09.00–midnight, spring & autumn 09.00–22.00, winter 09.00–20.00.*

**Café Ursula Aleksi** Aleksanterinkatu 13; ☎ 1314 4330; www.ursula.fi [5 F3]
Not such a peaceful location as other cafés, on busy Aleksanterinkatu ('Aleksi'), but you can venture to the

153

upstairs room to escape the street-level bustle. Ursula is owned by 6 non-profit organisations, & the proceeds from the café go directly to supporting underprivileged mothers, children & the elderly. *Open Mon–Fri 09.00–19.30, Sat 09.00–17.30.*

## TUCKING-IN IN TÖÖLÖ

If you've decided to stay in this upmarket neighbourhood northwest from the city centre, you need not be left out in the cold when it comes to filling your stomach with fine fare – the following are all heartily recommended.

Starting in the far north, **Maharaja** [1 A1] (*Mannerheimintie 21–23;* ✆ *444 436; mains €9.50–18.50; open Mon–Fri 11.00–midnight, Sat 12.00–midnight, Sun 12.00–22.00*) dishes up recommended curries. On the shores of Töölönlahti, by the Opera House, stands **Töölönranta** [1 B1] (*Helsinginkatu 56;* ✆ *454 2100; mains €17–25.20; open Mon–Fri 11.30–midnight, Sat 16.00–midnight, Sun 12.00–16.00*), an über-stylish place that commands a high price for its superb location but is recommended for inventive meat, fish and pasta dishes, or for a lazy drink on the summer terrace.

For pizza, head inland from the water to friendly **Ristorante Pizzeria Villetta** [1 A1] (*Ruusulankatu 8;* ✆ *498 960; mains €9.40–36, pizza €9.80–13.30; open Tue–Thu 10.00–21.00, Fri 10.00–22.00, Sat 12.00–22.00*), one of the city's best Italian eateries – great value and constantly recommended. Nearby is local favourite **Kuu** [1 A1] (*Töölönkatu 27;* ✆ *2709 0973; mains €12–23; open Mon–Fri 11.00–00.30, Sat 13.00–00.30,*

⌨ **Carusel** Merisatamaranta 10; ☎ 622 4522; www.carusel.fi [1 B5]
Wonderful seaside place down on the southern tip of Helsinki with a fantastic sun terrace & occasional live music. *Open daily 10.00–22.00.*

*Sun 13.00–22.00*), commended for honest Finnish dishes such as smoked salmon soup, fried Baltic herrings and reindeer fillet in port sauce.

Ornately decorated with roman style frescos, **Bar Teos** [1 A1] (*Runeberginkatu 61;* ☎ *454 3591; tapas* €*1.35–4.80; set menus* €*13.80–20; open Mon–Thu & Sun 15.00–01.00, Fri–Sat 15.00–02.00*) is the place for a broad selection of Spanish-style tapas and a glass of fine red wine or maybe a jug of sangria. If you've been scouring Helsinki in search of goat testicles (who hasn't?), you'll find them and other equally thoughtful dishes, many eminently more palatable, at **Motti** [1 A2] (*Töölöntorinkatu 2;* ☎ *409 659; mains* €*13–22; open Mon–Thu 11.00–midnight; Fri 11.00–02.00, Sat 12.00–02.00*). It's a touch pricey but its innovation and good-value lunch specials (€*7.60–8*) take some beating.

Finally, down in the south near Temppeliaukio Church, **Manala** [4 C1] (*Dagmarinkatu 2;* ☎ *5807 7707; mains* €*8.20–29.80; open Mon–Fri 11.00–04.00, Sat–Sun 14.00–04.00*) wins no Michelin stars but its reliable pizzas, grills and hearty stews are available long into the night. By the time you've finished, it could almost be breakfast time.

⌨ **Ekberg** Bulevardi 9; ☏ 6811 8660 [6 E5]
Helsinki's grand old dame, Ekberg is the oldest café in town (opened 1861) & although smaller than some rivals on the Esplanade remains a firm favourite for its civilised, convivial atmosphere where gentle chatter wafts across marble-topped tables. *Open Mon–Fri 07.30–19.00, Sat 08.30–17.00, Sun 10.00–17.00.*

⌨ **Engel** Aleksanterinkatu 26; ☏ 694 0403 [5 H3]
Situated directly opposite the Lutheran Cathedral on Senate Square, Engel could not be more on the main tourist trail & its prime location is equal measure blessing & curse. Solid range of tempting b/fasts, sandwiches & main meals, but the unique selling point is the open-air cinema that runs in the small courtyard through the summer months. *Open Mon–Fri 08.00–22.00, Sat 09.00–22.30, Sun 10.00–22.00.*

⌨ **Esplanad** Pohjoisesplanadi 37; ☏ 665 496 [5 F3]
My first experience of Esplanad came in the depths of winter, when I chattered from a fierce snowstorm to a warm wonderland of sweet-smelling delights. Have no doubt; you will find some of the most colossal cakes & pastries you could ever hope to see. Succumb to a monstrous meringue; you can walk it off later. *Open Mon–Fri 08.00–22.00, Sat 09.00–22.00, Sun 10.00–22.00.*

⌨ **Fazer Café** Kluuvikatu 3; ☏ 729 6702; www.fazer.fi [5 G3]
The main outlet of the Fazer confectionery brand, opened in 1891, exudes an opulent grandeur & relaxed demeanour that makes hours pass like minutes. Their delicious chocolate is second to none. *Open Mon–Fri 08.00–22.00, Sat 09.00–22.00.*

**Gran Delicato Café** Kalevankatu 34a; ✆ 694 0403 [6 C5]
Without a shadow of doubt, Gran Delicato serves the best freshly made sandwiches anywhere in Helsinki, & the precisely crafted cappuccino is unparalleled. Great service & cheaper than most as well. Find it a short westerly stroll from the Old Church on Lönnrotinkatu. *Open Mon–Fri 08.00–20.00, Sat 10.00–18.00, Sun 12.00–18.00.*

**Strindberg** Pohjoisesplanadi 33; ✆ 681 2030; www.royalravintolat.com [5 F3]
Next door to Café Esplanad is one of the most stylish places to take your *kahvi* – the summer terrace in the park is an ideal people-watching haunt. Finnish specialities such as Baltic herring & reindeer fillet feature heavily on the à la carte bistro menu. *Open Mon–Sat 09.00–22.00, Sun 10.00–22.00.*

## BARS AND PUBS

The distinction between pubs, bars and nightclubs is just as hazy as that which defines café-bars and restaurants. The section below includes places most akin to pubs, where you can pop in for a casual drink (a good beer or relaxed glass of wine) at any time of the day. If you want bars that are more part of the nightlife scene, see *Chapter 7, Bars and nightclubs,* page 168.

**Black Door** Iso Roobertinkatu 1; ✆ 680 2371 [7 F5]
Classic British-style pub with a wide selection of whisky & beer, & specialising in hand-pumped real ales. Authentic bar tables & stools, dim lighting & beer mats plastered across the walls. Occasional comedy nights. *Open Sun–Thu 11.00–02.00, Fri–Sat 11.00–03.00.*

🍺 **Hemingways** Hietalahdenranta 11; ✆ 270 7951 [6 C6]
Not overly British in style but comfy nevertheless. A good place for a coffee, pint or maybe a Havana whilst you watch sport from the snug armchairs or browse a tome from the library. To the west of the city centre, at the end of Bulevardi. *Open Mon–Sat 14.00–02.00, Sun 12.00–02.00.*

🍺 **Kitty O'Shea's Irish Pub** Keskuskatu 6; ✆ 8568 5670 [5 F2]
In the heart of the city, between Railway Square & Esplanade Park, Kitty's is a popular Irish boozer with the usual mix of Gaelic music & Guinness on tap – also a good variety of whisky. Dark-green décor, cosy booths & dozens of black-&-white photographs lend an air of authenticity. *Open Mon–Thu 12.00–midnight, Fri–Sat 12.00–02.00.*

🍺 **London Pub** Fredrikinkatu 46; ✆ 693 3016; www.delifox.fi [4 C3]
Near the Kamppi centre, this is an impersonation of a British boozer that misses the mark but is fine if you take that fact with a pinch of salt. Live music at weekends. *Open daily 15.00–03.00.*

🍺 **Marian Helmi** Snellmaninkatu 17; ✆ 135 6651 [5 H1]
With a wide range of Finnish & imported brews, this one's for beer lovers. Find it 2 blocks north of Senate Square. *Open Sun–Thu 16.00–02.00, Fri 15.00–03.00, Sat 16.00–03.00.*

🍺 **Molly Malone's Irish Bar** Kaisaniemenkatu 1c; ✆ 5766 7500; www.mollymalones.fi [5 F2]
With 3 bars spread over 2 floors, Molly's has been voted in the top 50 Irish pubs in Europe, & its atmosphere is the closest you'll get to the real thing in Helsinki. Live music every night. *Open Mon–Tue 15.00–midnight, Wed–Thu 15.00–02.00, Fri–Sat 15.00–03.00.*

🍺 **Old Skipper's** Laivurinkatu 10; ☎ 179 880 [6 E7]

Ahoy me hearties! Ancient mariners' tales & adventures on the high seas have inspired Skipper's, a welcoming local where you can sup a beer amid convivial chatter or fill your belly with hearty Finnish grub. Laivurinkatu is 2 blocks south of Iso Roobertinkatu, at the foot of Annankatu. *Open Mon–Thu & Sun 11.00–02.00, Fri–Sat 11.00–03.00.*

🍺 **Pub Gaselli** Aleksanterinkatu 46; ☎ 8568 5760 [5 F3]

Eleven beers & ciders on tap & over 40 bottled varieties in the fridge mean you'll never go thirsty in Gaselli. TV for showing big ice-hockey games. *Open Tue 16.00–01.00, Wed–Thu 16.00–02.00, Fri 16.00–03.00, Sat 18.00–03.00.*

🍺 **Punavuoren Ahven** Punavuorenkatu 12; ☎ 4780 3350; www.delifox.fi [6 D7]

Smoky, traditional boozer. *Open Sun–Thu 12.00–02.00, Fri–Sat 12.00–03.00.*

🍺 **Sir Eino** Eteläesplanadi 18; ☎ 8568 5770 [5 F4]

Another British-style pub, & the first to open on the Esplanade. Busy at all times, there's a good selection of beers, ciders & spirits, & hearty grilled meat dishes to soak up the ale. *Open Mon–Tue 16.00–01.00, Wed–Thu 16.00–02.00, Fri–Sat 16.00–03.00.*

🍺 **Sportpub Chelsea** Elielinaukio 5 [4 E2]

Run-of-the-mill sports bar underneath the Holiday Inn by Railway Square. Absolutely terrible name, which is why I boycott the place. *Open Sun–Tue 15.00–01.00, Wed–Sat 14.00–02.00.*

**St Urho's Pub** Museokatu 10; ☏ 5807 7707 [1 A2]

Possibly the best of the real pubs in Helsinki, with an excellent beer selection. Benefits from a discreet location away from the city centre, behind the parliament building. *Open Sun–Tue 15.00–01.00, Wed–Sat 15.00–03.00.*

**Teerenpeli** Vuorikatu 16; ☏ 0424 925 200 [5 G1]

Excellent pub near Kaisaniemi Metro station promoting its own brands from its Lahti brewery. They also have a cigar bar & whiskies imported from Scotland. Recently opened a second outlet near the Kamppi centre, which is more central if somewhat lacking in atmosphere. *Open Mon–Thu 12.00–02.00, Fri–Sat 12.00–03.00, Sun 16.00–midnight.*

# 7  Entertainment and Nightlife

As soon as Helsinki sheds its winter coat and the first shoots of spring peek into view, the city gears up for a summer of outdoor living. Pavement cafés stutter into life and by late May the terraces are bursting with people recharging their batteries under the sun's healthy glow. Come midsummer, there's hardly a spare seat to be found and the action spills over in the city's many parks. The elegant tree-lined Esplanade Park and the streets stretching towards Railway Square host much of the evening entertainment, but the waterside terraces by Töölönlahti and Kaivopuisto Park are as popular as anywhere. If you demand more than a simple glass of beer or bottle of wine, Helsinki offers something for all tastes; opera, theatre, ballet, jazz, rock or serious clubbing – you can pretty much take your pick and it will be close at hand.

Pick up a copy of *Helsinki This Week*, *SixDegrees* or *City in English* for the latest listings.

## TICKET OFFICES

Most venues sell tickets direct from their own box offices, but the following is a good bet for an online purchase.

**Lippupalvelu** ☎ 0600 10 800; www.lippupalvelu.fi. Central booking agency covering all major events in theatre, music, opera, dance/ballet, film, summer festivals & sport. Outlets in Stockmann & Sokos department stores.

## THEATRE

Finland has a thriving and heavily subsidised theatrical scene, which helps make performances affordable for the general public. Most productions in Helsinki are in Finnish or Swedish.

☺ **Finnish National Theatre** (Kansallisteatteri) Läntinen Teatterikuja 1; ☎ 1733 1331; www.nationaltheatre.fi [5 F1] The Finnish National Theatre was the first professional Finnish-language company, formed in 1872. Since 1902 it has resided in the beautiful Jugendstil building on the northern edge of Railway Square. With 4 stages, classic productions at the time of writing included Shakespeare's *A Midsummer Night's Dream* & Tennessee Williams's *A Streetcar Named Desire*. The theatre also hosts occasional touring productions.
☺ **Helsinki City Theatre** (Helsingin Kaupunginteatteri) Ensi linja; ☎ 394 01; www.hkt.fi [1 B1] The City Theatre's base in Kallio reflects its strong working-class roots. The company was formed in 1948 after the merger of the Helsinki Workers' Theatre (Helsingin Työväenteatteri) & Helsinki Popular Theatre (Helsingin Kansanteatteri) & took up residence in this theatre on the shores of Eläintarhanlahti in 1967.
☺ **Kiasma Theatre** Kiasma Museum of Contemporary Art; Mannerheiminaukio 2; ☎ 1733 6502; www.kiasma.fi [4 D1] Taking the museum's challenging modern art concept to the stage, Kiasma Theatre veers far from the mainstream with its mix of drama, dance, music, multimedia, film & video art.

🎭 **Swedish Theatre (Svenska Teatern)** Pohjoisesplanadi 2; ☎ 6162 1411; www.svenskateatern.fi [5 F4]
The Swedish-speaking community may be in the minority, but they have a beautiful old theatre on one
of the plum pieces of real estate in Helsinki, where the Esplanade Park meets Mannerheimintie. The
circular building, dating from 1866, is a city landmark & has been in constant use since its
construction. Architect C L Engel designed the first theatre to grace this site, as early as 1827. A stone-
built complex replaced Engel's wooden structure in 1860, but fire razed the so-called Nya Teatern (New
Theatre) just 3 years later.

🎭 **The Finn-Brit Players** c/o The Finnish-British Society, Puistokatu 1b A; www.finnbritplayers.com. This
Helsinki-based am-dram group has been staging English-language productions (on an irregular basis) since
the early 1980s, from musicals to murder mysteries & classics to comedy. Various locations around the city.

## MUSIC

### OPERA AND CLASSICAL

🎭 **Finnish National Opera** Helsinginkatu 5; ☎ 403 021; www.operafin.fi [1 B1] On the shores of Töölönlahti,
the opera house stages major domestic & international works as well as ballet performances & chamber
concerts. Highlights in 2006 included *Don Giovanni*, *Swan Lake* & *The Nutcracker*. Subsidised by the
government, ticket prices start from a ridiculously low €12.

🎭 **Finnish Radio Symphony Orchestra** www.yle.fi/rso. Performing in a variety of locations around the city
(Finlandia Hall, Temppeliaukio Church, University Hall, Hall of Culture), for the 2006–07 season the RSO
showcased Finnish classical music, Mozart's piano concertos & international classics through the ages. Tickets
€16–20.

☺ **Helsinki Philharmonic Orchestra** Finlandia Hall, Mannerheimintie 13e; ✆ 402 41; www.hel2.fi/filharmonia [1 B2] Based in the wonderful Alvar Aalto-designed Finlandia Hall, tickets for the Philharmonic are reasonable at €17.50, but for a real bargain you can watch the first half of a dress rehearsal for just €2! These performances usually start at 10.00 – check the website or ask in the Finlandia Hall InfoShop for details.

## JAZZ

Finland has a vibrant jazz scene, both traditional and contemporary. The summer Helsinki Jazz Festival is a popular event, but two venues keep toes-a-tappin' throughout the year. Nice!

☆ **Storyville** Museokatu 8; ✆ 408 007; www.storyville.fi [4 C1] Close to Töölönlahti, Storyville is popular with older jazzers & lets you swing with a decent plate of food as well as a cool drink. The large summer terrace stays busy late into the evening. *Jazz club open Mon–Sat 20.00–04.00, roof bar open Mon–Sat 18.00–04.00.*

☆ **UMO Jazz House** Pursimiehenkatu 6; ✆ 6122 1914; www.umo.fi [6 E7] This buzzing jazz-den is popular with a younger crowd & hosts Finland's only professional big band, the UMO Jazz Orchestra. *Open Wed–Thu 20.00–03.00, Fri–Sat 20.00–04.00, Sun–Tue as per live events.*

## ROCK, POP AND ELECTRONICA

Perhaps it's the fact that Finland is separated from mainland Europe by the Gulf of Helsinki, but the contemporary live music scene is pretty insular. Not many big Western names make it here, apart from arena-filling brand names such as Bryan Adams and Tracy Chapman. In 2006, the more contemporary likes of Mercury Rev, Mogwai, José Gonzales, ¡Forward, Russia! and Underworld made it to the frozen north, but they were the exception as opposed to the rule.

Finland's live scene is more varied than you might believe. Yes, there's a huge number of hairy death metal bands, but also a rich seam of more palatable indie, folk and electronica waiting to be discovered, and some atmospheric venues that would do any city proud. Notable festivals include **Koneisto** (see page 37) for electronica

## MUSICAL HERITAGE

A small nation Finland may be, but its contribution to the world of classical music and opera is significant. Here are a few of the biggest names.

**Jean Sibelius** (1865–1957) The most famous Finnish composer, celebrated far beyond his Nordic homeland and commemorated by Eila Hiltunen's Sibelius Monument (see pages 240–1).

**Aulis Sallinen** The so-called 'King of Opera' is credited with kick-starting the Finnish opera boom with his 1975 work *Ratsumies* (The Horseman). Performed around the world, Sallinen is also a distinguished composer of symphonic and chamber music.

and **Tuska** (*www.tuska-festival.fi*) for furious head-banging metal action. The biggest names tend to perform at the Hartwall Arena, whilst the more cutting-edge action is spread across a clutch of venues.

☆ **Club Liberté** Kolmas Linje 34; ✆ 272 6001; www.clubliberte.fi [1 B1] Live music across the spectrum, from hard rock to Finnish-Portuguese solo artists. They also offer big-screen sports action & free WiFi internet. *Open Tue–Sun 18.00–02.00.*

**Kaija Saariaho** Composing since 1982, Saariaho's works have premiered to audiences from London to Jakarta. Her first opera, *L'amour de loin*, scooped the renowned 2003 Grawemeyer prize and a cheque for US$200,000.

**Einojuhani Rautavaara** One of the world's leading composers of classical concertos, Rautavaara surpassed the great Sibelius in 2000 with the premiere of his eighth symphony, subtitled *The Journey* (Sibelius completed only seven such pieces).

**Magnus Lindberg** Born in 1957, Lindberg is still a whippersnapper but already stands as the latter-day Sibelius in the ears of many Finns. His encyclopaedic knowledge of classical music has raised his compositions to heights that others can only dream of.

☆ **Kuudes Linja** Hämeentie 13; www.kuudeslinja.com [1 C1] This small Kallio club is the best bet for live indie, soul & acoustic gigs, as well as some truly unclassifiable acts & regular club nights. Mostly Finnish bands but some international visitors. *Open Tue–Thu 21.00–03.00, Fri–Sat 22.00–04.00 Sun 20.00–03.00.*

☆ **Semifinal** Urho Kekkosenkatu 6; ✆ 7746 7424; www.tavastiaklubi.fi [4 C3] Tavastia's little brother showcases up-&-coming bands. *Open Sun–Thu 21.00–02.00, Fri–Sat 21.00–03.00.*

☆ **Tavastia** Urho Kekkosenkatu 4–6; ✆ 694 8511; www.tavastiaklubi.fi [4 C3] Finland's number-one rock venue, this mid-size club plays host to the biggest domestic names & the best alternative foreign acts who venture this far north. *Open Sun–Thu 21.00–02.00, Fri–Sat 21.00–03.00.*

## BARS AND NIGHTCLUBS

The best way to find out what's going down on the scene is to pick up a copy of the English-language publication *Helsinki Nightlife Guide* from a bar or club, or browse the more general *City in English* and *SixDegrees*.

☆ **Ahjo** Bulevardi 2–4; ✆ 770 4711; www.ahjoclub.fi [5 F4] Stylish venue in black & white at the KlausKHotel, pulling a cool crowd who glide around the glossy interior with considerably more grace than I could ever hope to muster. *Open Tue 16.00–01.00, Wed–Thu 16.00–02.00, Fri–Sat 16.00–04.00.*

♀ **Ateljee Bar** Yrjönkatu 26; ✆ 43 360 [4 E3] On the 12th floor of Hotel Torni, this small but smoky place is seldom patronised by locals but for visitors the sweeping views across the city (the best of which are from the ladies' room) make it worth a visit. *Open Mon–Thu 14.00–01.00, Fri 14.00–02.00, Sat 12.00–02.00, Sun 14.00–midnight.*

☆ **Bar Korjaamo** Töölönkatu 51b; ☏ 454 0117; www.korjaamo.fi [1 A1] An out-of-the-way location at the northern end of Töölönkatu keeps Korjaamo off the main city radar. But what a find! Resplendent in shockingly bright colours – the floor & walls of the bar are vivid pink – this pulls a mixed, artistic crowd with its blend of cool drinks & chilled tunes from DJs to live jazz. If you know your Finnish actors & actresses you could well see one or more of them here, some even working the bar. *Open Mon–Tue 11.00–23.00, Wed–Thu 11.00–midnight, Fri–Sat 11.00–02.00, Sun 11.00–16.00.*

☆ **Beatroot** Iso Roobertinkatu 10 [7 F5] Tiny, claustrophobic Beatroot is little larger than the average front room, but rich furnishings & quirky features, such as flip-down cinema seats bolted to the wall, make it a cool place to enjoy an eclectic mix of music. *Open Tue–Thu 18.00–02.00, Fri–Sat 18.00–03.00.*

☆ **Corona Bar & Billiards** Eerikinkatu 11; ☏ 642 002; www.andorra.fi [4 D4] 9 pool tables & 1 snooker table in this venue owned by film director Aki Kaurismäki. *Open Mon–Sat 11.00–02.00, Sun 12.00–02.00.*

☆ **Erottaja Bar** Erottajankatu 15–17; ☏ 611 196 [5 F4] One of the favourites on the alternative scene, dark & moody Erottaja has live DJs & weekend nights of some repute. *Open Mon 14.00–01.00, Tue–Thu 14.00–02.00, Fri–Sat 14.00–03.00, Sun 14.00–01.00.*

☆ **Helsinki Club** Yliopistonkatu 8; ☏ 433 20; www.helsinkiclub.com [5 G3] One of the larger clubs, with 3 separate areas & a constant shiny-happy crowd who value style over substance. Two blocks north of Esplanade Park. *Open Wed–Mon 22.00–04.00.*

☆ **Hevimesta** Hallituskatu 3; ☏ 174 395; www.hevimesta.com [5 H2] Helsinki, are you ready to ROCK!?! The city's only late-night heavy-metal karaoke bar is, somewhat surprisingly, right next door to the Lutheran Cathedral. *Open Wed–Sun 22.00–04.00.*

☆ **Ihana** Café Ursula, Kaivopuisto; www.ihana.info [1 C4] Down by the sea in Kaivopuisto Park, elegant Ursula hosts these Saturday-night shindigs throughout Jul & Aug. Recommended for clubbers. *Open Sat 22.00–04.00.*

☆ **Kafe Moskova** Eerikinkatu 11; ✆ 611 200; www.andorra.fi [4 D4] There's a clue in the name here. Harking back to the Russian era, Moskova promises no frills & decidedly frosty service – harsh strip lighting pierces the gloom enough to make out the stark Soviet-era décor. Another place owned by Aki Kaurismäki. *Open daily 18.00–02.00.*

## LATTE AND A LOAD OF WHITES

Helsinki's quirky individuality is a major part of its appeal, but it's also a guidebook writer's nightmare. However hard you try, some places just refuse to be pigeonholed. So whether you want to shoot some pool, have a sauna, send an email, buy some records, grab a coffee, do the washing, groove into the night or just have an honest drink, you'll be able to do all of these things (and more) at the following places.

**Café Tin Tin Tango** Töölöntorinkatu 7; ✆ 2709 0972 [1 A2]
Superb café, bar, sauna, bakery & self-service laundry in the Töölö district. Well recommended for its warming sun lounge & first-rate pastries, even if you don't have any washing to do. *Open Mon–Thu 07.00–midnight, Fri 07.00–02.00, Sat 09.00–02.00, Sun 10.00–midnight.*

**mbar** Mannerheimintie 22–24; ✆ 6124 5420; www.mbar.fi [4 D2]
'1013 mbar = 1 atmosphere = 1,013 bar/33.3 RPM' – so reads the catchy press blurb. Lord knows what it means but Helsinki's premier daytime internet café is also one of the city's coolest nightspots & the heartbeat

☆ **Mecca** Korkeavuorenkatu 34; 📞 1345 6200; www.palace.fi [5 F4] Cool cocktails & the trendiest DJs entertain a highly fashionable crowd in this complex that also serves swanky food (see page 147). *Open Mon–Tue 16.00–midnight, Wed–Thu 16.00–02.00, Fri–Sat 16.00–04.00.*

☆ **Oujee** Uudenmaankatu 28; 📞 044 592 21 00 [6 E6] Uudenmaankatu is the favoured haunt of the

of the Konisto electronic musical festival, featuring funk, soul, electro, house & deep techno. Centrally located opposite Kiasma Museum of Contemporary Art. *Open Mon–Tue 09.00–midnight, Wed–Thu 09.00–02.00, Fri–Sat 09.00–03.00, Sun 12.00–midnight.*

**Saunabar** Eerikinkatu 27; 📞 586 5550; www.saunabar.net [4 C4]
Yep, there's a sauna & a bar under one roof, as well as fine tapas, billiards, internet, evening DJs & occasional live music. Spur-of-the-moment sauna on Sun & Mon, when you don't need to book in advance. *Open Mon 15.00–22.00, Tue & Sun 15.00–01.00, Wed–Sat 15.00–02.00.*

**Vinyl Lounge** Yliopistonkatu 8; 📞 4780 3350; www.vinyl.fi [5 G3]
DJ record store by day, weekend cocktail bar by night. From laid-back down-tempo tunes to uplifting, melodic house music, this is the place to enjoy it with cocktails prepared from fresh fruits & juices, often with seasonal wild berries. *Open Wed–Mon 16.00–late.*

cliquey Helsinki media crowd, & many of them like to squeeze into little Oujee, which morphs from comfy after-work haunt to late-night disco den. *Open Fri–Sat 20.00–03.00, Sun 18.00–02.00.*

☆ **Rose Garden** Iso Roobertinkatu 10; www.clubrosegarden.com [7 F6] It's weekends only at one of Helsinki's premier underground dance music clubs. Techno, house, drum 'n' bass, leftfield disco & hip-hop. *Open Fri–Sat 22.00–04.00.*

☆ **Stockholm Diskotek** Simonkatu 8; ☎ 045 1103 210; www.stockholmdiskotek.com [4 D3] Monster club near the Kamppi shopping mall with 7 bars & 4 music rooms spread over 3 floors & 1,000m² — that's a lot of sweaty, writhing Finns to get friendly with. Disco, funk, soul, house, trance, hip-hop, techno & old-skool. They also run occasional club nights on the so-called 'love boat' overnight ferry to Stockholm. *Open Wed–Sat 22.00–04.00, Sun 23.00–04.00.*

☆ **The Stage Rock Bar** Iso Roobertinkatu 13; ☎ 608 211; www.delifox.fi [6 E6] If you like leather jackets, tight trousers & big haircuts, this is the place to get your rocks off or lick some killer riffs on the air guitar. *Open Sun–Thu 15.00–02.00, Fri–Sat 15.00–03.00.*

☆ **Underbar** Snellmaninkatu 13; ☎ 7429 8608; www.underbar.fi [5 H2] Two blocks north of Senate Square, Underbar is slightly away from the main action but attracts a mixed crowd with promises of funk, soul, rap, disco & hip-hop. *Open daily 15.00–03.00.*

☆ **Unity The Island** Uunisaari; www.clubunity.org [1 C5] 10 years of pioneering clubbing means Unity knows how to put on a good show, & every summer they put on at least one open-air night on the island of Uunisaari. The sun never sets, the music doesn't stop & the memories last at least until the following morning. Check the website for details.

## GAY HELSINKI

The gay scene in Helsinki is liberal and surprisingly extensive. Some of the venues listed below are popular with the straight crowd too, and the two communities exist side by side without any difficulty. The focal point of the scene is the annual Helsinki Pride carnival (see page 37). For more detailed information and current listings, take a look at www.ranneliike.net, www.z-lehti.fi and www.seta.fi.

☆ **Bar Stuff** Eerikinkatu 14; ✆ 608 826; www.stuff.fi [4 D4] Helsinki's newest venue offers 2 sleek bars with smooth glass, soft lighting & exposed brick walls. Internet & WiFi equipped. *Open daily 14.00–02.00.*

☆ **dtm** Iso Roobertinkatu 28; ✆ 676 315; www.dtm.fi [6 E6] dtm (Don't Tell Mama) is the largest gay café-cum-disco-cum-nightclub in the Nordic countries, with live floorshows & drag queen competitions. Chilled by day, you can sip a latte & surf free WiFi internet but the place really comes alive at night. Women's club HEHKU on Sat nights. *Open Mon–Sat 09.00–04.00, Sun 12.00–23.00.*

☆ **Fairytale** Helsinginkatu 7; ✆ 870 3226; www.fairytale.fi. This moody bar is so intimate you can only gain access by ringing the bell. Ding-a-ling! *Open Mon–Fri 16.00–02.00, Sat–Sun 14.00–02.00.*

☆ **Hercules** Lönnrotinkatu 4; ✆ 612 1776; www.herculesgayclub.com [4 E4] Dark & crowded, Hercules has live music shows & caters mainly (but not exclusively) to men. *Open daily 21.00–04.00.*

☆ **Lost & Found** Annankatu 6; ✆ 680 1010; www.lostandfound.fi [6 E6] One of the most popular late-night bars in town, & not just on the gay scene. Lost & Found welcomes everyone with open arms (the weekend queues indicate its reputation) & also hosts occasional live music & theatre shows. *Open daily 20.00–04.00.*

☆ **Mann's Street** Mannerheimintie 12a (2nd floor); ☏ 612 1103; www.herculesgayclub.com/mansku [4 E3] No city is complete without a gay karaoke bar for the more mature male crowd, & here's Helsinki's. Altogether now – 'It's raining men . . .' *Open Sun–Thu 14.00–02.00, Fri–Sat 14.00–04.00.*

☆ **Nalle Pub** Kaarlenkatu 3–5; ☏ 701 5543 [1 C1] All ages female pub in Kallio. *Open daily 15.00–02.00.*

☆ **Room Albert** Kalevankatu 36; ☏ 643 626; www.roombar.fi [6 C5] Snug, cosy bar with dark walls, friendly welcome & a small pavement terrace. *Open daily 14.00–02.00.*

## CINEMA

Helsinki has a broad range of cinematic options, whether you seek US blockbusters, contemporary world film or domestic offerings. All films are shown in their original language, with subtitles; international films are usually subtitled in English.

Finland's film industry, although small, has spawned two notable international names, brothers Aki and Mika Kaurismäki. Aki in particular has gained renown on the world stage; his film *The Man Without A Past* won the *Grand Prix* at the Cannes Film Festival in 2002 and was nominated for an Academy Award in the Best Foreign Language Film category in 2003. Far from celebrating his hometown, Kaurismäki's film-noir style often portrays Helsinki in a cold and distant light, and many of his characters express their disenchantment with the city. Perhaps Kaurismäki's most essential work is *Drifting Clouds*, the moving tale of a middle-aged couple faced with sudden unemployment that addresses some quintessentially Finnish characteristics.

During the Cold War years Helsinki's strong Russian heritage was exploited by a string of filmmakers who were unable to shoot on location in Moscow or St Petersburg. One of the most well-known examples was the 1983 thriller *Gorky Park*.

**Andorra** Eerikinkatu 11; ☏ 612 3117 [4 D4] The coolest cinema in Helsinki, popular with the film community. Shows mainstream works with a twisted, film-noir edge.

**Bio Rex** Mannerheimintie 22–24; ☏ 020 155 5800; www.biorex.fi [4 D2] Art Nouveau-style cinema in the elegant Glass Palace (Lasipalatsi) dating from the 1930s. Some first-run movies but emphasis on independent screenings.

**Finnkino** Tennispalatsi, Salomonkatu 15; ☏ 0600 007 007; www.finnkino.fi [4 C3] Finland's biggest cinema chain, the 14 screens at the Tennis Palace show all the major blockbusters. Located near Kamppi shopping mall.

**Maxim** Kluuvikatu 1; ☏ 0600 4444 [5 G3] Punters at Maxim appreciate the soft, wide seats. Popular with movie buffs, the 2 screens show mainstream, international & cult films. Central location between Esplanade Park & Aleksanterinkatu.

**Orion** Eerikinkatu 15; ☏ 6154 0201 [4 C4] Operated by the Finnish Film Archives, Orion is another hip place with a penchant for classic cinema & has themed seasons throughout the year.

## CASINOS

☆ **Grand Casino Helsinki** Mikonkatu 19; ☏ 6808 0380; www.grandcasinohelsinki.fi [5 F2] On the edge of Station Square, this glitzy place claims to be the only international casino in the Nordic countries & is the place to shoot craps or spin the roulette wheel. You can grab a meal whilst you fritter your cash, but don't expect any James Bond chic – the overall tone is more cross-channel ferry than Monte Carlo yacht. *Open daily 12.00–04.00.*

*Sibelius Monument*

# 8 Shopping

If you're toying with the idea of booking a five-star hotel, don't make a decision just yet – you might want to downgrade to something more affordable and spend the money you save in Helsinki's wonderful shops.

The big international chains can be found along Aleksanterinkatu and Mannerheimintie, where you can get the usual range of jeans, tops and underwear that you find in any European city. Similarly, shopping centres such as Kamppi and Forum offer an expansive but uninspiring range of fashions in shiny glass-fronted units staffed with chic and chirpy sales assistants. Out of town, the huge Itäkeskus shopping centre is the largest in all the Nordic countries, with 240 shops and plenty of restaurant and leisure opportunities.

Finnish design is well renowned, and rightly so. Some big names include Iittala, Marimekko and Artek, but the real joy is in discovering the city's individual boutiques. Glassware, ceramics, fashion and art spill out of the streets around Uudenmaankatu and Annankatu, at the heart of Helsinki's Design District. If you want something unique, this is the place to go.

When Finns aren't busying themselves designing achingly hip furniture and fashion, they're hard at it recycling everybody else's cast-offs. Flea markets and 'street style' are a huge part of many Helsinkiites' lives, and there are plenty of opportunities to pick up a slice of local style for rock-bottom prices, together with records, books and any amount of chintzy flotsam and jetsam.

Local crafts are ten-a-penny, some more worthy than others, and you'll have no problem picking up a souvenir fluffy reindeer or stuffed Santa to remind you of your trip. At the harbour end of Esplanade Park is the Market Square (Kauppatori), the tourist's favourite and accordingly expensive.

Prices for commonly available items are generally on a par with other northern European countries, meaning that there are no huge savings to be made, but expect prices to rise as you browse the more individual boutiques and Finnish design classics. If you're just here for a short break, bear in mind that weekend hours are usually short and many smaller shops don't open at all on Sunday.

## ART AND ANTIQUES

You might pick up a few bargains in Helsinki's flea markets, but these dedicated shops are usually bursting with wonderful pieces.

The city is home to over 70 art galleries with permanent and changing exhibitions, as well as plenty of opportunities to purchase unique pieces. By far the most enjoyable way of getting to grips with the choice is to pick up the Design District map and simply follow your nose. Marainkatu and the surrounding streets in Kruununhaka are home to most of the antique shops.

**Antikvariaatti Syvä Uni** Fredrikinkatu 55; ✆ 693 3939; www.kolumbus.fi/antikvariaatti.syva.uni [4 D4]
Wonderfully musty antiquarian bookshop, with sagging shelves stacked floor to ceiling. Also calligraphy &
paintings. *Open Mon–Fri 10.30–17.00, Sat 10.30–14.30.*

**Hietalahti Antique & Art Hall** Corner of Hietalahdenkatu & Bulevardi; www.hietalahdenkauppahalli.fi [6 C6] By
the Hietalahti flea market, the stalls in this elegant hall have a wide range of furniture & other *objets d'art.*
There's also a quiet upstairs café on the balcony.

**Old Times** Annankatu 12; ✆ 604 606 [7 F6] Silver, crystals, glassware & ornate lamps. *Open Mon–Fri
11.00–17.00, Sat 11.00–14.00.*

**POP-Antik** Iso Roobertinkatu 14; ✆ 040 581 5395 [6 E6] Specialising in toys of yesteryear – mechanical
trucks through to ragged old teddies. The owner lives upstairs, so if you just can't wait until the store opens
you can call her out of hours. *Open Mon–Fri 11.00–17.00, Sat 11.00–14.00.*

**Tomorrow's Antique** Hietalahti Market Hall, Hietalahdentori; ✆ 506 4320; www.tomorrowsantique.com [6 C6]
Strictly speaking, these aren't antiques but a unique chance to pick up design classics from the 1930s onwards
– tables, chairs, lights, etc. For example, an original 1961 Eero Aarnio Ball Chair is yours for just €4,500,
15% less than you would expect to pay for a new model. *Open Mon–Fri 10.00–17.00, Sat 10.00–15.00.*

## DEPARTMENT STORES

Two big boys dominate the department store scene.

**Sokos** Mannerheimintie 9; ✆ 010 76 65100; e helsinki@sokos.fi; www.sokos.fi [4 E2] Run-of-the-mill multi-
level store near the main railway station. *Open Mon–Fri 09.00–21.00, Sat 08.00–18.00.*

**Stockmann** Aleksanterinkatu 52b; ☎ 1211; 🖷 121 3632; www.stockmann.fi [4 E3] Finland's most famous department store, & the largest in the Nordic countries, is an adventure that demands investigation regardless of whether you want to buy anything. All the big fashion names are here, but the beautiful architecture & divine deli counters make Stockmann an essential Helsinki experience. Outlets also at Helsinki-Vantaa Airport & Itäkeskus Shopping Centre. *Open Mon–Fri 09.00–21.00, Sat 09.00–18.00.*

## DESIGN DISTRICT

In 2005, the city created the Design District to promote the strong Finnish pedigree for innovation and style. Focusing on Uudenmaankatu, Fredrikinkatu, Annankatu, Yrjönkatu and Erottajankatu, these are Helsinki's most stylish outlets, bursting at the seams with fashion, jewellery and slick interior design.

The listings below are just a select few – pick up a Design District map from the Helsinki City Tourist Bureau, or download it from www.designforum.fi/designdistrict_en, to see the full wallet-weakening choice. Look out for the distinctive black-and-white stickers in the shop windows.

### FASHION BOUTIQUES

**Cloth Gallery** Fredrikinkatu 31; ☎ 6124 1006; www.clothgallery.com [6 E6] Floaty women's fashions with a classic style – evening dresses, tops, skirts & suits. *Open Mon–Fri 10.00–18.00, Sat 10.00–16.00.*

**Hua** Eerikinkatu 4a; tel; 678 748; www.hua.fi [4 D3] Beautiful handmade dresses from China, jewellery, purses, bags & sandals. You can arrange a measuring or fitting time out of hours, & although it takes 3 weeks to make each dress, delivery can be organised. *Open Jun–Aug Mon–Fri 10.00–19.00, Sat 10.00–15.00; Sep–May Mon–Fri 10.00–18.00, Sat 10.00–15.00.*

**IVANAhelsinki Campus** Uudenmaankatu 15; ☎ 622 4422; www.ivanahelsinki.com [6 E5] The hub of Helsinki's fashion scene & one of Finland's most desirable labels, this is something of a cottage industry (employing just 8 people). New collections of their hand-crafted women's wear are hotly anticipated & the company upholds ethical design practices; no chemicals, dyes, fur or leather are used. *Open Mon–Fri 11.00–19.00, Sat 11.00–16.00.*

**Liike** Yrjönkatu 25; ☎ 646 265 [4 E3] This tiny place has a jumbled collection of fashion from young designers. *Open Mon–Fri 11.00–18.00, Sat 11.00–16.00.*

**Limbo** Annankatu 13; ☎ 644 060; www.limbo.fi [6 E5] Fun & flighty, Limbo's 2006 women's wear collection was inspired by trampish burlesque — seamed stockings & feather hats all round. *Open Mon–Fri 11.00–18.00, Sat 11.00–16.00.*

**Lux Shop** Uudenmaankatu 26; ☎ 678538; www.lux-shop.com [6 E5] Small boutique combining the best of new Finnish fashion with hard-to-find foreign labels. *Open Mon–Sat 12.00–18.00.*

**Marimekko** Pohjoisesplanadi 31; ☎ 686 0240; www.marrimekko.com [5 F3] The old lady of Finnish fashion, Marimekko is an essential part of the Helsinki shopping experience. As well as lovely clothes, they do classic printed fabrics (with striking floral patterns) & stylish home decorations. If you live in Finland this is probably over-exposed, but for everyone else it's a great & worthwhile novelty. This is just one of several stores in the city. *Open Mon–Fri 10.00–19.00, Sat 10.00–16.00.*

**Myymälä²** Uudenmaankatu 23; ☎ 050 404 3667; www.myymala2.com [6 E5] This organic collective of designers, musicians & artists runs a funky little boutique with individual clothes & jewellery, which also has gallery space for changing exhibitions. *Open Tue–Sun 12.00–18.00.*

**Popot Sneakerstore** Iso Roobertinkatu 7; ☎ 260 0080; www.popot.fi [7 F5] If you can squeeze into this tiny place on slightly seedy 'Iso Roba' you can pick up some fantastic trainers (many limited designs), including the elegant Finnish brand Karhu Originals. *Open Mon–Fri 11.00–19.00, Sat 10.00–15.00.*

## FURNITURE AND INTERIOR DESIGN

**Aero** Yrjönkatu 8; ☎ 680 2185; www.aerodesignfurniture.com [7 F5] New Finnish furniture & lighting, together with international classics from the 1930s to 1970s. Some of its lines have been in constant production for decades — try Eero Aarnio's famous Ball Chair, a snip at around €5,300. *Open Mon–Fri 11.00–18.00, Sat 11.00–15.00.*

**Artek** Eteläesplanadi 18; ☎ 6132 5277; www.artek.fi [5 F4] Beautiful collection of timeless classics by Alvar Aalto & other renowned international designers. Also glassware, fabrics & lamps. *Open Mon–Fri 10.00–18.00, Sat 10.00–16.00.*

**Aste90** Rikhardinkatu 1; ☎ 677 163; www.aste90.fi [5 G4] This quirky shop showcases limited edition & one-off pieces. *Open Mon–Fri 12.00–19.00, Sat 12.00–16.00.*

**Design Forum Finland** Erottajankatu 7; ☎ 6220 8130; www.designforum.fi/shop [7 F5] This showcase for Finnish design has bits & bobs of the best; not only the big names but also up-&-coming designers working with glass, wood, ceramics & textiles. The exhibition area has changing installations — my recent favourite was the *Kotilo*, a womb-like bed-space involving a softly lit padded wooden chamber & removable canopy. Difficult to describe, but this concept for budget-hotel accommodation was wonderfully relaxing. *Open Mon–Fri 10.00–19.00, Sat 10.00–18.00, Sun 12.00–18.00.*

**Formverk** Annankatu 5; ☎ 621 4611; www.formverk.com [6 E5] A comprehensive range of funky gear for your home, from giant Marimekko-patterned beanbags to groovy rubber draining racks & sleek towel rails for the bathroom. *Open Mon–Fri 10.30–18.00, Sat 11.00–15.00.*

182

**Funktio** Lönnrotinkatu 7; ✆ 607 207; www.funktio.com [4 E4] Decorate your house from top to toe – this is the kind of place that sells everything from bright plastic stools to spiral-shaped bookcases & curvaceous cutlery. *Open Mon–Fri 10.00–18.00, Sat 11.00–15.00.*

**Pentik** Mannerheimintie 5; ✆ 207 220 310; www.pentik.com [4 E3] Large Finnish chain specialising in soft furnishings, crockery & cutlery. *Open Mon–Fri 10.00–19.00, Sat 10.00–18.00.*

**Zarro** Fredrikinkatu 37; ✆ 603 806; www.zarro.fi [6 E5] Design with a difference, the majority of Zarro's kitchen, bathroom & office accessories are made predominantly from metal. *Open Mon–Fri 10.30–18.00, Sat 10.30–15.00.*

## JEWELLERY

**Alfred K** Korkeavuorenkatu 19; ✆ 622 2114; www.alfred-k.com [7 F6] Mostly working with silver, the craftsmen of Alfred K produce modern handmade jewellery as well as household decorations. Design your own piece & they can make it a reality. *Open Mon–Fri 11.00–18.00.*

**Atelier Torbjörn Tillander** Kluuvikatu 1; ✆ 686 0980; www.tillander.com [5 G3] Charming traditional creations by two sisters continuing a family goldsmith business. An opulent Russian influence can be seen in the ornate styles & use of rich gems. *Open Mon–Thu 10.00–18.00, Fri 10.00–17.00, Sat 10.00–15.00.*

**Galleria Koru** Fredrikinkatu 32; ✆ 321 5029; www.galleriakoru.com [6 D5] A collective of local designers & smiths run this workshop & put their contemporaneous wares directly into the on-site gallery. *Open Mon–Thu 10.00–18.00, Fri 10.00–17.00, Sat 11.00–14.00.*

## PORCELAIN, POTTERY AND GLASS

**Arabia Factory Shop** Arabiakeskus, Hämeentie 135; ✆ 0204 393 507; www.arabia.fi. Right – before you make any rash purchases, take note. This huge factory outlet sells all the standard ranges of Iittala glass & Arabia ceramics at specially discounted prices, meaning you can pick up some good bargains. There's a large area devoted to seconds, some of which are barely distinguishable from the items on sale in the city-centre showrooms. Take tram 6 from the city for the 20min journey. *Open Mon–Fri 10.00–20.00, Sat–Sun 10.00–16.00.*

**Bisarri** Annankatu 9; ✎ 611 252 [6 E5] A twinkling Aladdin's Cave of 20th-century art glass, ceramics & porcelain. *Open Mon–Fri 12.00–17.00.*

**Iittala Shop** Pohjoisesplanadi 25; ✎ 0204 39 3580; www.iittala.com [5 G3] There are several Iittala outlets around town but this is the flagship store, a stylish boutique full of gorgeous glass & ceramics. For the ultimate souvenir, pick up a renowned Aalto vase or one of Oiva Toikka's delicate glass birds. Temptation wherever you look. *Open Mon–Fri 10.00–19.00, Sat 10.00–16.00.*

## FOLK ART AND FINNISH CRAFTS

Finns produce some wonderful handmade crafts, which make much better keepsakes than the regular 'Suomi' T-shirts and reindeer tat. Together with the city markets, the various craft centres are the best places to search.

**Aarikka** Pohjoisesplanadi 27; ✎ 652 277; www.aarikka.com [5 G3] This swanky store bordering the Esplanade Park isn't really a craft centre as such, but they've been turning Finnish wood into stylish gifts & jewellery since 1954 & on that basis alone deserve your attention. *Open Mon–Fri 09.00–19.00, Sat 09.00–17.00, Jun–Aug Sun 12.00–17.00.*

**Anne's Shop** Fredrikinkatu 68; ✎ 445 823 [4 B1] If you're visiting the Temppeliaukio Church, pop across the road to browse a lovely selection of ceramics, woollens, Lappish dolls & (Rudolph lovers look away now) silky reindeer skins. *Open daily 09.00–17.00.*

**Artisaani** Unioninkatu 28; ✎ 665 225 [5 G3] Just next to the tourist office, Artisaani has tasteful porcelain, traditional knitwear & a small art gallery. *Open Mon–Fri 10.00–18.00, Sat 10.00–16.00.*

**HELSKY Taito Shop** Eteläesplanadi 4; ✎ 6877 5625; www.helsky.net [5 G4] Luxurious handicrafts – mittens, hats, shawls, scarves, jewellery, baskets & woodwork, in a swish city-centre showroom. Individualistic but expensive. *Open Mon–Fri 10.00–18.00, Sat 10.00–16.00.*

**Kiseleffin Talo** Aleksanterinkatu 28 & Unioninkatu 27, Senaatintori; www.kiseleffintalo.fi [5 H3] Designed by Carl Ludvig Engel, this stately building in the shadow of the Lutheran Cathedral was formerly the Kiseleff sugar factory & subsequently a wealthy merchant's house. Today it houses 20 wonderful boutiques of Finnish crafts over 2 floors in a vaulted hall. Clothes, dolls, puppets, ceramics, jewellery, home wares & a cosy café on the upper balcony – well worth a visit. *Open Mon–Fri 10.00–18.00, Sat 10.00–16.00, May–Sep Sun 11.00–16.00.*

**Marttiini** Aleksanterinkatu 28, Senaatintori; ✎ 633 207; www.marttiini.com [5 H3] Learn the secret of easy filleting at this atmospheric shop selling traditional *puukko* knives, made to a classic design using high-specification stainless chrome steel & decorative handles carved from Finnish curly birch. *Open Mon–Fri 10.00–18.00, Sat 10.00–16.00, May–Sep Sun 11.00–16.00.*

**Norsu Galleria** Kaisaniemenkatu 9; ✎ 2316 3250; www.norsu.info [5 G1] Looking like it slid straight from the pages of an interior design magazine, this high-class craft & exhibition gallery sells handmade items of glass, wood, ceramics, jewellery & textiles. *Open Tue & Thu–Fri 11.00–17.00, Wed 11.00–20.00, Sat 12.00–16.00. Other times by appointment.*

**Ryijypalvelu** Abrahaminkatu 7; ✎ 660 615 [6 C5] If the walls of your home seem a bit cold, then treat them to a traditional *ryijy*, a handmade woollen wall-rug. *Open Mon–Fri 10.00–17.00, Sat 10.00–16.00.*

**Secco** Fredrikinkatu 33; ✎ 678 782; www.seccoshop.com [6 E6] I'm not really sure where to list this place, but with a very strong design ethos this is as good a place as any. Secco recycles our everyday domestic & industrial waste to produce striking & stylish reincarnations — hence we have shoulder bags made from car seatbelts, jewellery from broken typewriter keys, handbags from car tyre inner tubes & so-called PCBeasts — funky animal shapes cut from scrapped computer circuit boards. *Open Mon–Fri 11.00–18.00, Sat 11.00–16.00.*

**The Friends of Finnish Handicrafts** Runeberginkatu 40; ✎ 612 6050; www.finnishhandicraft.net [1 A2] Attractive rugs & interior textiles inspired by nature. *Open Mon–Fri 12.00–17.00.*

## FOOD AND DRINK

Helsinki is so brim-full of cafés and markets serving the most delicious fresh fare, do we really need a separate section for food and drink? Probably not; but if you're looking for a special sweet treat or are pining for flavours from home, try these places.

**Behnfords** World Trade Centre Plaza, Keskuskatu 7b; ✎ 671 110 [5 F3] With little competition in the city Behnfords is pricey, but this is the place for homesick Brits & Yanks to find favourites like Kellogg's Corn Flakes, Hershey's Twinkies, HP Sauce or Jif peanut butter. *Open Mon–Fri 11.00–19.00, Sat 10.00–18.00.*

**Confectioner Alenius** Merikatu 1; ✎ 604 887; www.sokerileipuri.fi [1 B4] Quite simply the most decidedly decadent, seriously seductive & colossally calorific chocolatier you could wish for. Transactions are performed with a wonderfully antiquated cash register. *Open Mon–Fri 10.00–17.00, Sat 09.00–13.00.*

## MARKETS

If you've spent up in the Design District, or chic Finnish style just doesn't do it for you, then the markets are the place to be.

The Market Square (Kauppatori) is the main attraction, and busy from dawn until dusk. Rise early to see the fishmongers preparing the morning's catch and chatting over the first coffee of the day. Join them for a breakfast pastry or pancake before the early-bird tour buses roll up with their crowds of eager shutterbugs, all looking for the perfect souvenir. Summer sees the market stalls sagging under a rich bounty of strawberries, blueberries and lingonberries, eagerly gobbled by greedy locals and tourists alike. In winter the little café tents provide a cosy retreat from the chill air. They all display signs stating the inside temperature – just pick the warmest and thaw out in comfort.

Nearby, the Old Market Hall (Wanha Kauppahalli) is the most famous food market in the city, and a favourite place to pack a picnic before a trip to Suomenlinna. The historic hall is heady with the scents of cured meats, fresh baking and ground coffee. Away from the centre, locals favour the market at Hakaniemi.

Flea markets are big business, keeping the street-fashionistas one step ahead in their quest for individual style. If you choose to join them, arrive early and haggle for all you're worth but be prepared to strike a fair bargain. Many of the sellers are professionals and, although flexible, won't be taken for fools. Deal concluded, make sure you have cash – this is one of the few places Finns don't trade with plastic.

In the run-up to Christmas, festive markets swing into action – all twinkly lights, mulled wine and sleigh bells. In the land of Santa Claus, what better place to shop for gifts?

**MARKET HALLS** Attached to Helsinki's two principal market squares are beautiful and well-stocked indoor markets.

**Hakaniemen Kauppahalli** Hakaniementori; www.hakaniemenkauppahalli.fi [1 C1] On the northern edge of Hakaniementori, the ornate indoor market hall sells a similar line of fresh foods as the outdoor market square, but you can also browse clothing, souvenirs & design items or fill your belly with a hearty fresh-cooked meal. *Open Mon–Fri 09.00–18.00, Sat 08.00–16.00.*

**Old Market Hall (Wanha Kauppahalli)** Eteläranta 1; www.wanhakauppahalli.fi [5 H4] Helsinki's finest indoor market, the elegant Old Market Hall (Wanha Kauppahalli) is a classical hall dating from 1889, whose distinctive yellow-&-red brickwork makes it an easily recognisable harbourside landmark. Inside, it's a colourful treasure-trove of fresh fish, meat, food, bread & pastries. The melding aromas are wonderfully tempting, & fortunately you can savour them over a coffee or light lunch – salads, wraps, pizza or even a plate of sushi, should you desire. *Open Mon–Fri 08.00–18.00, Sat 08.00–16.00.*

## MARKET SQUARES

**Hakaniemi Market** Hakaniementori [1 C1] A 20min walk north from the Esplanade Park, or one stop from the main railway station on the Metro, this is where the locals who consider Kauppatori too 'touristy' do their shopping. Traders have been selling bread, fruit, vegetables, confectionery, berries & flowers for over

100 years. *Open Mon–Sat 06.30–15.00, first Sun of each month 10.00–16.00.*

**Kauppatori** Etelsätama [5 H4] Helsinki's most famous marketplace, with booths selling high-quality foods, handicrafts & souvenirs. Café stalls serve fresh coffee, warm cinnamon buns & giant jam-smeared pancakes, turning into cosy heated tents during winter. Find all sorts of postcards, hats, scarves & T-shirts. Reindeer skins are popular &, being a semi-domestic animal, there is no stigma attached to trading such products. Funnily, souvenirs here tend to be more expensive than in the shops (even Stockmann in some cases), so don't be too hasty. The main market operates only in summer, but fishmongers sell their fresh catches throughout the year. *Open May–Sep Mon–Fri 06.30–18.00, Sat 06.30–16.00, Sun 10.00–16.00.*

**FLEA MARKETS** Anything goes – mix chunky boots with hooped leggings, throw grandad's old jumper over your favourite band T-shirt or raid auntie's jumble for chic 1950s flair. Then just add a scarf, thickset belt and battered satchel and off you go.

**Hietalahti Flea Market** corner of Hietalahdenkatu & Bulevardi [6 C6] With a mixture of professional traders & individuals just cleaning out the clutter, this open-air gathering is Helsinki's best flea market & one of Helsinki's busiest shopping experiences. Clothes, music, art & a whole load of miscellaneous bric-a-brac. Do some serious bargain hunting, or just wander amidst the hustle & bustle to savour the atmosphere over an alfresco cup of coffee. *Open Mon–Fri 08.00–14.00 and Jun–Aug 15.30–20.00, Sat 08.00–15.00, May–Sep Sun 10.00–16.00.*

**Valtteri** Aleksis Kivenkatu 17. Large self-service flea market favoured by a trendy younger crowd. *Self-service market open Mon–Fri 10.00–19.00, Sat–Sun 09.00–15.00; traditional market open Wed & Sat–Sun 09.00–15.00.*

# MUSIC

Helsinki has a vibrant music scene, and a slew of specialist shops painting every colour of the sonic rainbow. You can browse secondhand and new vinyl and CDs at the following places.

**Black and White** Toinen linja 1; ☏ 701 3027; www.blackandwhite.fi [1 C1] Specialising in classic, prog & psychedelic rock. *Open Mon–Fri 10.00–18.00, Sat 09.00–14.00.*

**Digelius** Laivurinrinne 2; ☏ 666 375; www.digelius.com [7 F7] Helsinki's finest, Digelius is a sensational world music shop with over 20,000 items. Essential for any true music lover. *Open Mon–Fri 11.00–18.00, Sat 10.00–16.00.*

**Eronen** Laivurinrinne 2; ☏ 638 816; www.dubjazzsalsa.com [7 F7] Just next to Digelius, stocking reggae, salsa & classical discs. *Open Wed–Fri 12.00–19.00, Sat 11.00–16.00.*

**Fennica Records** Albertinkatu 36; ☏ 685 1433; www.fennicakeskus.fi [6 C5] Classic rock 'n' roll, blues & country. *Open Mon–Fri 10.00–18.00, Sat 09.00–14.00.*

**Lifesaver** Laivurinkatu 41; ☏ 630 051; www.lifesaver.net [6 E7] Soul, jazz, hip-hop, funk, dance & electronica. *Open Mon–Fri 12.00–19.00, Sat 11.00–17.00.*

**Popparienkeli** Fredrikinkatu 12; ☏ 661 638; www.popangel.fi [6 E7] Alternative rock (1960s & 1970s), soul, funk & Finnish music. *Open Mon–Fri 10.00–18.00, Sat 10.00–16.00.*

**Stupido Shop** Iso Roobertinkatu 20–22; ☏ 646 990; www.stupido.fi [6 E6] Pop, rock, alternative, dance, punk, dub, ska, hip-hop, funk & the best of Finnish. *Open Mon–Fri 10.00–19.00, Sat 10.00–17.00.*

## NEWSPAPERS, BOOKS AND MAPS

**Akateeminen Kirjakauppa** Pohjoisesplanadi 39; ✆ 121 4243; www.akateeminen.com [5 F3] Helsinki's academic bookstore is a wonderful place to while away a wet afternoon, browsing around 3 floors of wide-ranging titles. There's a large English-language section, comprehensive travel department & international periodicals. Designed by Alvar Aalto, like all his projects the architecture is striking — the store rises upwards around 3 rectangular balconies overlooking a central atrium. *Open Mon–Fri 09.00–21.00, Sat 09.00–18.00.*

**Suomalainen Kirjakauppa** Aleksanterinkatu 23; ✆ 696 2240; www.suomalainen.com [4 E3] Less intellectual in atmosphere than the Akateeminen, this run-of-the-mill shop nevertheless has a decent range of English-language titles. *Open Mon–Fri 10.00–18.00, Sat 11.00–23.00.*

## SECONDHAND SHOPS

**Fida Lähetystori** Iso Roobertinkatu 24; ✆ 612 1770 [6 E6] Everything from business suits to frilly dresses, armchairs to beer glasses & 7" records to bargain books. A treasure-trove of recycled clutter. *Open Mon–Tue 09.00–18.00, Wed–Fri 09.00–17.00, Sat 10.00–14.00.*

**UFF Second Hand** Iso Roobertinkatu 4–6; ✆ 603 755 [7 F5] The biggest store of the UFF chain, catering mostly to a young crowd who have the energy to sift wheat from chaff. *Open Mon–Fri 10.00–19.00, Sat 10.00–17.00.*

## SHOPPING MALLS

Helsinki has Finland's biggest and best shopping centres – try these for a quick mall-fix.

**Forum** Mannerheimintie 20a; ☎ 565 7450; f 641 584; e info@cityforum.fi; www.cituforum.fi [4 E3] Big & bustling, this place is slightly dated but its 120 shops & numerous fast-food cafés remain popular with locals. *Open Mon–Fri 09.00–21.00, Sat 09.00–18.00, Sun 12.00–18.00.*

**Itäkeskus** ☎ 343 1005; www.itakeskuskauppakeskus.fi. The largest mall in the Nordic countries, with nearly 240 shops, restaurants & entertainment attractions. Branches of Stockmann, Iittala & Marimekko. Fifteen minutes' ride on the Metro from the city. *Open Mon–Fri 10.00–20.00, Sat 09.00–18.00, Sun 12.00–18.00. Restaurants open daily until 22.00.*

**Kämp Galleria** Pohjoisesplanadi 33; www.kampgalleria.fi [5 F3] Located near Hotel Kämp, this posh & glitzy arcade has upmarket brands. *Open Mon–Fri 10.00–20.00, Sat 10.00–17.00, Jun–Aug Sun 12.00–16.00.*

**Kamppi** Urho Kekkosen katu 1; ☎ 742 98552; www.kamppi.fi/english [4 C3] Opened amidst much rejoicing in March 2006, this 6-floor monster in brushed steel & polished glass houses all the usual high-street suspects, plus bookshops, pharmacies, photographic shops & a huge supermarket. If you find yourself short of anything, this is the best place to start looking. *Open Mon–Fri 09.00–21.00, Sat 09.00–18.00, Sun 12.00–18.00.*

**Kluuvi** Aleksanterinkatu 9; www.kluuvi.fi [5 G3] Similar to Forum, another place with fast-food restaurants & high-street brands. *Open Mon–Fri 10.00–19.00, Sat 10.00–16.00.*

## SOUVENIRS AND GIFTS

You can probably pick up all the souvenirs you want in the markets and craft galleries. But there's one shop that I couldn't squeeze into any other category, and it seemed cruel not to include it.

## FIVE BEST SOUVENIRS

- Alvar Aalto's timeless Savoy vase
- A classic poppy-print *Unikko* bag from Marimekko
- One of Oiva Toikka's beautifully fragile glass birds
- Foodie delights – slabs of Fazer milk chocolate, the Sisu brand of *salmiakki* salted liquorice and lingonberry jam from Stockmann department store
- *From Finland With Love*, German author Roman Schaltz's hilarious if politically incorrect take on his adopted homeland

**Moomin Shop** Kämp Galleria, Pohjoisesplanadi 32; ☎ 622 2206 [5 F3]
As a Finnish friend once succinctly remarked, 'If you don't appreciate Moomins, you're a fool'. At this little shop in the swish Kämp Galleria, you can fulfil all your troll-like fantasies in one fell swoop; tea-towels, mugs, T-shirts, key rings or hats, you can get it all here. *Open Mon–Fri 10.00–20.00, Sat 10.00–17.00, Jun–Aug Sun 12.00–16.00.*

# 9 Activities and Sport

Finland might not be the world's leading light on the sporting stage, but that doesn't mean you can't work up a good sweat. The nation has a proud Olympic and athletic heritage, with some great facilities available for public use. From midnight golf in the midst of summer to Nordic walking in the depths of winter, you can find any number of ways to get active.

## BOWLING ALLEYS

**Kampin Keilahalli & Bar** Kamppi Centre 4th Floor; ☎ 020 712 1212; http://www.varaarata.com [4 C3] *Open Mon–Sat 10.00–late, Sun 10.00–20.00.*

## CANOEING

**Canoe Rent Center** Punavuorenkatu 22; ☎ 050 585 6000; www.canoerentcenter-finland.fi [6 D7] Arranges canoeing on the rapids of the River Vantaa at Vanhakaupunki or, for a more sedate paddle, at Kaivopuisto Park, as well as safaris further afield. Canoe-rental prices from €30 per day.

**Rastila Camping** Karavaanikatu 4; ☎ 321 6551; e rastilacamping@hel.fi; www.hel.fi/rastila. If you've decided to camp or stay in one of Rastila's cabins you can take a canoe out for around €5 per hour.

**Töölönlahti Venevuokraamo** Finlandia Hall; ☎ 040 530 9240 [I B2] Behind Finlandia Hall, on the shore of Töölönlahti, you can rent a simple pleasure boat for €9 per hour (May–Sep).

## CLIMBING

**Helsinki Climbing Centre** Erätie 3; ☎ 093 507 0710; www.kiipeilykeskus.com. Well-equipped indoor complex, north of the city near the airport. Instruction & solo climbing for the more experienced. Adult €10, equipment rental €6. Open Mon–Thu 08.00–22.00, Fri 11.00–19.00, Sat 09.00–18.00, Sun 11.00–21.00.

For outdoor climbing opportunities, check the forum www.slouppi.net.

## CYCLING

With abundant parkland, wild forest and a good network of dedicated paths, Helsinki is well geared up for cycling. If you pedal around the city, bear in mind that cycle paths follow the same flow as the road traffic and heading the wrong way could lead to a nasty tangle of spokes.

**Citybike** Pioneering scheme of free public bikes throughout Helsinki. There are 26 stands of cycles (you can't miss the green frames & solid yellow wheels) dotted around the city; simply drop €2 in the slot & off you go. Return the bike to any other stand & you get your deposit back. Head to the central stands in Esplanade Park to see the map of all other locations.

**Green Bike** Fredrikinkatu 31; ☎ 050 550 1020; www.greenbike.fi Centrally located, Green Bike rents street bikes (€13 per day) & mountain bikes (€20). Overnight rentals also available. *Open Mon–Fri 10.00–18.00, Sat 10.00–15.00.*

## FISHING

Fishing opportunities abound in Helsinki. There is no licence requirement for angling and ice fishing in Finland, but bait fishing requires a permit to cover both fishing rights and a general maintenance fee (*€5/10 per day/week and €6 per week respectively*). Permits can be bought at the following places, where you will also receive a map showing the best fishing locations.

**Rastila Camping** (see page 130)
**Salakala** Fredrikinkatu 31; ☎ 607 200 [6 E6]
**Schröder** Unioninkatu 23; ☎ 656 656 [5 G3]
**Stockmann** (see page 180) [4 E3]

For organised fishing trips, see page 98.

## FITNESS CENTRES AND SWIMMING POOLS

**Motivus Center** Simonkatu 9; ☎ 4153 3500 [4 D3] If your hotel doesn't have a gym of its own, there are several Motivus fitness centres around the city. Some cater only to male or female clients but this one, with solarium & sauna as well as exercise equipment, is unisex. *Open Mon–Thu 06.35–21.30, Fri 06.35–20.00, Sat 09.00–18.00, Sun 10.00–20.00.*

**Swimming Stadium – Uimastadion** Hammarskjöldintie 5; ℄ 3108 7854. By the Olympic Stadium, this outdoor complex is the most popular place during summer. 50m pool, children's play pool, diving area (5m, 7.5m & 10m), water slides, sauna & café. Adult/child €3/1.50, water slides €5. *Open mid May–mid Sep Mon–Sat 06.30–20.00, Sun 09.00–20.00.*

**Helsingin Urheilutalo** Helsinginkatu 25; ℄ 3488 6419 [1 C1] Gym, solarium, sauna & 25m indoor swimming pool. *Gym open Mon–Fri 06.15–22.00, Sat–Sun 09.00–21.00; swimming pool open Mon–Tue 06.15–20.00, Wed–Fri 06.15–08.00 & 14.00–20.00, Sat–Sun 09.00–18.00.*

## FOOTBALL

Football is far from Finland's number-one sport, and the international team consistently struggles to make an impact on the European and world stage. Despite this, there are some high-profile Finnish footballers: Jari Litmanen, Sami Hyypiä, Antti Niemi, Miakael Forssell and Aki Riihilahti have all graced the English Premiership. Club football in Finland takes place during the warmer summer months, but doesn't attract large crowds. HJK Helsinki is the biggest club, with experience of the European Champions League, but is currently facing stiff competition on the domestic front from the likes of FC Haka, FC Honka and Tampere United, the latter of whom clinched the 2005–06 league championship with a final day victory against HJK, who themselves would have claimed the title with victory.

## WINTER SPORTS

Finland's reliable snowfall and strong Nordic sports culture means there's no excuse to stay stuck indoors during the colder months. In fact, quite the opposite is true and Helsinki has first-rate facilities for the intrepid winter sports enthusiast.

The most popular activities are **cross-country skiing**, **snowshoe walking** and **Nordic walking** (walking quickly with ski poles), and the best place to start is the Nordic Fitness Sports Park (*Mäntymäentie 1;* ☎ *4776 9760; www.suomenlatu.fi/toolonlahti*). This purpose-built complex by the Olympic Stadium has a variety of forest and urban trails (from 2.4–22.6km), as well as equipment rental and tuition. Opening hours and the choice of activities depend on seasonal conditions, so call for details or contact the tourist office.

For downhill **skiing** and **snowboarding**, try **Talma Ski** (*Talmantie 341, Talma;* ☎ *092 745 410; www.talmaski.fi; opening hours are seasonal but generally Mon–Fri 13.00–21.00, Sat–Sun 10.00–18.00*), with seven dedicated slopes and a new 'snowskate' park. Situated near the town of Sipoo, 50km northeast of the city, take the train to Kerava from where there is a free shuttle bus.

A good bet for **sledging** or a spot of **slalom skiing** is the recreation area at Paloheinä, 12km north of the city. Take bus 66A from Railway Square to Paloheinä Hiking Lodge, where you can rent skis at Pakilantie 124. The journey takes 30 minutes.

In winter Helsinki becomes one giant alfresco **skating** park, with over 100 natural rinks where you can glide to your heart's content. However, unless you have your own gear you might want to try **Brahe Skating Rink** (*Helsinginkatu 23; ✆ 753 2932; adult/child €2/1, skate rental €4; open late Nov–mid Mar Mon–Fri 08.00–20.00, Sat–Sun 10.00–20.00*) in the Kallio district of town.

For maximum Finnish brownie points, take the plunge with a spot of brain-numbing **ice swimming**. Commonly known as *avanto* (meaning 'hole in the ice'), this is singularly the coldest thing I have ever done. Staring into the inky-black pool in nothing but a swimsuit induces a childlike regression – 'I don't want to do it!' – which is more than understandable given that you *will* gasp for breath, your heart *will* pound and your limbs *will* seize up. Back in the sauna, however, it feels great! In case you were wondering, it doesn't get any easier the second time. Funnily, the coldest part is not the water itself but the snowy 50m barefoot walk from the cabin to the pool – take sandals and it won't be half as painful. Believe it or not *avanto* is so popular it requires club membership at the best holes, but you can try it at **Rastila Camping** (see page 130) for the bargain price of €4.50.

For guided winter sports excursions, contact the Helsinki City Tourist Bureau (see pages 94–5).

**HJK Helsinki** Finnair Stadium, Urheilukatu 5; ✆ 7421 6600; www.hjk.fi. Playing games at the impressive Finnair Stadium, by the Olympic park complex, tickets for HJK games are good value at adult €8–15, child €2–3. HJK's small band of hard-core fans is a curious mixture of big-bearded rockers & 1950s-style teddy boys.

## GOLF

In the light summers golfers can tee-off late into the evening. Call ahead to the following places for exact availability and the latest green fees.

**Espoo Golf** Mynttiläntie 1, Espoo; ✆ 8190 3444; www.espoongolfseura.fi. Hosting Finland's biggest pro event, this championship complex also has a practice range & 3 par-3 holes.
**Helsinki Golf Club** Talin Kartano; ✆ 225 2370; www.golfpiste.com/kentat/hgk. Pleasant parkland course at Finland's oldest & most exclusive club, founded in 1932 & only 20mins from central Helsinki.
**Vuosaari Golf** Eteläreimarintie; ✆ 681 2210; www.vuosaarigolf.fi. Helsinki's newest championship course is laid out by the sea on the island of Vuosaari to the east of the city.

## HIKING

See the section *Natural Helsinki*, pages 246–62 and Nuuksio National Park, pages 263–4.

## ICE HOCKEY

Finland's number-one team sport, hockey is played all over the city during the winter months (*Sep–Mar*). On an evening stroll through Kallio you can often hear the throaty roar of beer-swilling supporters at an open-air game; the speed and ferocity is something to behold. Many of Finland's top players ply their trade in North America, but nevertheless meetings of Helsinki's two professional teams in the SM-liiga are always highly anticipated and bitterly contested affairs.

**HIFK** Helsingin Jäähalli; ✎ 4777 020; http://www.hifk.fi. The oldest & best-supported team, the 6-time Finnish champions play home fixtures in 'The Beast's Cave'. *Tickets* €10.50–31.50.
**Jokerit** Hartwall Arena, Areenakuja 1; ✎ 0204 1990; www.jokerit.com. Also 6-time winners of the Finnish league, the 'jokers' play in a bigger arena & have lifted the European Cup on 2 occasions, but attract less media interest. *Tickets* €13–33.

The easiest way to secure tickets for either team is via ticket agency **Lippupalvelu** (see page 163).

## PUBLIC SAUNAS

**Kotiharju Sauna** Harjutorinkatu 1; ✎ 753 1535 [1 C1] Helsinki's last wood-fired sauna is as close as you'll get to traditional **löyly** in the city. Located in Kallio, you can have a massage, sit out on the pavement & drink a beer (in summer *or* winter) & get scrubbed down by a ruddy-cheeked old washerwoman. Sauna €7, towel

## SACRED SAUNA

*Sauna on köyhän apteekk* (sauna is the poor man's pharmacy)

If there's one fact foreigners know about Finland above all others, it's that the Finns love sauna. For a population of a shade over five million, there are an astonishing 1.7 million saunas – that's one for every family and most single dwellers as well – and the cultural significance of taking the *löyly* (heat/steam) cannot be underestimated.

To appreciate the true context of Finnish sauna we need to leave the city far behind and head for the country. Nothing is more idyllic to the Finn than a summer escape to their lakeside cabin, and a sauna under clear skies. Listening to the birds sing and watching the sun set is fundamental to the experience – just light the barbecue, drink a couple of beers and cool off in the water. Total bliss!

Such gatherings are usually family events, and the essence of the ritual sheds light on Finnish attitudes to nudity – once you've seen Uncle Pekka and Auntie Piritta in all their glory, why worry about stripping off in front of a group of strangers? Brits and Americans often fret about this but none of the Finns do, so why should you? Despite common

€1.50. Open Tue–Fri 14.00–20.00, Sat 13.00–19.00, but the löyly continues until 22.00.
**Yrjönkatu Swimming Hall** Yrjönkatu 21; 🕿 3108 7401; www.hel2.fi/liv/eng/yrjonkatu.html [4 E3] These ornate Roman-style baths aren't especially Finnish but with a large pool on the ground floor & several saunas & steam

misconceptions, there's no sexual connotation involved in sauna and outside of family gatherings most sessions are single-sex only. In a mixed sauna the true Finnish gentleman maintains eye contact at all times…

The physics of what makes a perfect sauna and the intricacies of decorum are much debated, but all you need to remember is that the only etiquette is one of enjoyment. Come and go from the steam as you wish, cool off when you choose, eat a sausage or beat yourself gently with a moistened birch branch. The sauna is not a competitive environment, although the Sauna World Championships would have you believe otherwise, so just relax and enjoy.

The days when childbirth, meat curing and massage all occurred in the sauna may be a thing of the past, but the experience remains key to the Finnish existence. Illustrating Finland's edict of democracy and equality, many high-level political decisions have been made and business deals struck amidst the fragrant steam.

For the best *löyly* in Helsinki, try the wood-burning **Kotiharju Sauna** (see page 201), and should you ever get invited to a private gathering, accept at once – the experience more than outweighs your prudish embarrassment.

rooms set around an upper balcony, it's an atmospheric place to soothe aching muscles. Nude swimming means separate times for men & women, so check before going. Men should also know that Yrjönkatu features on the gay cruising scene. Swimming €4.50, swimming & sauna €11. *Open Mon–Fri 10.00–18.00, Sat 11.00–16.00.*

# 10 Walking Tours

## DISCOVERING HELSINKI ON FOOT

Helsinki is such a compact city that almost everywhere can be reached under your own steam, and the energetic may never need to set foot on a bus or tram. The heart beats around the central area running east to west between the Esplanade Park and Kamppi complex, crammed full of enticing cafés, stylish boutiques and many of the major tourist sights. Running north from here, the main artery of Mannerheimintie leads towards the elegant Töölö district, with the beautiful sea-inlet of Töölönlahti. Several major landmarks, including the Finnish Parliament (Suomen Eduskunta), Kiasma Museum of Contemporary Art and Olympic Stadium, lie in this direction. To the south, the peaceful residential areas of Eira, Ullanlinna and Kaivopuisto are a delight of leafy parkland, classical architecture and seafront promenades.

The unique archipelago location of Helsinki makes for several good circular tours, as well as a couple of longer routes that trace the coast. Explore individual areas or make your own combinations. Don't let winter put you off; on cold, crisp days with fresh snow crunching underfoot, there really is no better way to see the city.

Approximate durations have been given for walking at a casual stroll, but do not include any time spent browsing attractions, relaxing in cafés or arguing over directions.

## WALK I: SWEDISH THEATRE TO KAMPPI AND THE DESIGN DISTRICT

*Estimated time: 1¹/₂–2 hours*

At first glance this shopping-heavy tour might seem like one for the girls but don't switch off just yet chaps because it's not all credit-card-straining designer dresses and strappy sandals. Yes, Helsinki has a wealth of individual boutiques but you can flex the plastic equally well in timeless interior design shops, chic art galleries and some more 'alternative' venues. If you'd rather just spend your loose change, then hang fire until we reach one of the city's best flea markets.

Along the way are some fine sights; museums, galleries and a couple of classic cafés, stuffed full of sticky pastries and swirling with the aroma of freshly brewed coffee. These elegant meeting places are timeless institutions, an essential part of local life, and you don't need to shop to enjoy them.

A good place to start is the **Swedish Theatre** (Svenska Teatern) [5 F4] at the point where the **Esplanade Park** meets **Mannerheimintie**, lined with big-name high-street stores and noisy with the constant rattling of trams. Facing north, directly opposite the theatre is the **Stockmann** department store, the biggest of its kind in the Nordic countries. For some, this could well be the end of the walk already, such are the temptations of the delights found within.

Those with stronger willpower can continue, passing the statue of the **Three Smiths** [4 E3] that serves as a memorial to World War II, and on towards the **railway station** [4 E2]. Directly ahead of you, the peculiar curved building of brushed aluminium and sandblasted glass is **Kiasma – Museum of Contemporary**

**Art** [4 D1] whose installations are both baffling and beautiful in equal measure. Outside Kiasma is an equine memorial to **Field Marshal Carl Gustav Emil Mannerheim**, commander of the White Army during the Finnish Civil War of 1918 and subsequently President of Finland from 1944–46.

Crossing the road to which Mannerheim lent his name, the low two-storey building in crisp white is the **Glass Palace** (Lasipalatsi) [4 D2], housing a film and media centre, cinema and cafés. Constructed in 1936, it was designed to be temporary but is now considered to be one of the finest functionalist examples of its period.

If you haven't yet spotted the looming hulk of **Kamppi**, you're in for a shock because the enormous shopping complex dominates the backdrop behind the Glass Palace. Opened in March 2006, it marked the end of a lengthy project to bring a world-class mall to the heart of Helsinki, but serves a double purpose. Its sleek dark glass exterior hides a new underground transport hub for bus and Metro services. Helsinkiites love this as much as the glitzy shops and bars – no more alfresco queuing for buses in the midst of icy winters.

Skirt round either side of Kamppi, or straight through should you wish, and aim for the southwest corner of the complex. From here we need to cut across town through pleasant if unspectacular neighbourhoods to reach our next destination of note, so pay attention: on the corner of **Urho Kekkosen katu** and **Fredrikinkatu**, continue in a southwesterly direction along **Malminrinne** and into **Albertinkatu**, taking the first right to join **Lönnrotinkatu**.

At Lönnrotinkatu 29 is one of Helsinki's most romantically styled hotels. **Hotel Linna** [6 C5] is the former students' union building of Helsinki Polytechnic, notable for its distinct National Romantic style and detailed craftsmanship. Take a peek inside the beautiful vaulted reception area supported by columns of natural stone – a popular venue for a summer wedding.

At the end of the street, in **Hietalahdentori**, is **Hietelahti flea market** [6 C6]. Helsinki folk have embraced secondhand fashion like few others I know, and if you want to dress stylishly and for peanuts this is the place to do it. Bargain for all you're worth.

Turning eastwards, **Bulevardi** is one of the most beautiful streets in the city, which was home to some of the wealthiest and most cultured families of the late 19th and early 20th centuries. Apartments here still command a premium. Facing the eastern side of Hietalahdentori is Helsinki's former Technical College, whilst across Bulevardi to the right is the **Sinebrychoff Museum of Foreign Art** [6 C6].

On the corner of Albertinkatu, the neo-Renaissance **Alexander's Theatre** [6 D6] was constructed in 1879 to meet the cultural needs of Helsinki's growing Russian community. Inside, the 500-seat auditorium entertained the immigrant population until 1918, when it became the home of the Finnish National Opera. Since the Opera relocated to the shores of Töölönlahti Bay in 1993, the theatre has been used for occasional guest stage performances. Just after the theatre, **Le Petit Café** is a quaint and peaceful place to stop for coffee and cake, but you might want to wait because not far away is one of the old dames.

Turn right into **Fredrikinkatu** to enter Helsinki's **Design District**, choc-full of fashion boutiques, galleries and interior design gems. Personally, I have to stay out of this area due to overwhelming temptation and low resolve; but you carry on. The main concentration of shops is found on the north–south streets of Fredrikinkatu, Annankatu and Yrjönkatu, bounded by Bulevardi to the north and Iso Roobertinkatu to the south. It's a compact area so wander awhile and see what you discover.

If you prefer things a little grittier, drop down on to Iso Roobertinkatu, known as Iso Roba, home to some of Helsinki's more liberal gay bars and with a range of funky and alternative shops. Buy anything from super-cool trainers to hard-core porn or a handmade saddle for your horse.

When you've had your fill of shopping, head back up Annankatu to Bulevardi. Just before the junction, look out for Mountain Shop, which sells all sorts of serious gear for scaling vertical rock faces but displays a concerning message in the door – *Watch out for the steps!* About 100m to the left is **Ekberg**, Helsinki's oldest café and an oasis of sophisticated charm. Now is probably a great time to take the weight off your feet.

Leafy **Vanha Kirkopuisto** is home to poignant graves and memorials to Finnish and German soldiers who perished during the 1918 Civil War, as well as a memorial to Finnish volunteers who were lost in the 1919 Estonian War of Liberation – find the latter on the Yrjönkatu side of the park.

On the opposite side of the park and full of character is the **Old Church** (Vanhakirkko) [4 E4], another Engel masterpiece and one of Helsinki's few remaining wooden buildings. Rejoin Lönnrotinkatu, paying heed to the statue of

**Elias Lonnröt** opposite the church. Lonnröt was the famous collector of Finnish folk poems who compiled the national epic text the *Kalevala*.

For the best views in central Helsinki, detour down Yrjönkatu to the 12th-floor Ateljee Bar in **Hotel Torni**, Helsinki's first skyscraper, otherwise continue down Lönnrotinkatu back to our starting point at the Swedish Theatre.

## WALK 2: RAILWAY SQUARE AND AROUND TÖÖLÖNLAHTI BAY

*Estimated time: 1¹/₂ hours*

The vast majority of visitors to Helsinki arrive in the city at Railway Square (Rautatientori); if you take a bus from the airport, this is where you end up. Bustling and somewhat chaotic, the square may seem a long way removed from nature, yet a short northerly walk brings us to Töölönlahti, a sea-inlet lined with impressive wooden villas. Following the gentle curves of the shore, we return to the city via Finland's democratic heart, the Parliament House.

**Railway Square** [5 F2] is in many ways the heart of Helsinki, busy from dawn until dusk with the constant toing and froing of everyday life. There is some wonderful architecture here, not least the **railway station** itself and the **National Gallery** (Ateneum), on the south of the square, but also some latter-day monsters. In particular, the drab, modern offices with gaudy neon signs do little to nurture positive first impressions.

The grandiose main station building reflects Finland's National Romantic vision of the early 20th century. Commissioned in 1902, it was 17 years before the first trains rolled. After a lengthy period of construction, parts of the complex became a Russian military hospital during World War I before the Soviet-backed Red Army took up residence during the 1918 Finnish Civil War.

Facing the National Gallery, at the opposite end of the square, National Romanticism is also evident in the striking elevation of the **Finnish National Theatre** (Suomen Kansallisteatteri) [5 F1], although the incongruous electronic information sign does nothing to enhance the façade. In front of the theatre is a statue to Alexis Kivi (1834–72), Finland's tragically short-lived national writer.

Leaving the square by **Läntinen Teatterikuja**, to the left of the theatre, it is a surprise to emerge in a large park. Helsinki has been blessed with open space; this is **Kaisaniemi** [5 F1], the traditional working-class alternative to graceful Kaivopuisto in the south of the city. Kaisaniemi has retained its earthy atmosphere, and it is not uncommon to see vagrants (mostly harmless) sprawling on the grass, each clutching his *pussikalja*, a carrier bag full of beer bottles. The park can be edgy at night, so it pays to exercise caution.

Keeping the ornamental fountain on your right, watch out for the sculpture of a grazing elk mooching beneath the trees atop the grassy mound. Passing an area of the park that serves seasonally as either a football pitch or ice-hockey rink, you may be able to see the glass domes of the **University Botanical Gardens** peeking through the trees to your right.

All along here you can spot the trains drawing in and out of the main station, some heading to distant Lapland. Looking across to the water's edge, the districts visible to the east and north are **Hakaniemi** and **Kallio** respectively. Hakaniemi is home to the locals' favourite food market, whilst Kallio is the traditional workers' district; the solid granite, rocket-like top of **Kallio Church** [1 C1] stands tall above the surrounding rooftops.

Go uphill and cross the wide footbridge, from where it becomes evident just how much of central Helsinki is devoted to the spaghetti-like network of railway tracks and overhead wires. At the other side, if you fancy an alfresco coffee on a beautiful terrace, turn left. Little more than a cabin, the west-facing garden is packed long into the summer evenings and has beautiful views over sparkling **Töölönlahti**.

If coffee's not your thing head right past **Villa Kivi**, a writers' retreat, and follow the tree-lined road as it heads north. Come winter, the shallow bay freezes solid and you can follow the locals onto the ice for an unusual shortcut to the opposing shore.

This tranquil stroll brings you shortly to busy Helsinginkatu. Across the road are the **City Winter Gardens** [1 A1], and further beyond the stark-white modernism of the **Olympic Stadium** – follow Hammarskjöldintie to reach the 72m-high snorkel-like tower and the best views of the city. Allow an extra hour if you want to explore around the Olympic Park.

The less athletically minded can continue around Töölönlahti to the turf-roofed **Töölönranta Restaurant**, largely invisible from the main road thanks to its solid brick wall and extensive tree coverage. On the bay side, the sheltered terrace maximises its waterside location and is usually busy in summer. The original restaurant was lost to fire in 1987 and the current incarnation dates from 1996.

Next door is the **Finnish National Opera** (Ooppera) [1 B1], relocated in 1993 from its long-time location on Bulevardi. Although imposing from this aspect, the opera house has also been constructed sympathetically, being sunk into the slope to disguise its magnitude. It is much less incongruous when approaching from the opposite direction.

The area of parkland on the west shore of the bay is one of the city's most pleasing. Known as **Hesperianpuisto**, it is perennially popular with groups as disparate as joggers, martial artists and Indian drummers. Head away from the water towards Mannerheimintie, but remain in the park, and soon you arrive at one of Alvar Aalto's most recognisable works, the **Finlandia Hall** concert and convention centre [1 B2]. Originally planned as part of a grand development of public buildings along Töölönlahti, this was the only part of his scheme to be realised. The main auditorium is a breathtaking example of Aalto's minimalist style, visually pure yet with a rich acoustic depth; a guided tour is recommended. Finlandia Hall will host the **2007 Eurovision**

*Finlandia Hall*

## WALKING ON THE FRINGES

If you have either the time or inclination, there are another two worthwhile walks on the edge of the city centre that should not be ignored.

Katajanokka is a stately, peaceful island by the Market Square, famous as the home of the **Uspenski Cathedral** [5 K3]. Most visitors never get further than this fabled monument, but further investigation reveals some worthwhile finds. The streets around Luotsikatu are graced with Helsinki's finest Art Nouveau architecture, the excellent Restaurant Bellevue (see page 142) is the oldest Russian eatery in town, there are fine views across the North Harbour and towards Suomenlinna from the eastern tip, Carl Ludvig Engel's splendid Ministry for Foreign Affairs exudes elegant grace and the Katajanokka Ferry Terminal is the starting point for crossings to Tallinn and Stockholm. A leisurely exploration of Katajanokka takes about 1½ hours.

Meanwhile, on the east side of town is one of Helsinki's finest seaside walks. Starting from **Hietaniemi Cemetery** [1 A3], simply follow the coastal path in a northeasterly direction as it winds through beautiful parkland, past the official **presidential residence** (Mantyniemi) and the **Sibelius Monument** (see pages 240–1) before finally arriving at **Seurasaari** (see pages 256–8), the open-air island museum famous for its tame squirrels. The walk from Hietaniemi takes about an hour, but allow an extra 30 minutes if you want to walk from the city.

**Song Contest** after joke monster-rock band Lordi triumphed in Athens in 2006.

On the opposite side of Mannerheimintie are two of Helsinki's most significant landmarks. The palace-like **Finnish National Museum** (Suomen Kansallismuseo) [1 B2] is the best-known edifice of the National Romantic era and resplendently medieval in style. On the staircase by the front entrance, the cute statue of a brown bear pays homage to Finland's national animal.

A short way to the south is the stark, monolithic **Parliament House** (Eduskuntatalo) [4 C1], the only example of grand Classicism in Finland and unquestionably the country's most famous building. The severe, regular columns of the façade imbibe an air of authority. Two imposing statues flank the sweeping staircase; at the northern end is **Kaarlo Juho Ståhlberg** (1865–1952), the first President of Finland after independence in 1919, whilst at the southern end of the plaza rests **Pehr Evind Svinhufvud** (1861–1944), the fierce anti-communist campaigner who led the country between 1931 and 1937.

Traverse Mannerheimintie once again to skirt past **Kiasma, Museum of Contemporary Art** [4 D1] and drop down Postikatu to return to Railway Square.

## WALK 3: FROM THE MARKET SQUARE TO KAIVOPUISTO AND EIRA
*Estimated time: 1¹/₂–2 hours*

This route takes us around the beautiful southern headland of Helsinki, through stately Kaivopuisto Park and past several islands of the archipelago. With few shops, museums or galleries *en route*, this is one for those who want to experience the fresh air and sea breezes of outdoor Helsinki. Although it's hard to single out any one area of town in which to walk, this is possibly my favourite.

Starting out from the **Market Square** (Kauppatori) [5 H4] at the foot of Esplanade Park, you can grab a fortifying snack here or at the nearby **Old Market Hall** (Wanha Kauppahalli) [5 D2] before heading west along Eteläranta in the direction of the **Olympia Terminal** [7 J7], departure point for Silja Line ferries to Stockholm.

As the street curves away to the left, carry straight on up the hill towards the **German Church** (Saksalainen Kirkko) [7 H6]. Consecrated in 1864, the red-brick church served the 19th-century Germanic community. A romantic atmosphere pervades and this remains a favourite wedding venue.

At the top of the hill is **Carl Ludvig Engel's Observatory** (Tähtitorni) [7 H6], now shrouded in trees but at the time of construction (1834) the most dominant feature of the southern part of the peninsula. For maximum impact, the observatory was strategically located at the southern end of Unioninkatu, the longest straight-line street in the city. At the northern end is **Kallio Church** [1 C1], an equally powerful landmark in the working-class district of the same name. The observatory is still used by the Institute of Astronomy. If you stand with your back to the main gates, you can look all the way along Unioninkatu to the rocket-like church, some 2.5km away.

Continuing in a southerly direction, cross **Tähtitorninkatu** and follow the path between the large apartment blocks. The most majestic building of all is the granite-and-soapstone **Russian embassy** on Ullankatu [7 H7], hiding behind thick tree cover and complemented by its adjoining consular residences.

**Kaivopuisto** is an area of sedate refinement betwixt city and sea where little has changed in over a century. Ambling through leafy parkland redolent with summer's heady scents, the vibrant city centre seems far away. A gentrified peace epitomises the atmosphere, even more so on winter mornings when, muffled by snow, a beguiling silence blankets the neighbourhood.

Crossing Ullankatu to bisect the fine Jugendstil apartments, pass the **Catholic Church** (Katolinen Kirkko) [7 H8] and join **Iso Puistotie**, which leads to the park. The isolated wooden villa on the right is **Kaivohuone**, a former spa that was the hub of Helsinki's 19th-century upper-class social scene. It was much favoured by the Russian high societies, who for many years were prevented from travelling outside the empire. Today the spa plays host to a summer terrace and music club.

A little further on, to your left you will spot a rather small and unspectacular sculpture called **The Fishing Bear** (Kalastava Karhu). Somewhat forlorn, the lonely chap seems a pitiful acknowledgement of the Finns' national animal.

Leave the bear behind you and follow the path up and over the hill, keeping the wall on your right, and turn right on **Itäinen Puistotie**. Of all Helsinki's grand streets, this is one of the finest, but not for the traditional Jugendstil architecture so prominent in other areas. Here, amidst sprawling walled gardens and guarded by imposing gateways are some of the city's finest remaining examples of traditional villas. The oldest, at Itäinen Puistotie 7, dates from 1839. Popular with diplomats, some of the largest foreign embassies can be found in this area of the park.

216

Continuing on Itäinen Puistotie past the embassies of the US, France and Great Britain, drop down to the sea and join **Ehrenströmintie**. Sticking to the shoreline promenade, walk in a southerly direction around the headland. Ahead of you, the small wooden building with the sail-like canopy is **Café Ursula**, a haven for summer sun-worshippers and a cosy treat in the white, icy depths of winter. The British Ambassador has been known to take his coffee here, so it can't be bad – or could it be that he just loves the decadent pastries and live jazz?

If you can pull yourself from Ursula's clutches, heading west along the seafront you will spot **Ursa Observatory** (Ursan Tähtitorni) [1 C4] perched on a grassy knoll in the park. The observatory is occasionally opened for stargazing on clear nights and acts as a gathering place for student revellers during May Day celebrations.

Helsinki has an archipelago comprising over 300 islands, and you can visit several of them from here. One of the best is **Uunisaari**, only 200m from the shore but connected by boat during the summer months; it's worth a trip for the popular beach and café. In winter, this is one of the best places to experience walking on the frozen sea, although the wind that whistles unchallenged across the open plains of ice can equally well freeze your assets.

As you approach Uunisaari, you may see locals washing the city odours from their rugs with a series of large wooden drying racks and dangerous-looking mangles. Some see this long-standing social tradition as indicative of how well a Helsinkiite runs his or her home, and therefore by default their life in general.

All around the bay of **Uunisaarensalmi** are moored private yachts and cruisers, stretching as far as stylish **Café Carusel**. Yet another place popular with summer sun-worshippers, Carusel also hosts occasional live music. Behind the café is the jetty for boats to rocky **Pihlajasaari**, with attractive sandy beaches and, for the naturists among you, one of only two places in Helsinki where you can (legally) stew your plums in public.

Bid farewell to the sea and join **Merikatu**. Double back and head in an easterly direction before making a left turn into **Huvilakatu**, possibly the finest pure Art Nouveau street anywhere in the city and bisecting four uniform blocks that date from 1904–10. The colourful façades are characterised by gable motifs, towers, bays and a rhythmic roof profile.

Head left along **Pietarinkatu** and across to **Rehbinderintie**, which you follow to the right, aim for the distinctive spire of the **Mikael Agricola Church** (Mikael Agricolan Kirkko) [6 E8]. On the corner of Laivurinkatu and Tehtaankatu you can catch tram 3T back to the Market Square, or if you still feel energetic pick your way back on foot.

# 11 What to See and Do

Two of Helsinki's finest attractions are the Suomenlinna Sea Fortress and the island of Seurasaari, open-air museums that are key to Helsinki's culture – see *Natural Helsinki*, pages 256–61 for more details.

## MUSEUMS

### UNMISSABLES

**Design Museum (Design Museo)** *Korkeavuorenkatu 23;* ℡ *622 0540;* *www.designmuseo.fi. Open Tue 11.00–20.00, Wed–Sun 11.00–18.00, closed Mon; open Jun–Aug daily 11.00–18.00. Adult €7, student €3.* [7 G6]
Follow the stimulating history of artistic design and industrial art from the mid 19th century to the present day. Permanent displays and changing installations on themes such as the story of Finnish glass and interior design and fabrics, as well as touring foreign exhibitions.

**Finnish Architecture Museum (Suomen Rakennustaiteen Museo)** *Kasarmikatu 24;* ℡ *8567 5100; www.mfa.fi. Open Tue & Thu–Sun 10.00–16.00, Wed 10.00–20.00. Free admission Wed; adult €3.50, student €1.70.* [7 G6]

Helsinki has some fascinating architecture, as well as more than a few modern blots. Learn about the best ones, the pre-eminent Finnish architects, open design competitions that shaped the city's skyline and, perhaps most interestingly, plans for future development.

### Helsinki City Museum (Helsingin Kaupunginmuseoon) *Sofiankatu 4; ↘ 169 3933; www.helsinkicitymuseum.fi. Open Mon–Fri 09.00–17.00, Sat–Sun 11.00–17.00. Adult €4, student €2.* [5 H3]

The full gamut of Helsinki City Museum comprises a dozen attractions around the city, some better than others. At the main building near Senate Square, the Helsinki Horizons exhibit traces the city's 450-year history, with separate units devoted to the periods of Swedish, Russian and Finnish rule.

### Helsinki University Museum Arppeanum (Helsingin Yliopistomuseo Arppeanum) *Arppeanum, Snellmaninkatu 3; ↘ 1912 4071; www.halvi.helsinki.fi/museo/english/index.htm. Open Tue–Fri 11.00–17.00, Sat–Sun 11.00–16.00, closed Mon. Adult €4.20, child €2.50.* [5 H2]

Vast museum with medical, dentistry and veterinary exhibitions, as well as the history of the university and a mineral cabinet with fossils, rocks and meteorites.

### National Museum of Finland (Suomen Kansallismuseo) *Mannerheimintie 34; ↘ 4050 9544; www.kansallismuseo.fi. Open Tue–Wed 11.00–20.00, Thu–Sun*

*11.00–18.00, closed Mon. Free admission Tue 17.30–20.00. Adult €6, concession €4, under 18s free.* [1 B2]

This wonderful National Romantic castle-style museum charts the history of Finnish culture from prehistoric times to the modern era. The permanent collection has five sections; the Treasure Troves displays coins, silver and weapons; Prehistory of Finland is the country's largest archaeological exhibition; The Realm traces Finnish culture from the Middles Ages onwards; A Land and Its People shows life in rural Finland pre-industrialisation; and The Past Century addresses the development of the nation since independence in 1917. Temporary exhibitions are on display on the ground and third floors.

### Urho Kekkonen Museum Tamminiemi *Tamminiementie 6; ↘ 3108 7031; www.nba.fi/fi/ukk_museo. Open Wed–Fri 11.00–17.00, closed Mon–Tue; mid May–mid Aug daily 11.00–17.00. Adult €5, concession €4, under 18s free.*

Finland's most celebrated president was Urho Kekkonen. Pastel-pink Tamminiemi, near Seurasaari, was his official residence and is furnished as in Kekkonen's day. With fine Finnish art, design exhibits and a fascinating array of global curios that can only be collected from a lifetime in international politics, you can also see the famous sauna that played host to many a presidential summit meeting. Guided tours in English daily at 13.30.

## OTHER MUSEUMS

### Bank of Finland Museum (Suomen Pankin Rahamuseo) *Snellmaninkatu 2;* ↘ *010 831 2981; www.rahamuseo.fi. Open Tue–Fri 12.00–18.00, Sat–Sun 11.00–16.00, closed Mon. Admission free.* [5 H2]

Exciting multi-media presentations and the history of money, central banking and monetary policy might seem like a contradiction in terms, but that's what we've got here. The best bit is the fascinating section on the design of Finnish banknotes.

### Burgher's House (Ruiskumestarin Talo) *Kristianinkatu 12;* ↘ *135 1065; www.helsinkicitymuseum.fi. Open Jun–Aug & Nov–early Jan Wed–Sun 11.00–17.00. Adult €4, concession €2, children free.* [1 C2]

Part of Helsinki City Museum, this cute but unspectacular mustard-yellow place is Helsinki's oldest wooden house, dating from 1818. Halfway between Senate Square and Hakaniemi, the geography of Helsinki means that it isn't really on the way to anywhere. Unless you fancy a walk around this part of town, you might feel like you wasted your time.

### Cable Factory (Kaapelitehdas) *Tallberginkatu 1;* ↘ *4763 8330; www.kaapelitehdas.fi.*

Colossal just isn't the word for the cable factory, which began pumping out telegraph, electricity and telephone cables in 1912. Expanded between 1939 and

1954, construction was severely disrupted by World War II, but on completion the complex covered a staggering 56,000m². Keen eyes will readily see a similarity between the square-sided, monolithic bulk of this complex and the colossal mills of industrial England. The factory became a major part of the Nokia group after a merger in 1967, but when Nokia decided to move out in the late 1980s a controversial arrangement was hatched to convert the site for commercial use. Amidst widespread local opposition an alternative plan proposed the site be developed for cultural gain. So it is that today the Cable Factory is home to media companies, artists' workshops, galleries and theatre space – a vibrant cultural centre in the western Ruoholahti neighbourhood that's well worth visiting. There's also a contemporary café serving snacks and hot meals. Find the following museums at the Cable Factory:

*Finnish Museum of Photography (Suomen Valokuvataiteen Museo)* ℡ 6866 3621; *www.fmp.fi. Open Tue–Fri 09.00–19.00, Sat–Sun 12.00–18.00. Adult €6, concession €4, under 18s free.*
The most rewarding attraction in the complex is this huge sports hall-sized gallery tracing Finnish photography from the 1840s and incorporating regular temporary and foreign exhibitions.

*Hotel and Restaurant Museum (Hotelli ja Ravintola Museo)* ℡ 6859 3700; *www.hotellijaravintolamuseo.fi. Open Tue–Sun 11.00–18.00. Adult €2, concession €1*

Thankfully the admission price is the lowest of the three museums here, which is just as well given what's on offer. In a city boasting wonderful galleries, superb architecture and great outdoor activities, surely only chefs and hoteliers want to see antiquarian menus and plans of old country inns.

**Theatre Museum (Teatterimuseo)** ℡ 207 961 670; www.teatterimuseo.fi. Open Tue–Sun 11.00–18.00. Adult €5.50, concession €2.50.
Why just *learn* about Finnish theatre when you can *live* it? The museum calls itself a 'theatre park', presumably like a theme park but with fewer roller coasters and more greasepaint. Kids especially love its inclusive nature.

**Design Museum, Arabia Museum and Gallery (Arabian Museo)** Hämeentie 135; ℡ 204 39 5357; www.arabianmuseo.fi. Open Tue–Fri 12.00–18.00, Sat–Sun 10.00–16.00. Adult €4, concession €1.
Anything and everything to do with the famous Arabia ceramics factory, with permanent historical galleries and changing exhibitions on things like Moomin porcelain or Iittala home wares. Located at the Arabia factory in the northeast of the city suburbs, this is part of the Design Museum but don't confuse it with the main branch at Korkeavuorenkatu 23.

**Hakasalmi Museum (Hakasalmen Huvila)** Karamzininkatu 2/Mannerheimintie 13d; ℡ 169 3444; www.helsinkicitymuseum.fi. Open Jan–mid Feb & mid June–Dec

*Wed & Fri–Sun 11.00–17.00, Thu 11.00–19.00. Adult €4, concession €2, child free.* [1 B2]

When Helsinki's Procurator of the Senate, Baron Carl Johan Walleen, needed a summer residence this pretty waterside location must have seemed ideal. At least, maybe in 1843. Back then the Italianate villa was outside the town limits – today it's directly next to busy Mannerheimintie and very much in the city. The villa was bequeathed to the city in 1902 upon the death of Walleen's stepdaughter, Aurora Karamzin. Since 1912 it has been administered by Helsinki City Museum and now hosts an exhibition charting the development of Finnish society and specifically the changing social expectations across the generations.

### Helsinki Car Museum (Helsingin Automuseo) *Munkkisaarenkatu 12; ↘ 667 123; www.automuseo.fi. Open Jan–Mar & Oct–Dec Thu–Sun 12.00–15.00, Apr–Sep Tue–Sun 12.00–15.00. Adult €5.50, child €2.* [1 B4]

Classic vintage cars from around the world, including US models and limousines used by former president Urho Kekkonen. There's also Europe's largest exhibition of miniature model cars and, bizarrely, waxworks of famous Finns are dotted around the place.

### Mannerheim Museum (Mannerheim-museo) *Kalliolinnantie 14; ↘ 635 443; www.mannerheim-museo.fi. Open Fri–Sun 11.00–16.00, other times by appointment. Adult €8, concession €4, child under 12 free.* [7 K8]

11

C G E Mannerheim is Finland's most celebrated military figure, who rose to prominence during World War I and was the subsequent driving force behind the defeat of the Russian Red Forces during the Finnish Civil War of 1918. By the time of World War II Finland was closely affiliated to the German forces, and Mannerheim was appointed President of the Republic. With his considerable influence he was able to extricate Finland from the war as the sole nation on the losing side not to be occupied by foreign troops. The museum was Mannerheim's home and is preserved as such, with medals, uniforms and documents on display.

## Military Museum (Sotamuseo) *Maurinkatu 1;* \ *1812 6381;*
*www.mpkk.fi/en/museum. Open Tue–Thu 11.00–17.00, Fri–Sun 11.00–16.00. Adult €4, concession €2.* [5 K1]
Over 200,000 artefacts including tanks, guns, weapons, colours, uniforms and photographs covering Finland's history from Swedish territory, through to Russian rule, the struggle for independence and role in World War II.

## Museum of Technology (Tekniikan Museo) *Viikintie 1;* \ *728 8440;*
*www.tekniikanmuseo.fi. Open Jan–Apr & Sep–Dec Wed–Sun 12.00–16.00, May–Aug Tue–Sun 11.00–17.00. Adult €5, concession €1.*
For those whose brains turn with cogs, gears and levers, this is the place to learn all about industrial history, from wood processing to metal fabrication, power generation to computer technology. Located near the site of Helsinki Old Town at Vanhakaupunki.

**Post Museum (Posti Museo)** *Pääpostitalo, Asema-aukio 5h;* ☏ *020 451 4888. Open Mon–Fri 09.00–18.00, Sat–Sun 11.00–16.00. Adult €4, under 18s free.* [4 E2]
Finland's postal service is 365 years old and any philatelist should take a look at this tidy interactive exhibition in the main post office, with over 2,500 stamps from 200 countries.

**Power Station Museum (Voimalamuseo)** *Hameentie 163;* ☏ *3108 7064; www.helsinkicitymuseum.fi. Open Jun–Sep Sun 11.00–17.00. Adult €4, concession €2, child free.*
In the Vanhakaupunki district by the mouth of the River Vantaa, where Helsinki was born in 1550, this jolly red-brick watermill and turbine hall now serves as an interesting industrial museum that still produces a limited quantity of hydro-electric power.

**School Museum (Koulumuseo)** *Kalevankatu 39–41;* ☏ *3108 7066; www.helsinkicitymuseum.fi. Open Jan–May Wed–Sun 11.00–17.00, Sep–Dec first Sun of each month 11.00–17.00. Adult €4, concession €2, child free.* [6 C5]
Two lovely old wooden houses form a period museum with classrooms frozen in time from the 1920s. Take the kids along and astonish them with phrases such as: 'They didn't have computers in those days', 'Behave yourself or you'll get six of the best' and 'That dark piece of wood is called a blackboard'. Occasionally they hold free evening recitals of Finnish school songs.

**Sederholm House (Sederholmin Talo)** *Aleksanterinkatu 16-18; ↘ 169 3625; www.helsinkicitymuseum.fi. Standard opening hours Wed–Sun 11.00–17.00, but hours and admission prices dependent on exhibition. Adult €4, concession €2, child free.* [5 H3]

The oldest building in downtown Helsinki, dating from 1757, isn't particularly impressive from the outside but is used to house special exhibitions for the City Museum. In 2006, you could have learned about the legacy of Swedish and Russian rule or immersed yourself in the cartographic delights of Nordic maps.

**Sport Museum of Finland (Suomen Urheilumuseo)** *Olympic Stadium (Olympiastadion); ↘ 434 2250; www.urheilumuseo.fi. Open Mon–Fri 11.00–17.00, Sat–Sun 12.00–16.00. Adult €3.50, concession free.*

Helsinki's Olympic Stadium is worth a visit purely to admire the modernist architecture or take the panoramic view from atop the 72m-high tower, but for a sporty burst of history sprint round to the museum. In line with other parts of the ageing stadium it feels a bit cold and utilitarian in places, but the multi-media exhibits are nonetheless worthy of note. In the car park is a statue of Paavo Nurmi, not just Finland's greatest but one of the world's all-time distance-running legends.

*Olympic Stadium*

228

**Tram Museum (Raitioliikennemuseo)** *Töölönkatu 51a;* ☏ *169 3576;*
*www.helsinkicitymuseum.fi. Open Wed–Sun 11.00–17.00. Adult €4, concession free.*
[1 A1]
In the northwestern district of Töölö, the city's oldest tram depot presents the history of public transport in Helsinki. There's a rather underwhelming scale model of the city dating from c1870. Interesting for enthusiasts, otherwise just go next door and enjoy a drink in Korjaamo.

## GALLERIES

### UNMISSABLES
### Ateneum Art Museum – The Finnish National Gallery (Ateneumin Taidemuseo)
*Kaivokatu 2;* ☏ *1733 6401; www.ateneum.fi. Open Tue & Fri 09.00–18.00, Wed–Thu 09.00–20.00, Sat–Sun 11.00–17.00. Adult €5.50, concession €3, under 18s free.* [5 F2]
Finland's largest art collection is housed in a series of beautiful galleries displaying Finnish and international art ranging from 18th-century Rococo to 20th-century Expressionism. Famous names on show include Vincent Van Gogh, Paul Cézanne, Francisco de Goya, August Rodin and Paul Gauguin. The palatial Ateneum is one of Helsinki's architectural splendours. Completed in 1887, the main façade has three projections; the main one highlighting the museum, and two symmetrical side sections that accentuate what was formerly the art school. The four caryatids on the main projection symbolise painting, sculpture, architecture and graphic art.

### Kiasma – Museum of Contemporary Art (Nykytaiteen Museo Kiasma)
*Mannerheiminaukio 2;* ☎ *1733 6501; www.kiasma.fi. Open Tue–Sun 10.00–17.00. Adult €8, concession €6.50, under 18s free.* [4 D1]

If the Ateneum represents everything artistically mature and classical in a gallery, Kiasma is the teenage rebel who just loves to stir trouble. Controversy was sparked even before the gallery was constructed, when the commission was awarded to American architect Stephen Holl. In a country proud of its homegrown designs, some found this difficult to accept. The wonderfully modern Kiasma continues to challenge the accepted norm with installations that are beautiful, baffling and disturbing in equal measure. Multi-media installations feature heavily. Whatever your impressions of 'modern art', if nothing else a visit to Kiasma will certainly make you think. If it's all a little bizarre for your tastes, just soak up the sun on the superb summer terrace.

### Sinebrychoff Art Museum (Sinebrychoffin Taidemuseo) *Bulevardi 40;* ☎ *1733 6460; www.sinebrychoffintaidemuseo.fi. Open Tue & Fri 10.00–18.00, Wed–Thu 10.00–20.00, Sat–Sun 11.00–17.00. Adult €7.50, concession €4.50, child free.* [6 C6]

Finland's most significant collection of old masters was bequeathed to the city by Paul and Fanny Sinebrychoff in 1921. Collections ranging from the 14th to 19th centuries, together with glassware, silverware and furniture exhibits connected to Finland's contribution to European art. French, Italian and Dutch works feature prominently.

## OTHER GALLERIES
### Amos Anderson Art Museum (Amos Andersonin Taidemuseo) Yrjönkatu 27;
↘ 684 4460; www.amosanderson.fi. Open Mon–Fri 10.00–18.00, Sat–Sun
11.00–17.00. Adult €7, child free. [4 D3]

Finnish art, furniture and artefacts from the house of Amos Anderson, a benefactor who owned several printing presses and the largest Swedish-language newspaper of the day. Also changing exhibitions and art from the private collection of architect Sigurd Frosterus.

### Cygnaeus Gallery (Cygnaeuksen Galleria) Kalliolinnantie 8; ↘ 4050 9628;
www.nba.fi. Open Wed 11.00–19.00, Thu–Sun 11.00–16.00. Adult €4, child free. [7 J7]

Finland's oldest art collection, based around donations from Professor Fredrik Cygnaeus, concentrates mainly on 19th-century Finnish art. Located close to Kaivopuisto Park, in the leafy neighbourhood that houses some of the biggest foreign embassies, a visit here can easily be combined with a pleasant walk.

### Helsinki City Art Museum, Art Museum Tennis Palace (Helsingin Kaupungin Taidemuseo, Taidemuseo Tennispalatsi) Salomonkatu 15; ↘ 3108 7001;
www.taidemuseo.fi. Open Tue–Sun 11.00–20.30. Last admission 20.00. Adult €7, concession €5, under 18s free. [4 C3]

Originally built to house large car dealerships, this was for many years the national home of tennis in Finland. Illogically, during the 1952 Olympic Games the complex was used for basketball. Nowadays this fine example of Functionalist architecture houses temporary exhibitions for the Helsinki City Art Museum. Recent shows have been as diverse as Indian culture, contemporary Chinese photography, Japanese manga art and the stylistic development of men's underpants.

## MAJOR SIGHTS

**FINLANDIA HALL** *Mannerheimintie 13e;* ` 40241; *www.finlandia.hel.fi. Adult €4, concession €3.* [1 B2]
When Alvar Aalto designed Finlandia Hall, it was envisaged as the first piece in a development that would stretch along the shore of Töölönlahti Bay. The fact that the rest of the plan was never executed leaves the hall feeling somewhat isolated, a stark white modernist slab set against soft greens and blues, but immediately identifiable. Constructed between 1967 and 1975, the complex hosts major concerts, public events and conferences. The Finlandia Chamber, the 1,750-seat central auditorium, is as typically visually challenging as all Aalto architecture – acute angles and soft curves combine with a palette of stark black and white. The exterior of the building is clad in white Carrara marble – an expensive mistake. Totally unsuited to the harsh Finnish climate, the original marble was replaced in 1999 after considerable warping caused some tiles to fall off. Just seven years later the warping has started again, yet the Aalto Foundation refuses to consider any material not specified in the original design. In 2007, Finlandia Hall will host the Eurovision Song Contest, after joke-rock

band Lordi triumphed at the 2006 event in Athens. Guided tours last half an hour and are dependent on the usage of the hall – call for details.

## LUTHERAN CATHEDRAL (TUOMIOKIRKKO) [5 H2]

To the untrained eye Helsinki's iconic Lutheran Cathedral appears to be a wonderfully uniform creation, dominating Senate Square and its environs. However, in truth its history reveals a somewhat cluttered tale of changed plans and posthumous modifications. Designed by Carl Ludvig Engel, the architect responsible for much of the city's early 19th-century development, the original plans were drafted in 1818 and involved a central tower with prominent Greek cross, together with the striking Corinthian columns of the triangular gables that give the cathedral much of its identity. Originally called the Nicholas Church, after the Russian Tsar Nikolai I, construction began in 1830. By this time the aspect of the square had already been altered by the addition of the huge flight of steps on the northern perimeter. Engel died in 1840 before work was completed and by the time the cathedral was consecrated in 1852, architect E B Lohrmann had added four side towers to the structure and two separate pavilions

*Lutheran Cathedral*

11

on the side of the terrace closest to the square. After independence in 1919 the cathedral changed its name to the Great Church, finally settling on its current moniker in 1969. The interior of the cathedral is pure – a calm melding of white and pastel blue disrupted only by gold ornamentation surrounding the altarpiece. Although different in shape, the style is reminiscent of Engel's Old Church (see pages 244–5), which was used to serve the congregation whilst the cathedral was under construction. Three statues portray Luther, Agricola and Melanchthon, the three foremost clerics of the Lutheran reformation. Mikael Agricola was also the creator of the Finnish written language and translator of the New Testament. Below the main hall is the vast cathedral crypt. Its original purpose was to give a raised foundation upon which the main hall could be constructed, and for years it stood empty. Today it is used for concerts, exhibitions and some church services, and there is a little café accessible from Snellmaninkatu on the eastern side of the cathedral.

## MARKET SQUARE (KAUPPATORI) [5 H4]

Helsinki's bustling harbourside market square is the hub of the central tourist area, busy with coach parties and day trippers from the Tallinn ferries. The square's attraction lies less in the range of unspectacular souvenir stalls and more in its proximity to some of the city's most attractive buildings; together with the nearby Esplanade Park and Senate Square, this area forms the heart of architect Carl Ludvig Engel's vision for the new Helsinki of the early 19th century. At the eastern end, closest to the Uspenski Cathedral, is the Presidential Palace (Presidentinlinna), dating from 1820 and the first building in Helsinki to be built with Ionic columns and a projected gable. Moving westward, on the corner of Hetenankatu sits the Supreme Court (Korkein Oikeus), which was originally a two-storey sea captain's house but was altered in 1883 when the third storey was added and the façade altered to its current richly ornamented design. The Swedish embassy (Swedish Sveriges Ambassad) has one of the choicest pieces of real estate in the city, but this was never intended to be the case. Originally, in 1814, the site was earmarked by Engel for the new stock exchange, but became a private apartment before the Swedes snapped it up in 1921. They immediately changed the appearance of the building, giving it a style redolent of the Royal Palace in Stockholm. Arriving at the western extremity of the square, where Eteläranta forms the boundary with the Esplanade Park, Helsinki City Hall (Kaupungintalo) dates from 1833 and was originally built as a private members' club and hotel. Soon outdated, it was adapted several times and eventually reincarnated as the Town Hall in 1913.

In the square itself you can find a blend of colourful gift stalls, fresh food sellers and tempting alfresco patisseries, occasionally accompanied by winsome Russian accordion music. In the summer months, piles of fresh berries weigh heavy on overburdened trestle tables, whilst winter brings quiet and the promise of heated café-tents to banish the icy chills. In October, the annual Baltic Herring Festival celebrates everything about one of the Finns' favourite foods. If fish isn't your thing, the Old Market Hall (Wanha Kauppahalli) will provide everything you need.

## CONTEMPORARY ART BURNS BRIGHT

The vast area of waste land opposite the Parliament Building that stretches towards Railway Square is currently under development as part of a new entertainment complex, but the story runs deeper than the cranes and excavators would suggest. Originally home to a series of 19th-century railway warehouses, known as V R Makasiinit, the area had slipped away from the mainstream and found itself at the centre of the alternative arts scene – the dark atmosphere found favour for a range of cultural events. Whilst many saw individual spirit thriving in the heart of the city, the authorities only saw valuable real estate and the potential for making euros. Long and oft-heated debate ended with a decision to bulldoze the warehouses and construct a shiny new music hall; demolition was scheduled for 8 May 2006. On 7 May, a group of several hundred activists gathered at V R Makasiinit in a defiant act of protest. In the stand-off that ensued with armed police, trouble flared and, in a final blaze of glory, the warehouses were destroyed by fire. Arson was suspected and, according to the *Helsingin Sanomat* newspaper, the event was one of the most photographed in Finnish history.

**PARLIAMENT BUILDING (EDUSKUNTATALO)** *Mannerheimintie 30;* ☏ *4321; www.eduskunta.fi. Visitors' centre open Mon–Thu 10.00–18.00, Fri 10.00–16.00; free guided tours Jan–Jun & Sep–Dec Sat 11.00 & 12.00, Sun 12.00 & 13.00, Jul–Aug Mon–Fri 13.00, Sat 11.00 & 12.00, Sun 12.00 & 13.00. [4 C1]*

If you think that Helsinki's Parliament Building looks somewhat out of place, you'd be right. This hulking monolith is Finland's only example of monumental Classicism, with a sweeping flight of steps and a façade defined by severe-looking columns. Located on Mannerheimintie, by the southern point of Töölönlahti Bay, it holds a prominent position in the city. Built between 1927 and 1931 to plans by Johan Sigfrid Sirén, the complex is much larger than the façade suggests, comprising not just the main Chamber of Parliament but also the Hall of State, great committee chamber and impressive marble staircase. Monumental details and furnishings are evident throughout. At either end of the foot of the steps are statues to two of Finland's pre-eminent former presidents: Kaarlo Juho Ståhlberg and Pehr Evind Svinhufvud.

## RAILWAY SQUARE (RAUTATIENTORI) [5 F2]

The Railway Square affords most visitors their first glimpse of Helsinki, and if you're the type that judges a book by its cover then you might not be overly impressed. For whilst this ever-busy transport interchange has the fine railway station at its core, and boasts two other significant landmarks, it is today typified by late 20th-century architecture that owes more to functionality than aesthetics. Along the eastern side of the square in particular, dour grey concrete blocks squat above bars and restaurants, adorned by neon signs and advertising logos that do little to inspire you to hang around. But don't race off just yet. Turn to face the station and absorb this once-ridiculed symbol of Finnish architecture. When a competition was held in 1902 to find plans for the newly proposed terminus, the flood of entries bearing castle- and church-like motifs indicated the current fascination with National Romanticism, far removed from other transport hubs of the day. Mostly made from Finnish granite, the curved central section of the façade has been compared to the style of an Art Deco radio set. On either side of the entrance, two huge statues hold lamps that illuminate the square. Whilst the winning entry of Eliel Saarinen was subsequently toned down the structure remained controversial, but is now admired and cherished – the high-vaulted halls of the public areas are especially loved and remain favoured meeting points for Helsinkiites to this day. Although the first part of the station was completed in 1909, World War I and the Finnish Civil War delayed the arrival of the first train until 1919, by which time part of the complex had served as a headquarters and military hospital for Russian troops. The station is reputed to feature a private waiting room solely for the use of the Finnish president, the only one of its kind in the world.

Two famous institutions illuminate the respective polar boundaries of the square with equal flair. To the north, the chunky Finnish National Theatre (Kansallisteatteri) is a gem of National Romanticism dating from 1902 and featuring strong castle motifs. Built from local granite and steatite, the elaborately articulated roof features richly glazed terracotta tiles and copper cladding. At the southern end, the National Art Museum (Ateneum) dates from 1897 but presents a wholly different architectural vision. More uniformly classical, the Ateneum is much wider than the cube-like National Theatre, with three distinct storeys characterised by arched windows and the central hall with its busts depicting the great masters Raphael, Phidias and Bramante.

## SENATE SQUARE (SENAATINTORI) [5 H3]

Along with the Market Square, Helsinki's Senate Square is the city's most identifiable landmark. This was the focus of the town plan drawn up by Johan Albrecht Ehrenström in 1812. Designed to give the city a focal point befitting its new capital status, the style was influenced by the Russian desire to create a showcase at this western extremity of their empire, a 'mini St Petersburg' of sorts. Architect Carl Ludvig Engel was entrusted with designing the buildings that were to serve governmental, academic and ecclesiastical functions.

The first building of the composition to be constructed was a guardhouse on the northern side of the square, finished in 1819. In 1822, the most important governmental establishment in the plan, the Senate Building (Valtioneuvoston Linna), was completed on the eastern aspect. On the opposing western side, the main buildings of Helsinki University were designed as the symmetrical counterpart to the Senate Building and were completed some ten years later in 1832.

The square's dominating feature is the Lutheran Cathedral (Tuomiokirkko), construction of which began in 1830. A change in plans during the late 1830s led to the demolition of the guardhouse to make way for the immense flight of steps that lead to the terrace in front of the church. The alteration of the plans severely influenced the aspect of the entire square. Where hitherto the axis had run from east to west, the incorporation of the steps inexorably shifted this so that it was undeniably north to south. As a consequence, the early 18th-century merchants' houses running along the southern boundary of the square were adapted to rest more sympathetically with the overall surroundings. The finished article, resplendent with Engel's pastel yellow creations and the sparkling white bulk of the cathedral, forms one of the most coherent and beautiful early 19th-century European squares. In such a large-scale project sacrifices were inevitable, and to make way for new construction the original Ulrika Eleonora Church, built in 1727, was razed. Paving slabs on the western perimeter of the square mark the site of the church.

Today, as well as these architectural treats, there are numerous cafés, galleries and craft centres in the vicinity, and the square is used for large-scale public events and gatherings. Unsurprisingly, with so much to see, tourists flock here in their thousands. Try and visit at a quiet time; early morning is always best if you can drag yourself out of bed.

## SIBELIUS MONUMENT

Finland's most celebrated composer is Jean Sibelius (1865–1957), and this rather curious monument in the Töölö area of the city is one of Helsinki's most celebrated landmarks. In a small park sits a creation of around 600 stainless-steel tubes, of varying diameters and lengths, welded together to create one undulating entity. Ostensibly redolent of the pipes of an organ (although

*Sibelius Monument*

Sibelius never composed organ music) the design was adapted and softened to create an almost organic shape suggestive of a Finnish birch forest or the dancing aurora borealis. Each pipe was richly hand-textured by sculptor Eila Hiltunen and her assistant Emil Kukkonen. The project took four years to complete, by which time the overall structure measured over 10m in length, 8m in height and 6m in depth. The weight was 30 tons. For her endless hours of welding atop the pipes, Hiltunen had been rewarded with chronic bronchial asthma as a result of toxic metal fumes. But despite the monument's place in Finnish hearts, it could so easily have been a different story. Public opposition to the commission was incredibly strong, and not until the monument was finally unveiled did the outcry begin to subside. Nevertheless, to placate the most vocal protestors, a bust of Sibelius was also commissioned to create a more traditional memorial. Today, full-sized elements from the monument, used during the production process but discarded from the final composition, are displayed outside the UN offices of New York and Montreal, whilst a 1:5 replica is displayed at the UNESCO palace in Paris. Sibelius lived at Ainola, a large rural villa some 45km north of Helsinki; sightseeing trips can be arranged at the tourist office.

## TEMPPELIAUKIO (THE CHURCH IN THE ROCK) [4 B1]

The most-visited tourist attraction in central Helsinki is this weird and wonderful creation. Built in 1969, the church was blasted from a huge chunk of granite to create a structure with a saucer-like roof only just visible from the surrounding streets. In keeping with much construction work of the 1960s there's a fair amount of concrete, which gives a cold, stark feel, but the ingenuity of the interior demands respect. The walls comprise the jagged bedrock from which the church was hollowed, whilst a central window affording light to the hall circles the dense beams supporting the roof and gives a sense that the ceiling is floating above the hall. The church has strong acoustics and holds regular concerts. If you're visiting in winter, the snowfall that blankets the roof can from some angles render the church almost invisible.

## THE ESPLANADE PARK (ESPLANAD PARK) [5 G4]

This leafy boulevard between two of Helsinki's most stylish streets has always been one of the city's focal points since its inception in 1812. Lined with grand architecture, this is one of the key areas in the plan for the 'new' Helsinki, forming a uniform entity with the Market Square and sitting in close proximity to the splendid Senate Square. The park is a key hub of the city's social life, being a focal point for May Day celebrations and hosting other large-scale public events. It's also home to some of Helsinki's most famous cafés and restaurants, and for many the park is a favourite place to wine and dine. For others, the lure of designer boutiques and emporiums proves too strong to resist, whilst a significant number simply consider the Esplanade to be *the* place to see and be seen. To highlight its refined credentials, in winter the northern boulevard of Pohjoisesplanadi is one of the only streets in town to have heated pavements, presumably to spare the incongruity of getting snow on one's shoes.

The park has three notable statues. At the western end, close to the Swedish Theatre and Academic Bookstore, is a memorial to **Eino Leino** (1878–1926), a revered poet and writer. The striking sculpture features a plinth engraved with lines from the famous poet's elegy *Väinämöisen Laulu* (The song of Väinämöinen): *'Yksi on laulu ylitse muiden ihmisen aattehen hengen ankara laulu'* – One is the voice above all others; the stern voice of man's beliefs.

In the centre of the Esplanade stands Finland's much-loved national poet, **J L Runeberg** (1804–77). This monument to the author of the Finnish national anthem makes a striking landmark for finding the renowned **Hotel Kämp**, famous the world over for its opulent luxury and decadent indulgence (see page 112). So refined is the atmosphere that gentle classical music can often be heard floating around the immediate vicinity; such is the class of the local buskers. Next door to the Kämp, the flagship Marimekko store occupies the ground floor of the **Catani Building**, one-time home of the confectionery enterprise of the same name and complementary in style to its grand neighbour. On the park's opposing southern avenue, Eteläesplanadi, the **Savoy Restaurant** resides above the Finlayson and Papagena design shops. Another work by Alvar Aalto, this time in tandem with his wife Aino, the roof terrace has fine city views.

At its western extremity, the Esplanade runs into Market Square. Dividing the two is the **Havis Amanda Fountain**, an unofficial icon of Helsinki. In less liberal times, Havis Amanda's nudity was a source of disquiet amongst locals who considered her aura unsuitable. Perhaps this is what first attracted students to her svelte granite body, for nowadays she is the focal point of university May Day celebrations, when she receives a ritual wash to herald the dawn of summer.

## THE OLD CHURCH (VANHAKIRKKO) [4 E4]

If you walk along Lönnrotinkatu or Bulevardi, you can't help but be struck by the gorgeous wooden Old Church, sitting on the edge of a leafy park between these two streets. The church was built in 1826 to provide a temporary place of worship whilst the Lutheran Cathedral was under construction. Another design by Engel, there are very clear similarities with the main cathedral in Senate Square, from the white and pastel green colour scheme to the Greek cross atop a central dome. Originally, the Old Church was (unsurprisingly) called the New Church and contained the pulpit, pews, altar rail, chandeliers and organ from the razed Church of Ulrika Eleonora in Senate Square. Today, the only one of these items remaining is the pulpit. The interior is characterised by white columns and soft powder-blue walls, which act as a neutral backdrop to the bold altarpiece – *Jesus Blessing The Children* – installed in 1854 and the first monumental painting to be commissioned in Finland (from a Finnish artist) in modern times. Above the doorway, the impressive organ dates from 1869 and retains the majority of its original pipes. When the Lutheran Cathedral was completed, the New Church gracefully stood down and became the Old Church. Helsinki is well blessed with inspirational churches, but whilst others take the headlines, this wooden wonder remains my favourite. Fragile and atmospheric, it is also invariably deserted.